Carl Hiaasen

ALSO BY DAVID GEHERIN
AND FROM MCFARLAND

*Funny Thing About Murder: Modes of Humor
in Crime Fiction and Films* (2017)

Small Towns in Recent American Crime Fiction (2015)

*The Dragon Tattoo and Its Long Tail: The New Wave
of European Crime Fiction in America* (2012)

*Scene of the Crime: The Importance of Place
in Crime and Mystery Fiction* (2008)

Carl Hiaasen
Sunshine State Satirist

DAVID GEHERIN

McFarland & Company, Inc., Publishers
Jefferson, North Carolina

LIBRARY OF CONGRESS CATALOGUING-IN-PUBLICATION DATA

Names: Geherin, David, 1943– author.
Title: Carl Hiaasen : Sunshine State satirist / David Geherin.
Description: Jefferson, North Carolina : McFarland & Company, Inc., Publishers, 2019. | Includes bibliographical references and index.
Identifiers: LCCN 2018048526 | ISBN 9781476669441 (softcover : acid free paper) ♾
Subjects: LCSH: Hiaasen, Carl.
Classification: LCC PS3558.I217 Z63 2019 | DDC 818/.5409 [B] —dc23
LC record available at https://lccn.loc.gov/2018048526

BRITISH LIBRARY CATALOGUING DATA ARE AVAILABLE

ISBN (print) 978-1-4766-6944-1
ISBN (ebook) 978-1-4766-3459-3

© 2019 David Geherin. All rights reserved

No part of this book may be reproduced or transmitted in any form or by any means, electronic or mechanical, including photocopying or recording, or by any information storage and retrieval system, without permission in writing from the publisher.

Front cover images © 2018 iStock

Printed in the United States of America

McFarland & Company, Inc., Publishers
 Box 611, Jefferson, North Carolina 28640
 www.mcfarlandpub.com

To my favorite young readers:
Anna, Gino, Sofia, Maxine, Giada, and KK.
This one's for you!

Table of Contents

Preface 1
Introduction: Biography 3

1. Journalism 13
2. Nonfiction 25
3. Collaborations with Bill Montalbano 34
4. Novels for Adults 40
5. Novels for Young Readers 133
6. Literary Influences 163
7. Florida: Hiaasen's Muse 169
8. Humor and Satire 174
9. An Interview with Carl Hiaasen 180

Bibliography 189
Index 197

Preface

In 1982, I published a book on John D. MacDonald who at the time was one of America's most popular crime writers. He was best known for a series of mysteries featuring a Florida beach bum named Travis McGee, whom he used as a spokesperson to celebrate Florida's natural beauty and to bemoan its constant assault due to overdevelopment and overpopulation. That same year, Carl Hiaasen was a young investigative reporter for the *Miami Herald*. Over the next three decades, he too would become one of America's most popular and critically acclaimed crime writers. He would also assume MacDonald's mantle as a fierce advocate on behalf of saving what's left of Florida's natural beauty.

Hiaasen is a triple-threat author who has successfully made the rare jump from reporter to nationally known columnist; from columnist to bestselling author of comic crime thrillers; and then on to a third career as an award-winning writer of novels for young readers. His distinctive blend of crime, outrageous humor, and biting satire gives his books an appeal that extends beyond just mystery fans to include readers who love comic fiction as well as those interested in novels that address serious social and environmental issues.

I have previously written on aspects of Hiaasen's fiction in two of my earlier books: *Scene of the Crime: The Importance of Place in Crime and Mystery Fiction* (2008) and *Funny Thing About Murder: Modes of Humor in Crime Fiction and Films* (2017). This book gives me an opportunity to examine in greater detail his entire body of work, from his college satirical columns in the early 1970s up to his latest novels for adults and young readers. The book begins with a brief biography of Hiaasen followed by separate chapters devoted to his journalism, his nonfiction, and his early collaborations with Bill Montalbano. Chapters 4 and 5 consist of commentaries on each of his adult novels and novels for young readers. Chapters 6 through 8 focus on the major literary influences on his work, the critical role Florida plays in his

Peface

writing, and his use of humor and satire. The book concludes with an interview with Hiaasen conducted by phone in November 2017.

On a personal note, I would like to express my appreciation to Carl Hiaasen for providing me with copies of some of his earliest writings and for graciously answering my questions, especially for the interview included in this book.

Introduction: Biography

He may not have been born with a pen in his hand, but Carl Hiaasen knew from an early age he wanted to be a writer. At the age of four, he began reading the sports section of the *Miami Herald* to his father at the breakfast table. At age six, he asked his dad for a typewriter, which he got, a red manual model. He taught himself to hunt and peck and soon began banging out little stories and reports about neighborhood kickball and softball games which he passed out to friends. "I just thought it was the coolest thing in the world to be able to write a story," he says (Woods).

Carl Andrew Hiaasen (his Norwegian surname is pronounced HIGH-uh-son) is a third-generation Floridian. His grandfather, Carl Andreas Hiaasen, was born in a Norwegian farm community in Devil's Lake, North Dakota, in 1894 and didn't learn to speak English until he was fourteen. As a young boy he almost died in a blizzard, so it's not surprising that he eventually sought to settle in a warmer climate. In 1922, he moved to Fort Lauderdale, population 1000, and opened the first law practice in town. His son, Carl's father, later joined him in the practice of law.

Carl Andrew Hiaasen was born 12 March 1953 in Fort Lauderdale, the oldest of four children to K. Odel and Patricia (Moran) Hiaasen, a former English teacher who was raised in a strict Roman Catholic household in Chicago (her brother became a Paulist priest, her sister a nun). The family, which included two younger sisters, Judith and Barbara, and a younger brother, Rob, lived in Plantation, a small town a few miles west of Fort Lauderdale. (Rob, a journalist like his older brother, was one of five victims killed in a mass shooting at the office of the newspaper where he worked in Annapolis, Maryland in June 2018). The defining experience of Hiaasen's young life, one which would shape virtually all his writing, was growing up in a very rural place at the edge of the Everglades, just a short bike ride away from his home in Plantation. It was a magical place for a young boy:

Introduction

> We lived in a pretty isolated rural section of Broward County, Florida, on the edge of the Everglades. Where there is now an eighteen-lane highway, there was just a dirt road. We didn't even have a convenience store within five miles of my house until I was thirteen or fourteen. We had nothing else to do but get on our bicycles and ride until the pavement stopped—which wasn't that far. Then we would get off our bikes, and hide them in the bushes or trees, and go exploring, or collecting snakes or turtles, or fishing or boating. Kid stuff. Tom Sawyer stuff [Marcus 108].

He and his buddies Bob Branham and Clyde Ingalls would ride their bikes to an Edenic place that seemed to the young Hiaasen to be as exotic as the Serengeti. There they would fish and catch poisonous snakes to sell to dealers (poisonous snakes brought in more money than non-poisonous ones because dealers couldn't find that many kids dumb enough to try to catch them). But this childhood paradise wouldn't last forever. The dirt path they rode their bikes on would soon become a major highway lined with shopping malls. When the bulldozers began arriving, the trio fought back the only way they knew how, by pulling up surveyor stakes: "We didn't know what else to do. We were little and the bulldozers were big" (Stevenson xv).

"It is a very difficult thing for a kid to watch that unfettered part of your childhood being paved before your eyes," he says (Freeman). The anger at the utter devastation he witnessed has never left him, although he has put it to good use in his writing. The other dramatic blow to his idyllic life came a few months before high school graduation when his buddy Clyde Ingalls drove to the Everglades and ran a hose from the exhaust pipe into the car, killing himself at age seventeen.

Hiaasen says his friend was angry about a lot of things, including the Vietnam war which was raging at the time. But he was particularly angry every time he saw a bulldozer destroy a place he loved. "You can't have someone close to you die that young and not have it affect you," he says (Schindehette). Years later, he would dedicate his second novel, *Double Whammy*, to his friend and use him as the model for Skink, his most famous character.

"Humor was my salvation as a kid," he claims (Howard 136). He says he got his sense of humor more from his Irish Catholic mother's side of the family than from his father's Norwegian heritage, though he does credit his father with introducing him to Joseph Heller's comic masterpiece *Catch-22*, as well as to the early comedy recordings of Bill Cosby, Mike Nichols and Elaine May, and George Carlin. As a schoolboy, he got his first taste of the pleasures of being an author when his papers were read in class. And as the smallest kid in his class—he skipped first grade because he already knew how to read—

Introduction: Biography

he soon learned that if he got the bullies to laugh, they'd look for some other kid to pester.

Thanks to a mother who was a former English teacher, books were valued in the Hiaasen home and Carl became an avid reader. He remembers burning through the entire Hardy Boys series when he was in fourth grade. In junior high, he discovered Ian Fleming's James Bond novels, which he hid from his mother by slipping them into more acceptable reading material like *Field and Stream* and *Outdoor Life* magazines. Later on he read a pair of novels that affected him deeply: J. D. Salinger's *Catcher in the Rye* and Joseph Heller's *Catch-22*, which taught him that a book could make you laugh while dealing with a subject as serious as war. One other novel he read helped him decide about the kind of book he knew he didn't want to write: "I know *Silas Marner* at some level had literary value but you really truly want to hang yourself halfway through it's so freaking boring. When I decided I was going to be a writer, I wanted to be the other kind of writer that made people laugh and still had something to say" ("WSJ").

In junior high he wrote stories during long bus rides to school, and in high school he created a satirical newsletter called *More Trash*, which he ran off on a mimeograph machine in the school office. The newsletter was designed as an alternative to the rah-rah school newspaper that focused on the football team and the cheerleaders. He took potshots at the school administration, the service clubs, and all the institutional stuff of high schools in the sixties. He describes *More Trash* as "irreverent and smart-ass" (Kenen), which isn't surprising considering it was written by a person who confesses he "was always a pain in the ass" (Silet "Sun" 11).

The cool kids who previously never spoke to him liked the newsletter and would now come up to him in the hall and tell him how funny he was, which made him realize how rewarding it was to be able to make people laugh. His smart-alecky sense of humor, however, did come close to getting him into some trouble when in his farewell edition of *More Trash* he underlined seven letters which spelled out an obscene phrase beginning with the letter "F." The joke was meant for his friends, but when everyone else in school also caught it, he feared for a while he might have to explain to his father why he wasn't allowed to graduate.

He did graduate from Plantation High School in 1970 and that fall enrolled at Emory University in Atlanta. For a time he says he felt he might be expected to follow in the footsteps of his father and grandfather and become a lawyer like they were. His grandfather loved the law and practiced until he was ninety. His father, on the other hand, clearly didn't love it quite so much, and both encouraged him to do what he loved and do it the best he could no matter what. At one point he thought he might like to be a veterinarian, but then realized he would need to take more science courses than he wanted to. So in college he decided to become an English major.

During his freshman year at Emory, he married his high school sweetheart, Connie Lyford, and the following year became the father of a son named Scott. That same year he also displayed his prankish sense of humor by entering the "Miss Emory" pageant, which he lost. He also continued his journalistic pursuits, writing for *The Emory Wheel*, the campus newspaper. This was during the Vietnam War, a period he describes as "a Mecca if you were writing a column for a college paper" (Silet "Sun" 11).

At Emory he got his first taste of novel writing, only it wasn't his novel. In his freshman year, his writing professor asked him if he would like to help a young doctor named Neil B. Shulman shape some of his stories and reminiscences into a novel. He agreed, and the book, entitled *Finally.... I'm a Doctor*, was eventually published in 1976. The two collaborated on a second novel with the unusual title *What? ... Dead Again?* that was published three years later. A popular film based on the book, now re-titled *Doc Hollywood* and starring Michael J. Fox, was released in 1991. Although Hiaasen's name does not appear on the cover, he received 50% of the book royalties from the sales of *Doc Hollywood*.

After two years at Emory, he decided to switch his major to journalism. Emory didn't have a journalism program, so he transferred to the University of Florida in Gainesville. While there he became a columnist for the college paper, the *Independent Florida Alligator*. Hiaasen has described this period as "a poisonous time to be coming of age" (*Kick* xv), what with Nixon as president, the war in Vietnam accelerating, and criminal activities taking place in the White House that would soon lead to the Watergate scandal. "It was a hell of a time to go into journalism because you felt so inspired by what the *New York Times* and *Washington Post* were doing about Watergate," he said (Freeman).

Writing a column during such turbulent times was "a piece of cake" with each day providing a "wonderful new atrocity. It was a splendid opportunity for a columnist to learn the value of contempt, ridicule, and satire" (Pleasants 248). Mixing humor with outrage, he found, was a successful formula for a column. "I really tried to work hard at making the columns funny, so that even if people didn't necessarily agree with me, the humor was there. That's because it's a very hard thing to be funny about serious subjects, it's one of the toughest things you can do, but I enjoyed making people laugh" (Pleasants 249).

A pair of *Alligator* columns illustrate how he used humor. In one, written nine months before Nixon actually resigned, he imagines the President refusing to quit after being impeached, vowing to remain in the White House until the end of his term in 1977, confident that the only offense he can be charged with is loitering. In another, an end-of-the-year column, he handed out comic awards to newsworthy winners: he gave the 1973 Horse's Ass Award to Secretariat, the first horse in twenty-five years to win the Triple crown, because that was the only part of his anatomy that the other jockeys got a good look at all year.

He also worked as a student intern at the *Gainesville Sun*, covering local high school football games. In one story he reported that the kicker missed a last-second field goal that lost the game for his team. Early the next morning, he got an angry phone call from the kicker's mother who screamed at him and blamed him for ruining her son's life. He hung up and got an unlisted phone number. He also decided he no longer wanted to be a sports writer.

A second job—writing press releases for the University Police Department—taught him another valuable lesson. Riding around on duty with the campus police gave him an insight into how cops work, although the most serious crimes on campus tended to be bicycle thefts. The job also taught him what it was like to be on the other end of a reporter's calls: "I think it's a good experience for anyone who wants to be a journalist to sit there and answer questions from journalists" (Kenan).

Within a few days after graduating with a journalism degree in 1974, he began working as a general assignment reporter for *Cocoa Today* (now *Florida Today*), the precursor of *USA Today*, both of which were owned by Al Neuharth. After two years at *Cocoa Today*, the *Miami Herald* offered him a position at their Broward County bureau, near his childhood home. The job promised a boost in pay, a significant factor to a young man with a wife and child. Also, his father had just passed away (from complications of esophageal cancer at age fifty) and with his sisters away at college and his younger brother getting ready to go, coming home to be near his mother sealed the deal. He would eventually buy a house two doors down from the one he grew up in. (His mother died in 2016 at the age of eighty-eight.)

A few months later, the *St. Petersburg Times* offered him a job. To keep him, the *Herald* offered him a position at the Miami city desk. He started out

Introduction

there as a general assignment reporter, then moved to the *Herald*'s investigative team, researching and writing in-depth articles about corruption in the Bahamas, drug smuggling in Key West, and dangerous and incompetent doctors. The latter two were honored as finalists for the prestigious Pulitzer prize. In 1985, he became a regular columnist for the paper, which despite his growing success as a novelist he has continued to write ever since. Hiaasen's novelistic career began as a direct outgrowth of his investigative work. In that particular kind of newspaper work, he says, "You're up to your ass in files. You're putting together these big projects, but you're not writing every day. If you like to write, at the end of the day you're gnawing on your fingernails. I wrote because I needed to write" (Bowman "Carl"). And so in the early 1980s, while a still a member of the newspaper's investigative team, he and fellow *Herald* journalist Bill Montalbano teamed up to write a trio of crime thrillers; the first two drew heavily upon Hiaasen's reporting on the drug trade, the third was based on Montalbano's experiences in China.

Hiaasen's first solo effort as a novelist was *Tourist Season*, which came out in 1986. A cover blurb by John D. MacDonald and a glowing review by Tony Hillerman in the *New York Times* helped the debut novelist gain an audience. His next novel, *Double Whammy* (1987), is notable for the introduction of Skink, a former governor of Florida who lives like a hermit in the woods, who has become his most famous character, regularly making brief appearances in several later novels. With his fourth novel, *Native Tongue* (1991), he moved from Putnam to the prestigious publishing house of Alfred A. Knopf, where he began working with legendary editor Sonny Mehta. His very next novel, *Strip Tease* (1993), was the first to land on the *New York Times* bestseller list.

Between 1986 and 2002, Hiaasen published a total of nine novels, most of them bestsellers that made him famous and earned him widespread critical acclaim. He was admittedly surprised then when an editor asked if he was interested in writing a book for kids. His first reaction was, "Are you out of your freakin' mind? Have you not read any of my grown-up novels" ("BookExpo")? But at the time, his stepson was eleven and his nieces and a nephew were about the same age, certainly too young to read his adult fiction. He thought, "Wouldn't it be great to write a book that I could give to them without getting them taken away to the Division of Family Services" (Wappler). If the experiment didn't work out, at least he would have one book he could give to the kids in his family.

Hoot more than worked out: it sold well, won a prestigious Newbery

Introduction: Biography

Honor Award in 2003, and was chosen in 2005 as the selection for the "Read Together, Florida" project in which all Floridians are encouraged to read the same book. It was also made into a movie in 2006 and is now a popular reading assignment in middle-school classrooms around the country.

Hiaasen didn't originally plan to write more than one novel for young readers, but the success of *Hoot* inspired him to try another, *Flush*, which spent over a year on the *New York Times* bestseller list. He had now become a recognizable name in the field of Young Adult fiction. Inspired by his commercial success and by an outpouring of letters from young readers, he decided to continue writing more. Over the next decade he would alternate between both genres, and his output now totals nineteen novels, fourteen for adults and five for children.

Besides writing, the other major passion in his life is fishing, especially fly fishing. It is his escape and his salvation, so he tries to grab as much time on the water as he can. "It's not a reward," he says, "but an absolute necessity" (Burke "Last"). Being out on the water gives him a sense of peace. It also inspires him and reminds him why he writes what he does:

> I get the chance to fish some places in Florida that probably look much like they did one thousand years ago. I have to take my impressions away from those places to get pumped up about the recklessness with which many politicians go about dealing with what's left of our resources. It's hard for someone who doesn't have that connection to the natural world—that dazzling world where you're being totally immersed, emotionally and physically, in the life around you—to appreciate how precious it is. I don't think I could write like I do without the connection I have to the outdoors that fly fishing has given me [Santella 48].

Few of his readers may be aware of his national reputation as a fly fisherman: he is a six-time champion of the Islamorada Fall Fly Fishing Tournament and a multiple winner of the Mercury Outboards Bonefishing World Championship. His collection of flies was featured in an issue of *MidCurrent* and in 2012 *Fly Rod & Reel Magazine* named him Angler of the Year. Hiaasen says he would consider it a compliment to be described as a fisherman who happens to write.

Music is another of his interests. He's an amateur guitarist who likes to bang on the instrument when his writing is bogged down. He has even occasionally played some gigs with the Rock Bottom Remainders, the band of famous authors formed in 1992 (whose members have included Dave Barry, Stephen King, Amy Tan, Ridley Pearson, and Scott Turow among others). According to Barry—who has said that, "Playing guitar is the one thing Carl

Introduction

can't do well" (Freeman)—Hiaasen appeared on stage with his guitar teacher who kept shouting out the chords he was supposed to play.

He also numbers several famous musicians among his friends and fans. Jimmy Buffet wrote a song about Skip Wiley and collaborated with him on the film version of *Hoot*. Roger McGuinn became a friend after Hiaasen named a dog after him in *Sick Puppy*; Hiaasen later introduced him to the Rock Bottom Remainders, and he later became a regular member. Hiaasen also got to meet the Rolling Stones after learning that Keith Richards and Ron Wood were fans of his novels.

But no music-related friendship meant more to him than that with rocker Warren Zevon. They first met in LA in 1991, when Hiaasen was signing books during a promotional tour for *Native Tongue*, whose main character, Joe Wilder, was a big fan of Zevon's. Once notorious for his drunken escapades, Zevon by this time in his life was clean and sober. The two men formed a bond based on a shared sense of dark humor and a love of writing. They later even collaborated on three songs: "Seminole Bingo" and "Rottweiler Blues" appeared on Zevon's *Mutineer* CD in 1995; "Basket Case," one of the songs Hiaasen wrote for Jimmy Stoma in *Basket Case*, appeared on Zevons's CD *My Ride's Here* in 2002.

Hiaasen and his first wife Connie divorced in 1996. A few years later he met Fenia Clizer, who was managing a restaurant in the Keys where he would often eat alone and read a book. They married in 1999 and he became stepfather to her eight-year-old son Ryan by a previous marriage. A year later she gave birth to a son they named Quinn. Shortly afterwards, his older son Scott's wife gave birth to twins, making him both a new father and a grandfather in the same year. "I'm waiting for the call from Jerry Springer," he joked (Adams).

There's something of a Dr. Jekyll and Mr. Hyde quality about Hiaasen. Behind a boyish, affable exterior lurks a twisted imagination capable of creating bizarre characters and diabolical situations. He has been described as looking like "a tallish, lean, but graying college sophomore on summer break, driving an ice cream truck around the neighborhood" (Shacochis) and "a poster for the very normal, very straight, all-American male. If a casting director received his headshot, he would send him to read for a remake of 'My Three Sons'" (Hamill). On the other hand, Pete Hamill likened him to serial killer Ted Bundy in the sense that "his open-faced boyish appearance belies the sensationally dark sensibility that shows up in his fiction" (Rosenbaum 124). As Dave Barry said of his longtime friend, "It's a good thing he's

Introduction: Biography

able to write books and kill bonefish or else he might be an ax murderer. And a good one. And a likable one" (Patterson).

Hiaasen has been called "the Mark Twain of the crime novel" (Hillerman), the "Hieronymous Bosch of mystery writers" (Ott), and "a South Florida hybrid of Jonathan Swift, Randy Newman and Elmore Leonard" (Viertel). What these statements all have in common in an attempt to describe his blend of some of the traditional features of crime and mystery writing with an outrageous sense of humor that often has a biting sting to it.

It is his unique combination of crime, comedy, and satiric commentary that has brought him a readership that extends far beyond just fans of crime fiction. And far beyond just readers in Florida as his audience is now global wide. For many of these readers, Hiaasen is "America's finest satirical novelist" (Adams), "one of the most important writers of the last half century" (Burke "Last"), and "a great American writer about the great American subjects of ambition, greed, vanity, and disappointment" (Harris).

He is all of these things, but above all else, he's an entertainer. As Janet Maslin so simply and eloquently put it in describing his appeal, "The arrival of each of his new novels makes the world a slightly happier place" ("Everglades").

1

Journalism

Hiaasen the Reporter

Like many great novelists before him (Charles Dickens, Mark Twain, George Orwell, Ernest Hemingway, Gabriel García Márquez), and even several fellow crime writers (Laura Lippman, John Sanford, Edna Buchanan, Michael Connelly), Carl Hiaasen began as a journalist. Working as a reporter is great training for learning how to write effective prose and how to structure a story. Interviewing people also teaches one how to listen closely to the way people talk—good preparation for writing dialogue.

> All the senses you use covering a news story are the same senses you use when creating a scene for a novel. You have to bring the scene to life in the same way in fiction as you would when you go back to the newsroom and empty it out of your notebook into a story or a column. The training you get in a newsroom is very valuable for the writing of fiction, That's probably why so many novelists have come from a journalism background [Shackle].

Hiaasen began his professional journalism career at age twenty-one when he was hired by *Cocoa Today*. It was a heady time to become a reporter: the Watergate scandal was breaking and Nixon was about to resign. "I didn't go in thinking, 'I want to work for *The Washington Post* and bring down a crooked president,'" he says. Instead, he thought, "There are stories like this all over the place, and wherever I'm working I want to be able to turn over rocks and shine a spotlight on these cockroaches" (Bonner).

Some of the small-town stuff he had to cover drove him crazy. For example, one of his first assignments—interviewing Adam West, TV's original Batman, while he was struggling to fit into his costume before an appearance at a local mall—might have given him second thoughts about his chosen profession. On the other hand, working for a small newspaper did provide many valuable experiences for a fledgling journalist with talent and ambition, and he enjoyed the opportunity to write feature stories for their Sunday magazine as well as news reports.

In 1974, he joined the *Miami Herald* as a general assignment reporter and later a feature writer for *Tropic*, the paper's Sunday magazine. But his most serious work was as an investigative reporter. In 1979, he and fellow reporter Patrick Malone teamed up with two-time Pulitzer Prize winner Gene Miller in investigating and writing an eight-part series entitled "Dangerous Doctors: A Medical Dilemma." (The series was edited by William Montalbano, who would later co-author three crime thrillers with Hiaasen.)

The opening installment, written by Hiaasen, begins in dramatic fashion: "Dr. David Romano had one of his surgery patients wheeled out of the hospital while her fractured pelvis was still mending. He drove her to his apartment, had sexual intercourse with her, then took her back to the hospital. Today, Dr. Romano practices medicine in Tampa" ("Dangerous" 2). What follows is a disturbing account of incompetent doctors and a medical board that is too slow, too forgiving, and too protective of fellow doctors to do anything about them. Over a five-year period, the Florida Board of Medical examiners, composed of ten doctors and one layman, received 1561 complaints but revoked only ten medical licenses. The series won the 1979 Heywood Broun Award from the Newspaper Guild and was a finalist for the 1980 Pulitzer Prize in Public Service; it also resulted in a statewide effort to replace the board of doctors with a Department of Consumer Protection.

Hiaasen learned a valuable lesson about writing by working alongside Miller: a newspaper story had to be accurate and factual, but it didn't have to be bland. Effective use of color and detail could add human interest and impact to even the most routine story:

> Gene believed that no matter what kind of project we were working on, the whole trick is impact. And there is no impact without any involvement of your readers. You have to get them involved in a story. If you can't get them past the jump, you've failed not only as a writer but as a journalist. That was Gene's point, and he was right. It made for a hell of a lot more interesting newspaper [Stanton 22].

In 1980, he and two other reporters (Richard Morin and Susan Sachs) under the direction of editor James Savage spent five months examining thousands of documents and conducting more than 200 interviews for a series about the lucrative marijuana smuggling operation in Key West. The eye-opening six-part report on their findings, entitled "Key West: Smuggler's Island," appeared in March 1980 and exposed not only the extent of the drug trade but the related corruption it produced: law enforcement agencies unable or unwilling to stop it as well as prosecutors who failed to prosecute. The series prompted Florida Governor Bob Graham to appoint a special prosecutor to investigate the *Herald*'s findings and earned for Hiaasen and his fellow team members the honor of being named as finalists for the 1981 Pulitzer Prize for Local Investigative Specialized Reporting.

Hiaasen considers a series of articles he wrote in 1982 with fellow *Herald* staffer Brian Duffy entitled "North Key Largo: The Last Stand" to be his proudest accomplishment as a journalist. The pair spent two months poring over documents and interviewing planners, developers, environmentalists, and county officials regarding plans to build some fifteen condominium and hotel developments on 12,000 acres of unspoiled wilderness in North Key Largo, fifty miles south of Miami. The environmental consequences of such a massive development that was projected to house as many as 45,000 residents would be devastating: not only would the last pristine stretch of unspoiled land in the Keys be bulldozed over, the development would pose a major threat to John Pennekamp Coral Reef State Park, second largest living reef system in the world. Also threatened would be the nearby habitat of six endangered species, among them the Southern Bald Eagle and the 50 to 100 American crocodiles living there.

How could this be allowed to happen? Hiaasen and Duffy uncovered evidence of futile efforts by local agencies who were powerless to stop it, serious conflicts of interest, and local government's lack of ability or desire to control development. Developers routinely dredged, cleared, and excavated without getting required approval. Much of the reporting focused on Port Bougainville, a 406-acre development with 2806 planned housing units, the largest project ever started in the Keys. Hiaasen and Duffy found that state, county, and regional officials required by law to review the plans for the development never even saw them until the reporters showed them copies. It turns out that the original plan, which was approved in under two minutes several years earlier, allowed for alterations due to "changing market conditions." This gave a green light to the developers to proceed unchecked for years.

As a result of the series, Governor Bob Graham called for an investigation into the matter. One month later, state officials sued to gain an injunction to halt the Bougainville project. The following day, the developer agreed to halt all construction and submit all site plans to a comprehensive review. Eventually the whole project went bust after the bank foreclosed on the developer and the project went into receivership. The state later began purchasing vast tracts of North Key Largo for preservation. In a final victory for nature, demolition of what was left of the abandoned Port Bougainville project began to take place in 2016.

Hiaasen took justifiable pride in *The Herald*'s role in setting into motion actions that led to the demise of the project. "That's why I have great affection for the newspaper," he says. "All that's going to be preserved, so my grandkids can go there and take a boat along the shoreline and still see the bonefish and the tarpon and the wildlife that are there now. That's ten times more important than anything else you can do" (McMahon 98). In one of the first columns he would later write for the paper, he describes the now abandoned site as looking not like a painting by Cezanne, as the advertising for the project had promised, but like "Salvador Dali on a bad day" (*Kick* 361). He concluded this way: "Each officious drone who said yes to this extravaganza ought to be forced to spend a day on North Key Largo, walking the property with his own children. Explaining the scars, the rubble, the whole atrocious legacy" (*Kick* 363).

In 1984, Hiaasen and fellow *Herald* reporter Jim McGee spent five months investigating drug smuggling and corruption in the Bahamas, which resulted in a six-part series the two wrote, "A Nation For Sale: Corruption in the Bahamas," that appeared in September of that year. The series focused on the major role the Bahamas play in the smuggling of drugs into Florida (as much as 40% of the Florida-bound cocaine and marijuana pass through the islands) and the inevitable corruption that infects every strata of society all the way up to the Prime Minister himself.

Being a member of an investigative team, where every article is heavily edited and lawyered, had its challenges.

> Every shred of subjectivity is beaten out of that work, and it has to be, because you are dealing with many cases [with] high libel potential. You are dealing with serious allegations against people. You are disciplined and trained to take yourself out of every sentence in that story. Your point of view should be the last thing that hits the readers, but you should still be able to make a strong point [Pleasants 250].

Because so much of his time during this period was spent investigating, he had to find other outlets for his writing. He wrote several feature stories for *Tropic*, the *Herald*'s Sunday magazine, which gave him an opportunity to write more freely in his own voice:

> You bring a whole different approach to it on the bigger stuff—the pace of the storytelling, the way information is parsed out—you don't have to go for the inverted pyramid lead. You've got a long time to tell a story and build drama and employ some of the devices of literature in getting people engrossed whether it's a feature story or a heavy, important story [Stanton 21].

"Killer: The Life and Death of a Cocaine Cowboy" (3 Jan. 1982) is a chilling account of a Cuban thug from Union City, New Jersey, named Miguel

1. Journalism

Miranda who failed to show up to begin serving a ten-year sentence for distributing cocaine and heroin. For the next eight years, he lived the good life as a federal fugitive under the less-than-watchful eyes of the Miami police. Not that he was hard to find: he openly rode on Lear Jets, had his picture taken with Frank Sinatra, and was even arrested once (under a pseudonym) for carrying a concealed weapon, but after posting bond he simply walked away. During this time he was also smuggling mountains of cocaine into Florida, and over the final eighteen months of his life, before finally being gunned down by the police, he committed ten brutal murders.

On the other hand, "The Bird Snatchers" (10 Oct. 1982), a richly detailed feature about the illegal smuggling of exotic birds into the U.S., is written in a far more humorous style, which is apparent from its opening line: "Blame it all on Fred, the wiseacre cockatoo who upstaged TV's detective 'Baretta'" (9). While the illegal trafficking in rare birds is serious, Hiaasen's style exploits the subject for some smiles, as in this description of the efforts to obtain fake documentation for the export of such birds into the U.S. as "the underground Polly-want-a passport business" (10) or his conclusion that "As long as the parrot-on-every-patio trend continues, the smuggling and theft of these magnificent birds is likely to thrive" (12).

Hiaasen's colleagues are unanimous in their praise of his journalistic talent. "Carl is a hell of a digger," said reporting partner Brian Duffy (who would later become editor of *U.S. News & World Report*). "He loved to get that telling detail, whether from the fifth re-interview of a source or from a mind-numbing government document" (Weeks 90). Jim Savage, Hiaasen's editor on several investigative pieces, praised him as "the most talented journalist I've worked with" (*Kick* xvii) and observed that, "He can build a story, like a craftsman builds a house. He could see from the start what one quote, what illustrative anecdote the story would need, whereas the rest of us would be gassing about for weeks" (Freeman).

Hiaasen, the Columnist

In 1985, Hiaasen was offered the position of columnist for the paper, which he readily accepted and which, despite his later success as a best-selling author of novels for adults and young readers, he continues to write. His columns initially appeared three times a week in the Metro section. He later cut back to two appearances weekly, and when the size of the columns on the

Metro page shrunk to 600 words, he moved to the Op-Ed page where he was allowed greater length. It was also a better home for the columns which over the years had gradually transformed into more traditional opinion pieces.

Not every journalist is up to the daunting challenge of turning out a column on a strict deadline two or three times a week. Columns must have topical urgency, express a clearly stated opinion, and immediately engage the reader, all in the limited space of 600–700 words. The special challenge Hiaasen faced was moving from the discipline of investigative reporting, where every line is scrutinized by editors and lawyers and all subjectivity is purged from the prose, to a column where he would be free to say whatever he wanted and in whatever style he chose.

Hiaasen was ideally suited to the challenge: he had some previous column-writing experience in college; as a person who always had strong opinions, he was comfortable following the first commandment of a good column: "You're not being paid to sit on a fence and scratch your chin and say, 'On the one hand this' and 'On the other hand that,'" he notes. "You're getting paid for your opinion. So don't be a candy-ass about it" (Leopold); as an investigative reporter, he was a firm believer in the principle that when a person in a position of public trust does something wrong, no matter which political party he belongs to, it should go in the newspaper; and finally, having already begun to, in his words, "cut loose and have some fun" (Silet "Sun" 68) in the writing of his first solo novel, *Tourist Season*, he had already found a distinctive satiric voice that would prove to be ideally suited to a column.

Hiaasen wasn't hired to be a humor columnist. Dave Barry, whose column began appearing in the *Herald* two years earlier, famously filled that role. He would instead be a combination watchdog and advocate, extolling the virtues of honesty, decency, accountability, and common sense among those in charge of the public good and attacking all those who fail to live by those virtues. But since humor had always been important to him, he employed it generously in his columns, both to make them as entertaining to the reader as he possibly could, but also as a way of ridiculing individuals and actions he felt deserved it.

The columnist has the best job at the newspaper, says Hiaasen, because he can "cherry pick the best stories and just take off on them. You have the luxury and also the duty of writing what everyone else is thinking but that can't be in the news story because it's not objective. You're getting paid for your opinion" (Richards). Fortunately, he has plenty of strong opinions which he isn't afraid to express, no matter the consequences.

1. Journalism

While a column lacks the staying power of a novel or even a feature-length piece of reporting, it has an immediacy that books cannot have. "Day-to-day journalism is hard to beat for immediate feedback and the high that comes from pounding out something on deadline," he insists (Kenan). It also allows a writer to develop an emotional connection with the reader. Newspaper columnists run the risk of preaching only to the choir, but when that choir hasn't found its voice or its voice isn't being listened to, it can be comforting for them to read someone who can articulate their concerns in such an effective way.

In this unfortunate current age of "fake" news and "alternative" facts, Hiaasen is strictly old-fashioned, a devout adherent of former U.S. Senator Daniel Patrick Moynihan's famous dictum: "Everyone is entitled to his own opinion, but not to his own facts." His columns are as fact-based as his newspaper articles. Typically he begins with an actual news event or published story and then expresses an opinion that is supported by research and bolstered by quotations, statistics, and other evidence.

His primary focus is divided between Miami politics and state-wide issues. In many instances, however, though the issues are local the relevance is universal. Scoundrels are everywhere, dumb politicians are dumb politicians no matter where they live, and environmental issues are everybody's concern. He often addresses national issues that have a Florida connection (the Elián González custody case in 2000, the contested Florida vote count in the presidential election that same year, the BP oil spill in the Gulf of Mexico in 2010), and since moving to the Op Ed page he has expanded his scope to include a wider range of issues. For example, he was one of the first to satirize the presidential ambitions of Donald Trump; in a 2011 column, he has the future President defending his record—"I'm not a racist. What I am is an egotistical gasbag who will say or do anything for attention"—and his hair—"No orangutans were harmed during the weaving of my toupee" (*Dance* 309).

Hiaasen's favorite column subjects won't be a surprise to readers of his fiction: political corruption, cronyism, and ineptitude; the various threats to Florida's natural environment, especially the state's unbridled growth; the many faces of human absurdity. These are the subjects that fuel his passion, ignite his ire, and inspire his novels, and he is relentless in sounding the alarm whenever he feels it is necessary.

Hiaasen never picks on the little guy. He aims his rants at the big shots who violate the public trust. He names the offenders, hangs colorful nicknames on them ("Howard the Rat," "Loophole Lucien," "Mayor Loco"), ridicules them with comic putdowns, (he says that what one golf-loving elected official knows about leadership "wouldn't fill the dimple of a Titleist" (*Paradise* 281)), and describes them in memorable ways (he calls one mayor of Miami "a pernicious little ferret").

He saves his strongest venom for the Florida legislature in Tallahassee, whose members he has vilified over the years as "nitwits," "stooges," "yahoos," "clowns," "knuckleheads," "prepaid toadies," "spineless blobs," "grandstanding boneheads," and "low-wattage trolls" for their dishonesty, incompetence, wasteful spending, inept oversight, and nonsensical laws. He began a 2011 column with this apology: "I once referred to a past legislature as a festival of whores, which in retrospect was a vile insult to the world's oldest profession." The current "lackluster assemblage in Tallahassee," he went on to declare, cannot be fairly compared to anything "except a rodeo of phonies and pimps" (*Dance* 126). Its insane antics once provoked this suggestion: "One way to save Florida tons of money, and loads of embarrassment, would be to abolish the Senate" (*Kick* 165).

Among his pet peeves are publicity-hungry politicians who come up with dumb ideas that grab headlines but defy logic and common sense. For example, he dubs Governor Bob Martinez "Bladder-Buster Bob" for proposing drug-testing for all first-time applicants for a Florida driver's license. He doesn't just scoff at the idea, he details the common-sense reasons why such a proposal would accomplish little (among other things, applicants would know in advance the date of the test and the proposal would affect only sixteen year olds and retirees moving to the state).

He routinely castigates zoning boards that continue to mindlessly approve the building of malls even when a study shows that there is a glut of 25 million square feet of shopping space in a tri-county area: "Any idiot could have predicted that not all these malls could make money—any idiot except the ones who approved them: the elected officials" (*Kick* 344). His frustration at the legislature's decision to authorize random drug tests for state workers, but then to exempt themselves from having to pee in a cup, prompted him to offer to pay for drug tests for all 160 state senators and representatives. (The offer was ignored). When the legislature takes up the subject of hurricane preparedness, decades of experience leads him to declare: "We all know what that means; absolutely nothing" (*Dance* 111).

His other major theme is the ongoing assault on Florida's natural environment. A plan to turn a 35-acre city park into a Grand Prix race track is but one example of the kind of thinking that infuriates him: "I guess the city commissioners couldn't help themselves. They saw this luscious hunk of bayfront not making money, just sitting there being a park, and they couldn't stand it. The shakes set in, then drooling; an uncontrollable urge to bulldoze. Apparently shrubbery was not the kind of green that Bicentennial Park was meant to sprout" (*Kick* 314).

The columns provide a factual background for much of what Hiaasen satirizes in his fiction; they also illustrate many of the comic and satiric techniques he employs so effectively in those books. One strategy common to both is to begin with a factual news item—e.g., state medical examiners have acknowledged secretly removing parts of the brains of executed prisoners for use in laboratory studies of aberrant behavior—and then spin out a comic story about doing the same thing with the brains of state politicians.

The brains will be preserved in a mixture of formaldehyde and Johnnie Walker Red and made to feel right at home by being tested in an expensive suite on the top floor of the Tallahassee Hilton. One neurologist argues that because politicians' brains are smaller than those of other humans, they won't cost much to store, though he does admit he's having trouble recruiting experts to work on the project: "Doctors who wouldn't think twice about examining a bank robber's brain won't set foot in the same lab with a state senator's" (*Kick* 159). He does promise not to attempt to duplicate a previous study which found that when a U.S. Congressman's brain was placed beside a stack of $50 bills, it began quivering and inching closer to the cash.

Hiaasen's columns also illustrate his ability to grab the reader's attention right from the opening sentences: "Well, they don't call it Old Sparky for nothing. Florida's infamous electric chair went haywire again Tuesday, and Pedro Medina caught fire" (*Kick* 199); "The Romans managed to build 53,000 miles of road without once celebrating the accomplishment by dressing up in frog costumes" (*Kick* 337); "Like many other Americans, every time I take my family to a national park, I find myself thinking: *Wow! If I only had a gun...*" (*Dance* 245); "If P. T. Barnum were alive to watch the Metro Commission in action, he'd probably revise his famous axiom. Not only are suckers born every minute, they invariably get elected to political office" (*Kick* 324). He tempers his outrage with humor, and is especially effective in using biting ironic wit to make a point, as in this commentary about the historic treatment of the Seminoles in Florida:

> Look at all the terrific things Florida has done for them. Remember when we took those millions of acres of ranch land off their hands, just so they wouldn't have to be bothered with platting, zoning and development rights? Why, we even resettled the

tribe in the Everglades, where the land was under water, so they could concentrate on more lucrative enterprises such as alligator wrestling [*Paradise* 411].

His humor often tends toward the absurd. For example, a proposal to stage a horse race on the beach gets him thinking about some added attractions, like having a celebrity "scoop-up" between races or holding a "Dodge the Muffin" contest for the kiddies. He also comes up with a new directive spelling out proper etiquette at University of Miami football games: "Alcohol should be used only in moderation at the Orange Bowl. 'Moderation' is hereby defined as the upright consumption of beer and/or hard liquor from cans, bottles, flasks, jugs, coolers, carafes, decanters, pitchers, crocks, urns, bowls, tureens, canteens, wineskins and 55-gallon drums" (*Paradise* 320).

While there is a direct connection between Hiaasen's columns and his fiction—fellow columnist Pete Hamill once observed that, "If you think of the columns as drawings and the novels as paintings, they make up an absolutely coherent and consistent world view" (Seymour)—there are some key differences between the two. As a columnist, he is bound by facts, and there are limits as to how much he can exaggerate the truth for comic purposes. In the novels, he is free to make up facts and exaggerate at will. And since a novel offers a much larger canvas, there is more room for his humor. Most important of all, he can devise satisfying punishments for his villains. In his columns, he can only hope that his targets get convicted of their crime or defeated in the next election. In the novels, he is judge, jury and executioner, and the fate he creates for his characters plays a key role in his satiric takedown of them.

A good example of this is his treatment of Geraldo Rivera, a TV personality notorious for his sensationalist approach to the news. Any "newsman" like him who "gets so excited by the sight of his own face on camera that he darn near hyperventilates" is an affront to serious journalists like Hiaasen (*Kick* 111). In a column, however, the most he can do is ridicule him and hope for an end to his "self-serving hokum." In his fiction, however, it's a whole different story. In *Skin Tight*, he creates a fictionalized version of Rivera named Reynaldo Flemm, whom he gleefully makes fun of in hilarious detail. But he can do more than simply ridicule him: he has him die during a tummy-tuck procedure at the hands of a plastic surgeon he's hoping to expose on camera. In a final bit of poetic justice, his naked body ends up at a medical school in Guadeloupe where students who have no idea who he is can practice their skills on him.

Three collections of Hiaasen's columns have been published—*Kick Ass*

1. Journalism

(1999), *Paradise Screwed* (2001), and *Dance of the Reptiles* (2014)—giving readers of his fiction an opportunity to enjoy an aspect of his writing they may be unfamiliar with. While many of the columns are too topical and too local to be of much interest to outsiders, others still retain their sting, and several of the subjects he rails against will be familiar to readers outside Florida. Betrayal of the public trust is not just a local issue, and politicians who roll over compliantly "at the whiff of money" or who value profit over the environment can be found virtually everywhere.

How has he managed to produce a regular column for over three decades while at the same time also writing nineteen novels? "Easy," he jokes. "You write every waking hour and have no life" ("Biography"). In fact, the two careers satisfy different needs: "I do the column because it is important," he says. "I do the books because it's therapy" (Pleasants 262). They complement one other, with the journalism feeding the imagination, which inspires the fiction. Journalistic discipline also helps: "I was taught to write on a deadline," he says. "Instead of having six weeks to write a poem, I had an hour and a half to write 400 words" ("Biography"). Setting aside a day or two each week for the column still leaves plenty of time for his fiction.

Hiaasen's long and distinguished career as a columnist has earned him his profession's highest honors: the Denver Press Club's Damon Runyon Award in 2004 and the Ernie Pyle Lifetime Achievement Award given by the National Society of Newspaper Columnists in 2010. In 2011, he also received the Florida Lifetime Achievement Award in Writing.

But as the years have gone by, it's only inevitable that a "here-we-go-again" feeling has occasionally crept into his work. But while he confesses he sometimes gets tired of the whole enterprise, he carries on, in part out fear that because of cutbacks in the newspaper industry, he won't be replaced if he quits. He also feels a strong sense of duty: "I go through periods all the time when I say, to hell with it; I don't want to do it anymore. I'm tired, I can't do that and the books at the same time. But then you get this mail, and people seem to really depend on you in the morning over their breakfast cereal to at least say what they have been thinking and ranting and raving about" (Pleasants 252).

He considers it a privilege to be able to write a column in the newspaper he grew up reading, and appreciates the opportunity it gives him to make a difference in a place he loves. He knows he can't solve the problems he writes about singlehandedly. All he can do, he says, is to keep holding "the corruption up to the light and, if the people decide that's how they want their state run, then that's their decision, but at least they should know what's going on" (Williams 15).

And so the man once described by an editor at the *Herald* as "the voice of every person who is fed up with pompous politicians and corruption, who hates to see Florida raped and pillaged" (Cheakalos) happily intends to continue what has turned into a lifelong crusade to "Turn over rocks. Dig out the truth. Kick ass" (*Kick* xiii).

2

Nonfiction

Team Rodent: How Disney Devours the World *(1998)*

In 1998, Hiaasen was invited by Random House to contribute to The Library of Contemporary Thought, a new series of short nonfiction books aimed at giving writers an opportunity to explore topics of interest to themselves and their readers. The series would include such authors as Jimmy Carter on aging, Pete Hamill on journalism at the end of the twentieth century, Anna Quindlen on how reading changed her life, and Stephen Jay Gould on science and religion in the fullness of life. Hiaasen chose to write about a subject he certainly has strong feelings about in a book provocatively titled, *Team Rodent: How Disney Devours the World*.

Hiaasen had previously expressed some negativity toward Disney World in his writings. In his 1991 novel, *Native Tongue*, he attacked the Magic Kingdom indirectly. The novel features a theme park called the Amazing Kingdom of Thrills that was built by Francis X. Kingsbury as competition to Disney World. Despite his contempt for Disney, which is shown by the pornographic tattoo on his arm depicting sex between Mickey and Minnie Mouse, he nonetheless mimics the company's successful formula of fakery. His rodeo ride is located in a corral with brown-dyed dirt, balsa fence posts, and polyethylene cowshit. And his version of the Magic Kingdom's nightly pageant embraces Disney's feel-good philosophy by sugarcoating Florida history with cheery farm workers break-dancing in a sugar-cane field and a bikini-clad Seminole princess dancing a sexy lambada.

A 1995 column began with this pronouncement: "Well, Disney kicked us in the coconuts again" *(Paradise* 19). His complaint was prompted by Disney's announcement that it was building a $750 million expansion of Walt Disney World by adding a fourth theme park, the Animal Kingdom. One objection was that Disney was delivering yet another cruel blow to South

Florida's tourism by further monopolizing the tourist dollar: "Even folks brave enough to come here won't be able to afford it after Mickey and Minnie finish rifling their pockets" (20). Although he admits that sabotage is an ugly word, he offers one helpful suggestion. Because Disney's new Animal Kingdom has excluded all of Florida's own native species, he encourages visitors to the park to bring along a little friend—a Bufo toad, a walking catfish, maybe even a box of fire ants—to "enhance" the menagerie. Better still, how about an alligator? "What would you pay to see Donald Duck up to his feathery butt in alligators?" he asks (20).

In a 1998 column about the actual opening of the new Animal Kingdom theme park, Hiaasen playfully satirizes Disney's efforts to sanitize every little thing. Since this is Disney's first experience with real animals rather than the animatronic kind whose behavior can controlled, he provides a helpful list of officially scripted Disney explanations for park tour guides. For example, animal scratching and licking must be called "grooming." The inevitable poop produced by a thousand animals must always be described as "droppings." No animal ever dies; they are "lethargic," "inactive," or simply "napping." And they never mate, they only "wrestle" or "frolic" or "romp." The advice ends with this directive: "Now go out there and give these wonderful folks an authentic true-life jungle experience, droppings and all" (*Kick* 157).

Hiaasen's opening salvo in *Team Rodent* is aimed at what he sees as the detrimental effect Disney has had on his beloved state. The company unquestionably has pumped untold millions of dollars into the state economy and provided thousands of jobs, but most of the tourist dollars never leave Central Florida. And although Disney's parks encompass a 43-square-mile area, except for the occasional buzzard victim of road kill one never sees any evidence of the real Florida. Once inside the park, visitors are subjected to "a sublime and unbreakable artificiality" (80). Outside the park, thanks to all the tacky businesses that have grown up eager to get their hands on whatever crumbs Mickey and Minnie leave, all one sees is "an execrable panorama of suburban blight" (5).

> But Disney's most detrimental effect is on Florida's image of itself: The absolute worst thing Disney did was to change how people in Florida thought about money; nobody had ever dreamed there could be so much. Bankers, lawyers, real-estate salesmen, hoteliers, restaurateurs, farmers, citrus growers—everyone in Mickey's orb had to drastically recalibrate the concepts of growth, prosperity, and what was possible. Suddenly there were no limits. Merely by showing up, Disney had dignified blind greed in a state pioneered by undignified greedheads [4].

This new way of thinking resulted in the disappearance of most of the real Florida as developers begin plowing under every inch of the state's natural beauty they could in pursuit of the almighty dollar.

The sheer magnitude of the Disney Empire is truly breathtaking; in addition to a dozen theme parks around the world, it includes several movie studios (Walt Disney Pictures, Touchstone, Miramax), TV networks (ABC, ESPN, the Disney Channel, A&E, the History Channel, Lifetime) as well as numerous radio stations, hotels, housing developments, even a cruise line. According to Hiaasen, "Disney touches virtually every human being in America for a profit" (10).

But more than its immense size, it's how the company uses its power that concerns Hiaasen. "Disney is so good at being good that it manifests an evil; so uniformly efficient and courteous, so dependably clean and conscientious, so unfailingly *entertaining* that it's unreal, and therefore is an agent of pure wickedness" (18). To Hiaasen, Disney is really in the business of "superimposing its own recreational-based reality" (19) in order to project an "overpowering brand of make-believe" (44). The message in all of this is that "America's values ought to reflect those of the Walt Disney Company and not the other way around" (9).

In his fiction, Hiaasen loves to expose the fake and phony in our culture. No one is guiltier of promoting fakery better than Disney. For example, nature is apparently never quite beautiful enough for Disney. Florida's lakes, which are often tea-colored from cypress bark, don't fit into the company's vision of reality, so they must be drained and cypresses removed so that the new improved blue-water lakes can be more pleasing to tourists. Disney isn't so much exploiting nature, says Hiaasen, as striving to improve on it, "constantly fine-tuning God's work" (18).

Sometimes, however, Disney is guilty of overreach. Hiaasen cites the example of the company's plan to build an amusement park with a history theme called "Disney's America" in Virginia. The location of the project—just a few miles from the Manassas National Battlefield, site of the battles of Bull Run—sparked local opposition concerned that this time it wasn't Nature but American history that Disney sought to "polish up and market as a fun ride" (23). Civil War historians and others, aghast at the prospect that "Mickey and Minnie soon would be dancing on the graves of Civil War heroes" (24), forced Disney to abandon the project.

Team Rodent isn't entirely one-sided. Hiaasen doesn't deny that Disney has brought joy to countless millions of children around the globe. He also credits the company with forward-thinking in its decision to provide health insurance to partners of gay employees despite the threat of a boycott from Southern Baptists. Visitors to its theme parks and associated tourist attractions can be assured that nobody "provides a safer, more closely supervised brand of carefree than Team Rodent" (49). He even confesses that whenever he and his wife took their young son to Disney World, he always seemed to have a blast.

But Disney didn't get to be the Florida behemoth it is today without the complicity of one of Hiaasen's favorite targets, the Florida legislature. In the 1960s, the legislature "blitheringly" agreed to give the company whatever it wanted, and what it wanted was absolute autonomy. Under the title of the Reedy Creek Improvement District, Disney was granted the power of a private government with the authority to create its own building codes and hire its own inspectors, maintain its own fire department, and levy taxes. (In his book *Married to the Mouse*, Richard E. Fogelsong said the agreement turned Disney World into a "Vatican with Mouse ears" (5).) The company was even given the power, which it hasn't yet used, to build its own international airport and a nuclear power plant.

Disney is the happy recipient of plenty of free publicity thanks to the many press junkets it often arranges, but much of the blame for that resides with the journalists themselves. "Disney's publicists don't invite people like us to the Magic Kingdom for the pleasure of our company," Hiaasen points out (63). It's hard to believe any reporter's argument that free food and lodging don't compromise the reporting "when you see the stampede of foam-flecked Fourth Estate freeloaders at a Disney dinner buffet" (61). To the Atlanta columnist who insisted that all that free booty couldn't possibly influence her reporting—"What could you say bad about Disney anyway?" she announced—all one can say is she should get a copy of Hiaasen's book.

Team Rodent reads like a collection of extended Hiaasen columns. The eighty-two-page book is divided into nine chapters, each focusing on a different aspect of the Disney empire. It is solidly grounded in Hiaasen's own reporting, supplemented by personal experience, courts records, and a variety of published magazine and newspaper reports. As is the case with most of his columns, Hiaasen's anger is filtered through his typical comic style. For example, after reporting an incident in which a fully grown African lioness (named Lala after a character in Disney's *The Lion King*) had escaped from a roadside zoo near Disney World, Hiaasen indulges in this comic fantasy: "Sweet Jesus, just imagine: the hot-blooded 450-pound namesake of a Disney cartoon lion, bounding down Main Street U.S.A. (perhaps during the nightly SpectroMagic Parade!) and with one lightning swipe of a paw taking down Goofy or Pluto, or maybe one of those frigging chipmunks" (36).

The book also contains a generous helping of Hiaasen's typically witty phrases and descriptions: he dubs Disney's private-security force "Goofy's gendarmes" (35) and dismisses its infamous strict clothing and makeup rules as an "Aryan-android dress code" (19). He ridicules Disney's attempt in its Animal Kingdom park to recreate an African animal reserve on 500 acres with this snarky retort: "Typical Disney: Honey, I shrunk the Serengeti!" (68).

Not surprisingly, Disney wasn't happy with *Team Rodent*. Rather than address any of Hiaasen's criticisms, company spokesperson John Dreyer simply brushed off the book as "leftovers that have been heated up for a third time. He's continuing his fiction here" (Allen). But when he added, "I think he's afraid he would come here and have a good time," it casts doubts as to whether he even read the book in light of Hiaasen's admission in it that he and his family made several enjoyable visits to the park. When asked if Hiaasen would now achieve his longtime dream of being permanently banned from Disney World, Dreyer said that would never happen: "We welcome him," he said. "We'd even make him and his family grand marshals of a parade."

Tragically, the death in 2016 of a two-year-old boy who was snatched by an alligator and killed while playing at the edge of a lagoon at Disney's Grand Floridian Resort confirmed one of Hiaasen's fundamental concerns about the company. There were no signs anywhere warning guests of danger, despite the fact that in the ten-year period prior to the attack, workers had secretly removed over 250 of the animals from Disney properties. Wild alligators don't fit the Disney image, so instead of acknowledging the reality of danger on its property, the company simply pretended it didn't exist. It took the death of a toddler to force Disney to erect warning signs to prevent such a terrible thing from ever happening again.

The Downhill Lie *(2008)*

In 2005, after a thirty-two-year break from the game, Hiaasen made the foolish decision to begin golfing again. He took the game up as a young boy for two reasons: it allowed him to spend more time with his dad and it excused him from having to attend Sunday Mass with the rest of his family. But a few years later, as a twenty-year-old college student with a wife and small child, he had neither the time nor the money to continue playing. He quit the game in 1973.

Jump ahead thirty-two years. Hiaasen and his family had recently moved to Vero Beach from the Florida Keys, where one of his favorite pastimes was bonefishing. There being no bonefishing in Vero Beach and in need of "an unhealthy obsession" (18), he allowed himself to be talked into playing golf again. Why in the world would he again take up a game he never excelled at and one he confesses had dealt him mostly failure, angst, and exasperation. The answer: "I'm one sick bastard" (4). But a sick bastard with a sense of humor who is willing to make himself the butt of the joke.

The opening line of the preface—"There are so many people to blame for this book that it's hard to know where to begin"—sets the comic tone for what follows. He blames an old buddy for getting him golfing again, his good friend and fellow author Mike Lupica for conning him "primarily for his own sick amusement" into keeping a journal of the experience that forms much of the book, his editor for being "no help at all" in insisting he continue to write "no matter how rotten I was playing," and several "other good people who declined to intervene and put an end to my misery."

For readers of *The Downhill Lie: A Hacker's Return to a Ruinous Sport*, it's certainly a good thing that Hiaasen's return to the game wasn't a triumphant one. Who wants to read about a guy gloating about his success? Hiaasen's constant sense of failure as he (in his words) "thrashes," "lurches," "mangles," "chokes," "bungles," "slaughters," and "flails" his way around a golf course makes it far easier for the reader to identify with him. The frustrations of failure are a whole lot funnier than success would be.

Hiaasen has two strikes against him before he even begins: his Norwegian heritage and his writerly profession. Possessor of a "wintry Nordic soul" (68), he is a confirmed glass-half-empty kind of guy. Add to this the perfectionist bent of an author and he certainly lacks the proper temperament for golf. The entire effort proves to be a totally frustrating experience to a person who admits that as a writer he labors over every word and every line of dialogue until he gets it just right.

Ironically, what makes golf so frustrating for Hiaasen is the very same quality that makes him such a successful author. No one keeps score in writing. He can tinker with a chapter fifteen or twenty times, as he admits he sometimes does, until he gets it exactly right. The only thing that counts is the final version. In golf, however, at least to its honest players, there are no mulligans, no do-overs. Like it or not, you must count every sliced drive, shanked iron shot, and pulled putt.

Hiaasen's experiences—taking lessons, getting fitted for clubs, searching for the perfect driver, reading every golf magazine published, and ordering every cheesy gimmick that promises success on the links (swing aids, pills to help you focus, and a Q-Link, a gadget you hang around your neck that promises to fortify your "biofield" and improve mental acuity)—will undoubtedly be familiar to every duffer who has tried to master the game. His commentary on golf books, especially those instructional manuals that promise to improve your game, will also resonate with die-hard golf fans. Not all such books work for him. For example, he suggests that the title of Tiger Woods's *How I Play Golf* ought to be changed to *In Your Dreams, Sucker*. More to his liking is *Harvey Penick's Little Red Book*, the best-selling book in sports history, which he describes as rambling fondly "like your favorite uncle sipping bourbon on the veranda" (68). And many of his funniest lines—"Why doesn't someone invent a tee that you can slit your wrists with?" (24) and "The shank is to hackers what the clap is to porn stars" (134)—are directed mainly at fellow golfers.

But there are plenty of rewards for the non-golfer too, thanks to Hiaasen's trademark sense of humor. For example, after discussing the latest technological advances in golf-club design—shafts and clubheads designed by "finite-element analysis" to achieve the greatest "moment of inertia"—he puts it all in terms that any reader can understand: "The last thing I wanted was a driver that came with an instructional manual. I can't assemble a toy train track without leaving blood on the floor" (27).

With little to satirize, Hiaasen is able to free up his inner jokester, resulting in book that is chock full of funny lines. He's especially inspired in the creation of hilarious similes, most of them applied to himself: he paws through golf magazines "like a junkie in a medicine cabinet" (70); as for his golf game, he swings like "a vertigo patient, threshing wheat"(130), putts "like a caffeinated chimpanzee" (147), and has been known to unravel "like a crackhead at a Billy Graham crusade" (5) when he plays poorly.

Golf, however, does offer more than constant disappointment. Even the self-flagellating Hiaasen has to admit that a good shot "is a total rush, possibly the second most pleasurable sensation in the human experience" (203). It also produces priceless memories. Some of the more touching sections of the book are those that involve memories of his father, who died unexpectedly when Hiaasen was only twenty-two.

He began golf as a way of spending more time with his dad, but as an "impatient, hot-headed and self-critical" kid (98), he could never find a way to love the game the way his father did. Looking back now, he says he doesn't regret a moment spent golfing with him, but does regret his tantrums and sulky behavior. "Every time I hit a bad shot I acted like it was the end of the world," he confesses. "And I think I wasted a lot of moments and a lot of afternoons with him that I wished I could have just done over again and behave a little better and enjoy them for what they were" (Tanber). One memory he particularly cherishes is watching his father "swing a driver with a sweet, fluid rhythm at which I could only marvel" (98).

The book ends on a high note as Hiaasen accompanies his six-year-old son Quinn on a three-hole golf scramble. Watching Quinn's "500-watt smile" after he drills a putt reminds him that despite all his own tribulations, "this really is a great game. Truly it is" (207). One reason for that is golf isn't always just about how you play. It can also be about fathers and sons: "I see warmer days ahead, when a certain young player might want his old man to join him for nine holes after school. For some reason he enjoys watching me hit the ball, so I suppose I'll bring my clubs. What the hell" (202).

Hiaasen may never be the first-rate golfer he wishes he could be, but his book provides ample evidence that he could be one heck of a golf writer. He captures the graceful swing of Ernie Els by describing it as "the Perry Como of golf swings, smooth and oh-so-easy" (110). He admires the way Tiger Woods shapes his golf shots "as gorgeously as Eric Clapton bends the notes on a Stratocaster" (113), but notes that after making four bogies in a row, the look on his face "would have made a suicide bomber wet himself" (112).

The Downhill Lie will appeal to both sports enthusiasts as well as to fans of Hiaasen's trademark sense of humor. What it probably won't do is inspire many to take up the game of golf.

The theme of fathers and sons is also prominent in an essay Hiaasen published twenty years earlier entitled, "Last of the Falling Tide." It begins with a trip he took with his father and grandfather to the Florida Keys for the first time when he was six years old. Inspired by a photo of his father taken in Key West when he was thirteen, Hiaasen imagined the place to be a "mystical, Oz-like destination: a string of rough-cut jewels" (71). It turned out to be every bit as enchanting as he hoped it would be. But soon much of it would be gone. Like the rest of the state, the Keys he remembered so vividly from that first trip fell victim to man's "unrelenting hunger to dredge, subdivide, pave, build, and sell" every inch of paradise possible (73).

The essay ends with a trip Hiaasen took his own young son Scott on to the Keys when he was a young boy. Sadly, he had to spend much of the time telling Scott how beautiful it once was, "before the greedy bastards ruined it" (77). As battered as the Keys are, however, they still have the power to "enchant and seduce," and his son, like three generations of Hiaasens before him, fell in love with the place. More importantly, like his father he became angry about the destruction of something so precious. And as long as people continue to get angry about that, Hiaasen hopes, they will fight to save what's left of it.

3

Collaborations with Bill Montalbano

In the late 1970s, Hiaasen was reporting about the cocaine wars that had broken out in Miami. One day Bill Montalbano, the *Herald* editor he worked with on his articles, suggested that the two of them ought to write a novel about the subject just for fun. Montalbano's wife wanted a swimming pool and he wondered whether they could make enough money from a novel to buy one. Their first collaboration, *Powder Burn* was published in 1981, and Montalbano's wife got her swimming pool. The two of them then decided to write two more thrillers together.

Writing a collaborative novel is a tricky business. For one thing, both writers have to write in the same homogenized voice, which requires each partner to suppress his own individual style. In addition, the book has to be carefully plotted out in advance, so each author can work independently on separate chapters, which became even more an issue when Montalbano's duties as a foreign correspondent often had him traveling. Fortunately, Hiaasen and Montalbano had similar editing sensibilities and thick enough skin that they could edit one other's work and still remain friends. They were so successful in blending their styles together that is it difficult to identify who wrote what. Readers of Hiaasen's later solo novels will find little evidence of the absurdist humor or sharp satire that would later become his trademark.

Powder Burn resembles one of those classic Alfred Hitchcock films like *North by Northwest* where an innocent man get sucked into a perilous predicament he must extricate himself from. It all begins with a shocking scene of senseless violence. T. Christopher Meadows is an accomplished architect living in Coconut Grove, Florida. One day, purely by chance, he bumps into a former girlfriend he hasn't seen in six years who's visiting Miami with her five-year-old daughter. After a brief conversation, they bid farewell. Moments later, Meadows is horrified to see the woman and her daughter

3. Collaborations with Bill Montalbano

mowed down by a speeding red Mustang. And then he watches in disbelief as a passenger in the car that was chasing the Mustang gets out and calmly mows down the two men in the disabled car with a machine gun. Then the killer turns and fires at him, hitting him in the leg.

As an architect, Meadows has an eye for detail and an ability to draw, which enables him to produce an accurate sketch of the shooter, which the police use to identify him as a CIA-trained Cuban gunman named Mono. Unfortunately, Mono has also been able to identify Meadows, which leads to a pair of hair-raising escapes. After nearly being electrocuted when his pool is booby trapped by Mono, Meadows decides to get out of Florida for his own safety. But at the airport garage where he parks his car, Mono suddenly appears again, this time armed with a knife. During a scuffle in a vacant stairwell, Meadows miraculously manages to fight off his assailant and in the process stab him in the chest.

His troubles now come from a new direction. Mono dies of his wounds, and the police are able to gather enough evidence to arrest Meadows for his murder. Octavio Nelson, the Miami cop he has been working with, is angry with Meadows because Mono's death has jeopardized a three-month investigation aimed at identifying the ringleader of a major drug operation, a man known only as *el Jefe*. Nelson makes a deal with Meadows: if he can draw sketches of Mono's two henchmen and *el Jefe*, Nelson will forget the murder charge. Nelson drops him off at the funeral home where Mono's viewing is being held, and sure enough Meadows manages to get a good look at Mono's henchmen and the elusive *el Jefe*. But when he leaves to report to Nelson, the cop is nowhere to be seen. Fearful that he has been used simply as a decoy to catch *el Jefe*, he decides to go underground and go after *el Jefe* by himself.

The second half of the novel is devoted to Meadows's plan for revenge, which he constructs with the deliberate care an architect like himself would take. It involves his participation in a late-night pickup of a shipment of drugs dropped into the Everglades from a low-flying plane and the risky theft of a bag of cocaine from an attorney's desk during a party at his house. The mild-mannered architect who previously didn't "know cocaine from coconuts" (226) now displays another side of his personality, "something leaner, tougher, something that tasted of recklessness and danger" (216), as the narrator rather melodramatically puts it. Watch out, *el Jefe*.

In the end, Meadows proves to be a capable action hero who, with the help of his girlfriend Terry and a former Pittsburgh Steeler football player, sets a trap that snags *el Jefe*. He is revealed to be a prominent Cuban-born

Miami banker with big dreams of operating his drug empire from a seat in the United States Senate, which he hopes to purchase with cocaine money. As the narrator says, in a sarcastic line that sounds like Hiaasen likely wrote it, "anything was possible—wasn't it?—in the land of free enterprise" (252).

Hiaasen's reporting on the drug wars provided the dramatic background for the story he and Montalbano came up with. Because of its location, Miami became the center of the drug trade, with an avalanche of marijuana from Jamaica and cocaine from Colombia coming by land, sea, and sometimes, we learn, even smuggled in the corpse of a three-month-old baby. But the inevitable breakdown of the onshore-offshore agreement between the growers in Colombia and Cuban distributors in Miami, with each side now trying to control both ends, results in a free-fire zone of unprecedented violence that often claims innocent bystanders like Meadows's former girlfriend and her daughter.

Trap Line (1982) also draws upon Hiaasen's reporting on drug smuggling and police corruption in Key West. Breeze Albury is a local fishing captain whose troubles begin when someone cuts the lines to over 300 of his crayfish traps, which are then swept away. It turns out that it was a message sent by the local drug-smuggling organization known as the Machine which wants his help in transporting a group of Colombian illegal immigrants from the Bahamas to Florida. Crosses and double crosses ensue, with events eventually leading to his interception of a shipment of marijuana headed to Key West which he holds for ransom until the Machine pays him the $50,000 he was promised for the transfer of the Colombians.

One highly suspenseful scene takes place in the dark of night as Albury brings his boat as close as he can to a tiny island in the Bahamas where he is supposed to pick up the twenty Colombians he's being paid to transport back to Key Largo. Complicating matters are the unexpected presence of several additional passengers and the disappearance of one who suddenly slips under the water while making his way to the boat, forcing Albury to dive into the inky sea in an unsuccessful attempt to rescue the man. Then a Bahamian Royal Defence Force gunboat appears, forcing Albury to beat a hasty retreat while trying to avoid slamming into a dangerous reef. Only a skilled sailor like Albury would know how to lure the pursuing gunboat into the reef, disabling it, though not before a volley of machine-gun fire rakes his fleeing boat.

In the end the good guys win. Albury gets his money and his revenge on those responsible for his ordeal and for breaking his son's arm, endanger-

3. Collaborations with Bill Montalbano

ing his dream of becoming a major league pitcher. A major subplot described the efforts of a special prosecutor, Christine Manning, who was sent by the governor to clean up corruption in Key West. With the help of a group of local gays who are fed up with the police chief's homophobia, she manages to gather enough evidence to get seventeen indictments against the chief and six of his officers.

While it's difficult to identify with any certainty which parts of the novel are Hiaasen's, there is at least one incident that will become a signature feature of his fiction. Albury finds the man who sabotaged his traps and devises a cleverly appropriate punishment for him. He drops him off on a small island used by the University of Miami to study rhesus monkeys. There are now over a thousand monkeys on the island who are fed every third day. Between feedings, all the monkeys do is fight and fornicate. As Albury's boat leaves, he hears the monkeys "shrieking their hatred for the intruder" (167) in their midst.

A Death in China (1984), the most accomplished of the three novels the duo wrote, offers the twin pleasures of an engrossing mystery and a spy thriller along with the added attraction of an exotic setting: Communist China. It's also the least representative of Hiaasen's own work. Material gleaned from Hiaasen's investigations into Florida's drug trade provided the criminal background for the first two novels the duo wrote. This time, the background material comes from Montalbano's experiences in Beijing where he was bureau chief for the Knight-Ridder newspapers from 1979 to 1981.

Tom Stratton is a professor at a New England college who is visiting Beijing on a tour of Communist China with a group of fellow art historians. Shortly after arriving, he's surprised to bump into a former professor of his, David Wang, who has come to China at the invitation of his brother Wang Bin, who many years earlier remained behind instead of leaving for America like his brother. Wang Bin has since risen through the Communist Party ranks to become deputy minister of art and culture. Tragically, however, David Wang dies of a sudden heart attack shortly after meeting his brother at Xian, the site of the Emperor Qin Shi Huangdi's fabled army of life-sized terracotta soldiers.

Wang Bin asks Stratton to accompany his brother's coffin back to the U.S., but when Stratton discovers that David Wang's coffin has been welded shut and his passport is missing, he decides to stay in China and try to figure out what's going on. After discovering evidence suggesting that Wang Bin might be involved in the smuggling of several of the terracotta soldiers into the U.S., he becomes embroiled in a series of harrowing adventures that include being beaten, shot in the leg, and locked in a closet with a deadly cobra. Eventually, Stratton and Wang Bin's beautiful and rebellious young daughter Kangmei, with whom he has become romantically involved, are forced to flee for their lives and head for the safety of a commune she knows located a thousand miles from Beijing.

This results in an exciting but improbable subplot when Stratton recognizes that the commune is the very same village where he was involved in a secret intelligence mission during the Vietnam war eleven years earlier that resulted in the deaths of five other members of his squad. The lone survivor, he was able to escape only by stabbing to death a pregnant peasant woman, the memory of which has haunted him ever since. But now he gets a chance at redemption when he jumps into a raging river to save the lives of a two young children who had fallen in. As he's being hailed for his bravery, one of the locals accuses him of being the American who shot him during his previous visit to the town. But thanks to another villager, whom Stratton recognizes as a twelve-year-old boy whose life he spared eleven years earlier, who returns the favor and declines to identify him as the American his accuser said shot him, he is free to leave.

Stratton can now return to the matter of solving the dual mysteries of Wang's death and the identity of the mastermind behind the smuggling of the priceless terracotta soldiers into the U.S., which he does in heroic fashion. In the end, he returns to his quiet life as an art history professor in New England, where he awaits the arrival of Kangmei, whose safe passage to America he secured by arranging for the return of the stolen terracotta soldiers to China.

Despite its improbabilities, the novel has many virtues: it's tightly plotted with plenty of foreign intrigue; the portrait of China and its people under Communism is filled with fascinating details; there are several heart-pounding close calls and daring escapes; and it offers the added attraction of a love story between the daring American and the beautiful young Chinese woman.

Taken for what they are—potboiler thrillers—all three novels offer many pleasures to the reader. Though handicapped by the built-in limitations of collaborative authorship and the primacy of plot over characterization, Hiaasen and Montalbano deliver suspenseful, action-packed tales set against richly detailed and authentic backgrounds. *The New York Times* reviewer hailed *Powder Burn* as a "smoothly written book, natural in its dialogue,

3. Collaborations with Bill Montalbano

expertly plotted, with a most attractive hero" (Callendar). Roz Shea praised *Trap Line* for its combination of "fast action, likable characters, and a plot that twists and turns like a speedboat through a mangrove swamp." *A Death in China* was called "an imaginative thriller" in *The New York Times* (Mitgang) and *The Washington Post* described its pace as "fast and unrelenting" and its landscapes as "exotic and well-presented" (McLellan).

The collaboration taught Hiaasen several valuable lessons about plot, characters, and the business of publishing. He also met Esther Newberg, the literary agent he's still with. But due to Montalbano's foreign travels and both authors' desire to write something more personal, the collaboration came to an end. Hiaasen says he now felt free to "cut loose and have some fun" (Silet "Sun" 68), which he certainly did with his first solo effort, *Tourist Season*.

Montalbano went on to join the *Los Angeles Times* in 1983. For seven years he served as their Rome bureau chief before moving to London to head the bureau there. He also wrote a pair of solo novels, *The Sinners of San Ramon* (1989) and *Basilica* (1998), before dying of a sudden heart attack in 1998 at age fifty-seven while walking to his London office.

4

Novels for Adults

Tourist Season *(1986)*

Tourist Season begins with the gruesome discovery of the body of Sparky Harper, president of the Greater Miami Chamber of Commerce, which is found stuffed into a suitcase floating in a canal. The legs have been cut off, his face has been slathered with suntan oil, and he's dressed in a brightly flowered print shirt and baggy shorts. An autopsy determines that death was caused by a five-inch toy rubber alligator that had been jammed down his throat. Adding to the mystery is a note addressed to the Chamber of Commerce that is later sent to the police:

> Welcome to the Revolution.
> Mr. B. D. Harper's death was a milestone. It may have seemed an atrocity to you; to us, it was poetry. Contrary to what you'd like to believe, this was not the act of a sick person, but the raging of a powerful new underclass [22].

The note was signed *El Fuego, Comandante, Las Noches de Diciembre.*

A second note later appears, addressed to the wife of a visiting Shriner from Evanston, Illinois, who went missing a few days earlier. Also signed by *El Fuego,* this one is even more ominous:

> Welcome to the Revolution. Sorry to disturb your vacation, but we've had to make an example of your husband. Go back North and tell your friends what a dangerous place is Miami [53].

It now becomes clear that this is more than a case of a serial killer on the loose: it's an attack on tourists and tourism in Florida.

At the same time, another missing person case develops. Skip Wiley, popular columnist for the Miami *Sun,* has mysteriously vanished after his car was found abandoned on the highway. Wiley wrote provocatively and eloquently about many important local issues, including the commercial assault on Florida by its boosters and developers. Here's what he once wrote

4. Novels for Adults

about Sparky Harper, the late Chamber of Commerce head, a "proud pioneer of the shameless, witless boosterism that made Florida grow" (29):

> If there has ever been a more myopic, insensitive, and avaricious cretin to lead our Chamber of Commerce, I can't recall him. Sparky Harper takes the cake—and anything else that isn't nailed down. He is the Sultan of Shills, the perfect mouthpiece for the hungry-eyed developers, hoteliers, bankers and lawyers who have made South Florida what it is today: Newark with palm trees [24].

Wiley is well known for his offbeat ideas (he once launched a write-in campaign to get porn start Marilyn Chambers an Oscar) and erratic behavior (he once peppered his living wall with gunshots after watching the governor on television promoting more growth in Florida). Does his disappearance have any connection to the murders?

Enter Brian Keyes, a former colleague of Wiley's on the *Sun* who now works as a private investigator. He realized he wasn't cut out for the newspaper business after finding he couldn't bring himself to interview the grieving parents of a four-year-old girl who had been kidnapped and murdered. He fabricated quotes for a heart-breaking story about the girl's murder and then submitted his resignation. Now his former boss at the paper hires him to find Wiley.

What follows next is Hiaasen's version of Joseph Conrad's *Heart of Darkness*, the story of a man named Marlow who travels to the heart of Africa in search of Mister Kurtz, an idealist who has reportedly gone mad in the jungle. After learning that Wiley's family once had a cabin in the Everglades, Keyes rents a canoe and like Marlow heads up the river into the wilderness. At first, the setting is tranquil, but when his canoe paddle is stolen, he is stranded overnight and the mood darkens.

What he learns the next day is deeply disturbing. He finds Wiley, who now reveals that he is *El Fuego*, leader of *Las Noches de Diciembre*, the person responsible for the kidnapping and murders of Sparky Harper and a pair of tourists. He also meets Wiley's trio of associates: Viceroy Wilson, former star fullback for the Miami Dolphins, now an anarchist dedicated to "kicking the living shit out of whitey" (102); Tommy Tigertail, a young Seminole who is bankrolling the operation with money the tribe has earned from its popular bingo parlors; and Jesus Bernal, an Ivy League graduate devoted to right-wing terrorism.

Wiley tells Keyes he plans to continue killing tourists as a way of scaring away "all the morons who thundered into Florida the past thirty years and made such a mess" (103). He wants Keyes's help in publicizing his cause while keeping his role in the terrorist activities a secret. To convince him he means business, he forces him to witness a truly horrific scene: he orders one of his associates to toss a local woman in her sixties he's kidnapped into the water where a hungry North American crocodile is lurking. The scene convinces Keyes that he's now "face to face with raw insanity" (104). The man he once knew as a moral crusader for Florida's future has turned into "the worst Kurtz I ever saw" (100).

Wiley's terrorist acts become increasingly outlandish. To the recorded sound of Pat Boone crooning the theme from the movie *Exodus*, he drops a bunch of shopping bags from a helicopter on to a boatload of travel writers who have come to Florida intending to sing its praises as a tourist destination. They end up scrambling in horror when they discover the bags are filled with 200 snakes, many of them poisonous. The coup de grâce is his plan to kidnap Kara Lynn Stivers, the beautiful nineteen-year-old Orange Bowl Queen.

The novel ends in dramatic fashion on Osprey Island, a small uninhabited coral island in Biscayne Bay where Skip Wiley has brought the kidnapped Orange Bowl Queen. He intends for the two of them to die when at dawn the island is scheduled to be leveled by 800 pounds of dynamite to prepare the terrain for a planned sixteen-story luxury condominium complex. Wiley hopes the tragic death of Kara Lynn, symbol of American Beauty, alongside the equally tragic death of all the other living creatures on the island will awaken the good people of Florida to the magnitude of their sins.

Wiley, however, is surprised by the unexpected appearance of Brian Keyes, who in classic heroic fashion arrives in the nick of time to save the damsel in distress. In the end, Keyes, Kara Lynn, and Wiley's girlfriend Jenna, whom he has brought along to use as leverage to save Kara Lynn, escape the island shortly before the detonation. As they make their way across the bay to safety, they look back to witness one final heroic act: despite having been shot in the knee by Keyes, Skip Wiley has dragged himself up a tall pine tree in a desperate attempt to shoo away the island's lone bald eagle that is perched there before it too is destroyed. The novel ends with the sound of the signal for the dynamiting to begin followed by Keyes's whispered prayer: "Please fly away."

Creating several characters with ties to the same newspaper gives Hiaasen an opportunity to make *Tourist Season* in part both a tribute to journalism as well as a satire on some of its worst practices and practitioners. Cab Mulcahy, managing editor of the *Sun*, is an example of the best the profession offers, a dedicated, principled man who'd "gone into newspapers for all the right reasons, with all the right instincts and all the right sensibilities" (190). He deals with talented but difficult writers like Skip Wiley (who once fired a speargun at another editor), a meddling publisher who thinks the *Sun* is a good newspaper because it carries Ann Landers and Dagwood Bumstead, and incompetent reporters with grace and dignity.

Wiley's girlfriend Jenna, who was formerly Keyes's girlfriend, is correct when she describes the two of them as two sides of the same coin. Keyes is a decent guy who recognizes there's a line he can't cross and leaves journalism behind; Wiley is a man of principle but unfortunately he does cross a dangerous line that has tragic consequences for several innocent victims. He can be seen as an example of what can happen to a person who becomes so outraged at the damage he sees being done to his beloved state that he goes crazy. (Hiaasen points out that Wiley is not based on himself; he did not begin writing his own column until he was halfway through *Tourist Season*.) "There ... is ... no ... other ... way," Wiley insists, except "Murder, mayhem, and madness—the cardinal M's of the newsroom" (166). But terrorism is not the only alternative. He could have used the anger and outrage to inspire him to a more creative response. He could have transformed his "moral rage into comic art," as novelist Philip Roth once described satire (119). That's the path Hiaasen took: writing fiction, he says, "keeps me from going completely around the bend" (Jones "More").

Ricky Bloodworth, a third member of the *Sun* staff, is one of two comic characters held up to ridicule in the novel. A clueless and incompetent reporter, he dreams of being hired by *The New York Times*. As a journalist, however, he's a disaster: he puts words into the mouth of an interview subject and then passes them off as direct quotes; he so sloppy that in a piece he writes about *Las Noches de Diciembre*, he makes the inexcusably careless error of calling them *Las Nachos*, turning the dangerous terrorist outfit into something of a joke. In what will become a Hiaasen trademark, he gets his comeuppance in absurd fashion: he steals a package from *Las Noches* meant for a cop and opens it while sitting on a toilet; the package contains a bomb which explodes, singeing the tip of his penis and shearing off all his fingertips.

Jesus Bernal, one of the members of Wiley's terrorist group, is another comic screwup. A Dartmouth grad, the son of an accountant, he was born in Trenton, New Jersey. Somehow or other, he ended up as a member of a rabid anti–Castro terrorist group. As a supposed munitions "expert," he proved to be a colossal failure: his first two bombs detonated prematurely; his third killed the wrong victim. Banished from the group by its leader, who called him "the worst bomber I ever saw. You couldn't blow up a balloon" (216), he's later given a second chance with the group, this time as defense minister (mainly because of his Ivy League typing skills). But his ineptness continues: he mistakenly drops six tons of anti-Castro leaflets on Kingston, Jamaica, instead of the intended target of Havana. He gets one more chance to prove himself after becoming a member of *Las Noches*, but his targets—one of his bombs, which he plants in the cup on a golf course green, kills three golfers; another kills eight greyhounds during a race—don't seem to have much to do with scaring away the tourists.

Disillusioned with the methods of *Las Noches*, he decides to go out on his own as "the Reggie Jackson of South Florida terrorism, a free-agent superstar-assassin" (295). His first target is Al Garcia, a Cuban-American cop leading the search for Skip Wiley. He kidnaps him, takes him to a secluded spot, and shoots him in the side. Then he orders him to jump in the water and swim to Cuba where he can atone for his sins by joining the underground to "fight the devil in his own backyard" (305). Only the timely intervention of Brian Keyes, who had been tailing the two men, saves Garcia's life after he shoots Bernal.

The comic highlight of the novel is Hiaasen's hilarious spoofing of the Orange Bowl half-time show hosted by popular television personality John Davidson. The garish spectacle opens with the appearance of four hundred professional young people "who all look like they just got scholarships at Brigham Young" (338), followed by an array of Broadway characters in full costume: "bewhiskered cats, Yiddish fiddlers, gorgeous chorus girls, two Little Orphan Annies, three Elephant Men, a Hamlet, a King of Siam, and even a tap-dancing Willy Loman" (339). Then comes a reenactment of legendary stage scenes, each compressed to eighty-five seconds. The grand finale is a holographic tribute to Ethel Merman accompanied by the singing of her trademark song, "Give My Regards to Broadway."

Tourist Season shares the same rambunctious comic spirit as *The Monkey Wrench Gang* (1975), Edward Abbey's famous novel about environmental terrorism. His quartet of eco-terrorists—a rich Albuquerque doctor, a former Green Beret medic in Vietnam, a Mormon riverboat guide with three wives, and a nice Jewish girl from the Bronx with an M. A. in Classical French Literature—embark on a rollicking guerrilla campaign of destruction aimed at halting the damage being done by man and machine to the air, water, and natural beauty of the desert Southwest. Unlike Skip Wiley, however, they take care to avoid any human casualties, focusing instead on cutting down billboards and power lines and blowing up bridges and dams. Their aim is "constructive vandalism" inspired by the slogan, "God Bless America. Let's Save Some of It."

(Hiaasen says he didn't actually read *The Monkey Wrench Gang* until a friend gave him a copy following the publication of *Tourist Season*. He then read everything else Abbey wrote. "I certainly felt that we were some sort of kindred souls in the way we looked at what was happening to a place we cared about," he has said. "He was terrific" [Weich].)

Skip Wiley is more symbol than fully developed character. He represents the outlaw hero, the madman who speaks the truth. It's impossible to overlook the evil deeds he does, but unlike the villains in Hiaasen's later novels, he's pure of heart. Hiaasen will soon direct his satiric scorn at those who represent the kinds of evil Skip Wiley was in his misguided way trying to warn the public about.

Hiaasen is still feeling his way as a novelist. He sometimes allows the columnist in him to have the upper hand by including some extended speeches that slow the narrative flow to a crawl. For example, after Brian Keyes tracks down Wiley on a beach in the Bahamas, he ends up as a captive audience for the terrorist's soapbox orations. Wiley begins by offering another colorful description of Florida—"Brian, what is Florida anyway? An immense sunny toilet where millions of tourists flush their money and save the moment on Kodak film" (166)—but then proceeds to lecture Keyes on the subject of his Asshole Quotient theory. According to him, the quality of life declines in direct proportion to the number of assholes per square mile: by his reckoning, Miami has 134 per square mile, the worst A.Q in America, beating out Aspen, Colorado, and Malibu, California. He concludes by reminding Keyes that during the hour they have been talking, "41.6 morons moved into the state of Florida. They are arriving at the rate of a thousand a day. One thousand each and every day! There is *no place to put them!* The land is shriveling beneath us, the water is poison, the air is rancid" (171).

Elsewhere, Hiaasen begins one chapter with a two-and-a-half page account of Florida history; the following chapter opens with three whole pages devoted to Wiley's final column, in which he explains the motives behind his actions, which have already been made crystal clear to the reader. While the message is perhaps worth repeating, Hiaasen will in the future become much more adept at incorporating such material in a more effective manner.

Tourist Season got a helpful boost from an enthusiastic review by Tony Hillerman in *The New York Times*. While noting that Hiaasen "leaves you grinning a lot" and that reading him "is fun," Hillerman went on to praise the novel as a "remarkable example of what talented writers are doing these days with the mystery novel" ("Tourists"). Skip Wiley and his crazy campaign to save Florida were also famously memorialized by Jimmy Buffett in "The Ballad of Skip Wiley."

Double Whammy *(1987)*

Double Whammy is private-eye tale with a fishy twist. Like Brian Keyes, R. J. Decker is a newspaperman-turned-private eye (he was formerly a photographer) who is hired by a wealthy professional fisherman named Dennis Gault to investigate cheating on the competitive bass-fishing circuit. Professional bass fishing is the fastest-growing outdoor sport in America, with tournaments now offering prizes of $75,000 and more. Gault suspects that Dickie Lockhart, one of his fellow competitors and star of his own popular TV fishing show, has been cheating by secretly stashing fish he has previously caught and using them to win the competition. Gault offers Decker $50,000 to confirm his suspicions.

Decker decides he needs to hire a local guide in order to learn more about the bass-fishing phenomenon, so he is directed to an oddball named Skink who lives nearby. The man makes a memorable first impression. In his late forties, early fifties, he stands six-foot-six, has blindingly white TV anchorman teeth, and wears Marine-style boots and a luminous orange rain suit (even though it isn't raining). His silver-flecked hair hangs in a braided rope down his back, and sometimes he also wears a flowered shower cap. To top it all off, he lives on roadkill, scraping up dead opossums and armadillos off the highway or snatching a freshly killed seagull from the grill of the truck that hit it. All of this reminds Decker of the banjo music from *Deliverance*, which "got louder every time he took a good look at Skink's face" (33).

After a pair of murders—that of a pro fisherman Decker is surprised to learn had been hired by Dennis Gault to investigate Lockhart before he was and a former newspaper reporter who had been helping him snoop around— he isn't so sure getting himself killed over a dead fish is such a great idea. On the other hand, the fact that somebody has become homicidal over a largemouth bass is perversely appealing to him, so he decides to continue on.

At this point, Hiaasen interrupts the narrative to tell the story of a man named Clinton Tyree. Readers of Hiaasen's newspaper columns would be familiar with his scornful attitude toward the Florida legislature, which he once famously called a "festival of whores." Hiaasen imagines what might happen if an honest man—a handsome former second-team All-American college football player, a decorated Vietnam vet, and an avid outdoorsman—ever managed to get elected as governor of Florida. That man was Clinton Tyree, who "to the utter confusion of everyone in Tallahassee ... turned out to be a completely honest man" (107). He refuses all kickbacks and publicly dismisses a group of land developers who try to bribe him as "submaggots, unfit to suck the sludge off a septic tank" (108).

Not everybody considers him a hero. To the people who count in Tallahassee, i.e., the ones with money and power, he's "a dangerous pain in the ass," so they conspire to get rid of him. Even though he's widely hailed, even getting his picture on the cover of *Time* magazine, this means nothing "as long as his colleagues kept voting to surrender every inch of Florida's beach-front to pinky-ringed condominium moguls" (109). Finally, after one particular stunning defeat (his was the only vote against selling a nature preserve to a development corporation whose primary stockholder he learns was his running mate, the lieutenant governor), he simply disappears. He eventually turns up in a small town with the lowest voter registration per capita in the state where no one will recognize him. And he changes his name to Skink.

The reader now knows what has turned Clinton Tyree into such an eccentric hermit. But is he a harmless eccentric, or a dangerous sociopath? Some of his actions suggest the latter. On a flight to New Orleans with Decker to attend a fishing competition, he causes a disturbance. Later, when Decker returns to the motel room he is sharing with Skink, he finds a half-naked woman wrapped from her shoulders to her ankles in fishing line lying on the floor. She tells him that the culprit was Skink, who never said a word the whole time he was wrapping her up, he just kept singing the Moody Blues song "Nights in White Satin" over and over. How nuts is this guy?

Things turn really dark when Decker discovers the body of Dickie Lockhart in the Louisiana lake where the fishing competition was held. The killer added a diabolical twist: a fishing lure known as the Double Whammy was dangling from Lockhart's lower lip like a Christmas ornament. Decker fears that Skink, who had earlier suggested shooting Lockhart, might be the killer.

When Decker returns to Miami, he gets another jolt: the primary suspect in Lockhart's murder isn't Skink, it's him. Al Garcia, a Miami homicide detective and a longtime friend, who previously appeared in *Tourist Season*, receives a warrant from the Louisiana authorities for Decker's arrest for the murder of Lockhart. Decker is shocked when he learns that his client, with the help of his sister, has set him up and is attempting to frame him for Lockhart's murder. He now has something more important to do than investigate cheating in a fishing tournament; he has to save his own skin by finding the real killer.

It doesn't take long for Garcia to determine that Gault is a liar and his friend Decker is innocent. The two of them join forces with Skink and Jim Tile, a black Florida highway patrolman who served as one of his bodyguards when he was governor and who has remained a trusted friend, to smoke out the truth about Gault and the three murders now connected to the case. All this, however, is merely a set-up for the farcical spectacle that is the main business of the novel.

The central figure in that spectacle is the Reverend Charles Weeb, founder of the First Pentecostal Church of Exemptive Redemption, the first in a long line of phonies, frauds, and hypocrites Hiaasen will lampoon in his novels. Weeb isn't an ordained minister, doesn't have a church, and isn't even Christian (his family is Jewish). His special talent, healing crippled animals, broadcast regularly on his popular TV show, *Jesus in Your Living Room*, is also a fraud, as is the story he concocts about his poor (invented) sisters who he says were sold to a Chinese slavery ring: the heart-warming pictures of the two unfortunates (which he clipped from *Playboy* magazine) he displays during the broadcast under the caption "WHAT HAS SATAN DONE WITH THESE ANGELS?" is a proven moneymaker. Another big moneymaker is Dickie Lockhart's popular *Fish Fever* show on the Christian Outdoor Network, which he also happens to own.

Weeb's real crime in Hiaasen's estimation is not that he's a fraud, but that he's also responsible for bulldozing a large parcel of land on the edge of the Everglades near Fort Lauderdale (a place similar to where Hiaasen and his buddies played when they were kids) in order to build condominiums. Lunker Lakes (a lunker is a large fish), which offers "Christian town-home living at its finest" (259), is projected to eventually grow to 29,000 units. Like so many of Hiaasen's villains, Weeb has zero appreciation for nature's beauty. Looking out over the Everglades only inspires this response: "Reminds me of the fucking Sahara … except with muck" (121). All water represents to him is money, so he has canals dredged everywhere (which he insists must be called straight, narrow lakes) so he can sell "waterfront" property to gullible customers.

The units aren't selling fast enough, however, so Weeb comes up with a scheme to boost sales: he'll hold the biggest fishing competition in the world at Lunker Lakes and name it after the late Dickie Lockhart; he'll invite the best bass anglers in the world to compete for a cash prize of $250,000; and he'll televise the event live on his Christian Outdoor Network and invite a thousand prospective buyers to attend in person.

But then things start to go sour for Weeb. First of all, he discovers that Lunker Lakes is built on a poisonous landfill that has turned all the fresh water into a toxic stew, killing all the fish. He now must secretly truck in thousands of fresh bass so the competition can go on as scheduled. What he doesn't count on are the combined efforts of Skink and his trio of henchmen to gum up the works even more.

Jim Tile and Al Garcia register for the competition under the name of the Tile Brothers. When they arrive, Weeb isn't happy to see a Cuban and a black man in his planned lily-white community and dubs them "the spic and spade brothers." For their part, just to have some fun, the two men begin performing like a comedy team, with Tile speaking in Spanish and Garcia talking jive. But they have a more serious role to play: they intend to secretly plant a twenty-nine pound bass named Queenie that Skink has adopted as a pet in the lake to ensure that they win the competition.

The location where they stash Queenie—at the edge of an earthen dike that separates Lunker Lake Number Seven from the Everglades—becomes the symbolic site of the battle between the forces of good and evil in the novel. Skink calls it "the moral seam of the universe.... Evil on the one side, good on the other" (353). Hiaasen's description of the place emphasizes the dramatic contrast between the two worlds:

> Water glistened on both sides of the dike. Under a thin fog, Lunker Lake Number Seven lay as flat and dead as a cistern; by contrast, the small pool on the Everglades side was dimpled with darting minnows and waterbugs. The pocket was lushly fringed with cattails and sawgrass and crisp round lily pads as big as pizzas [349].

But unbeknownst to Tile and Garcia, one of Dennis Gault's henchmen spots their activity from a helicopter flying overhead and reports the location to his boss, who intends to get the fish for himself. He beats Tile and Garcia to the site and hooks the great fish, who puts up a valiant battle and in the end becomes an agent of justice: she pulls Gault overboard and into the propeller of his boat, which grinds him up like a garbage disposal.

Meanwhile, Skink gets his revenge against Weeb in another way. Earlier in the novel, Skink was savagely beaten by a trio of teenage thugs who attacked helpless transients simply for the thrill of it. The real reason for the attack, however, was to give Skink one more oddball characteristic that Hiaasen could use for comic purposes: the attack resulted in Skink losing his left eye, which he replaces with a glass eye he takes from a stuffed barn owl. Now, as luck would have it, Weeb's associate who has been charged with finding someone Weeb can "heal" on live television stumbles upon a blind man wearing sunglasses who tells him his name is Skink. He's hired and given a script to memorize, but at the moment when his blindness is "healed," instead of taking his sunglasses off and reading the banner announcing the Lunker Lakes Bass Blasters Classic, he instead shouts, "Squeeze My Lemon, Baby." Then he winks and the glass eye pops out of his head and bounces on the stage, sending the audience fleeing. So much for Weeb's reputation as a healer.

The rest of Weeb's empire comes crashing down when the Tile Brothers claim the first-place prize for reeling in the largest (and only) catch of the day, a fourteen-ounce bass. Then Jim Tile arrests Weeb for fraud. Only one task remains. Queenie is trapped in the toxic water and will die unless Skink can rescue her in time. He does, and carries the sluggish fish up and over the dike into the fresh water on the other side. The novel ends with the soft sound of the fish swimming away.

As a comic bonus, the novel also includes another memorable weirdo in the person of Thomas Curl, Gault's hired killer. While trying to track Decker down in order to kill him, he is attacked by a pit bull that clamps itself onto his right hand. He kills the animal with a screwdriver but is unable to loosen the dog's jaws. Desperate, he takes a hacksaw and cuts off the animal's body, leaving his hand looking "like a football with ears" (284). He names the dog's head "Lucas," shoves Gaines Burgers into its clenched jaw, and murmurs to it affectionately as if it were a new puppy. As the head starts to rot and begins buzzing with the sound of flies swarming around it, Curl's infection intensifies. When he threatens to shoot Decker, Decker asks him to first take a picture of him with a camera he has secretly rigged to explode when the shutter button is pressed. The explosion puts an end to Curl's misery in typical Hiaasen fashion by blowing *his* head off.

In addition to addressing his favorite topic—the continuing destruction of Florida by mindless development—Hiaasen takes some satiric potshots at two other targets—the twin perversions of the purity of fishing and preaching. To an avid amateur fisherman like Hiaasen, who as a young boy fished for bass in the Everglades from a floating inner tube, the very idea of a big-business professional fishing circuit is absurd. By the same token, a preacher addressing the faithful can be a genuine spiritual experience, but not when money attracts TV evangelists like Weeb to the profession, turning what was pure into cynical fakery, all in the service not of the Almighty but the Almighty Dollar.

Though Skink's character dominates the proceedings in *Double Whammy*, he was originally intended to play a minor role. Hiaasen found himself liking him more and more and decided to give him a bigger role. Like Skip Wiley, he's a bit crazy, but his heart is in the right place. Unlike Wiley, he doesn't harm innocent people; those he attacks deserve it. Also, unlike Wiley he doesn't get up on a soapbox to pontificate or offer lengthy justifications for his behavior. Once we know his background, we understand why he acts the way he does. He's a man of principle (Hiaasen calls him a "moral compass") whose actions speak for themselves. "He's the sort of character I wish existed in real life," Hiaasen says, "and it's one of the great joys of the novel, being able to turn him loose and have him kick some butt" (Pleasants 268).

Skink serves as Hiaasen's avenging angel. Some of his actions are more symbolic than realistic, like firing his pistol at airplanes bringing prospective Lunker Lakes buyers to Fort Lauderdale. Others are more personal, like barbecuing a pet poodle belonging to the man who was once a leading salesman of units at the development Skink as governor failed to stop and which prompted his resignation. Now as ex-governor, Skink can, like Hiaasen in his role as novelist, act as his own judge, jury, and executioner. For example, as he pilots a boat along the Intracoastal Waterway, he slows to a crawl when he approaches a manatee zone. But when a nearby boatload of partygoers ignore his repeated warning to slow down, he takes matters into his own hands: he pummels several of the passengers and then fires three shots into the hull, sinking the boat.

Hiaasen says he modeled Skink in part on his childhood friend Clyde Ingalls, whose suicide at age seventeen made such a powerful and lasting impression on him. (The novel is dedicated to his memory.) But, he confesses, "The other part of Skink is me.... He does things I wish I could do" (Burke "Last").

Double Whammy represents a noticeable advance in Hiaasen's narrative mastery. Where the momentum in his first novel was periodically interrupted by speeches and lengthy stretches of exposition, the pace of the narrative in his second novel never falters. Hiaasen is able to tell several stories almost simultaneously, artfully switching back and forth between scenes. Like a skilled film editor, he knows how to quicken the pace of the story by using shorter scenes and rapid cuts. And instead of exposition, he relies almost entirely on character and action to propel the narrative.

Though Hiaasen once admitted that *Double Whammy* was a twisted little book and said he was proud he was even able to get it published, he needn't have worried about the reception it would receive. Allan J. Hubin, founder and longtime editor of *The Armchair Detective*, said the novel "might be the wildest mystery story I've ever read, with at least one outrageously memorable character and a narrative like none other, with bizarre and comic scenes generously arrayed along the route." The *New York Times* reviewer singled out Hiaasen's skill in grabbing the reader's attention: "He does it in *Double Whammy* on the very first page and he doesn't let go until virtually every one of the book's bizarre characters gets his or her just deserts in a final scene that would have movie audiences bursting into cheers." He ends with this injunction: "Climb aboard, bubba. Strap yourself in. You gonna like this ride" (Walker). Other reviewers found appropriate fish metaphors to sing its praises: one called it "a raucous, mordant whopper of a South Florida fish story" (Trimborn); another said the novel "strikes with all the force of a hawg bass on amphetamines" (Morris). After just two solo efforts, Hiaasen's fledgling career as a novelist was off to a promising start.

Skin Tight *(1989)*

Mick Stranahan is a former investigator for the Florida State Attorney's Office, now on disability retirement. He lives alone in an old stilt house on the shallow tidal flats of Biscayne Bay. One day a stranger appears at his door. Suspicious about the man, Stranahan, who has been hiding in the dark ever since hearing his boat approach, kicks a stool across the floor, causing the stranger to pull out a pistol. Stranahan then grabs a stuffed marlin head from the wall and runs its bill through the man's chest, killing him. The manner of death may be ludicrous, but the threat was serious. Somebody wants him dead. Who? And why?

The only clue he has is a case he worked on four years earlier involving the disappearance of a young college student named Vicky Barletta, who vanished after leaving the office of a plastic surgeon named Dr. Rudy Graveline, who had just performed a nose job on her. The connection to that case becomes stronger when a famous TV journalist named Reynaldo Flemm and his producer arrive from New York looking for an interview with him about

4. Novels for Adults

the young woman's disappearance. They were recently contacted by Maggie Gonzalez, Rudy Graveline's nurse, about what really happened to the missing woman. When Stranahan later learns that Gonzalez told Graveline that he was resuming his investigation onto the incident, he concludes it was Graveline who hired the man who tried to kill him. What he doesn't know is that Graveline has hired a second killer to finish the job.

The man he hires is named Chemo, another unforgettable product of Hiaasen's twisted imagination. Born Blondell Wayne Tatum, he was orphaned at age six when his parents, members of a religious cult that believed in vegetarianism, UFOs, and not paying income taxes, were gunned down in a shootout with the FBI. He was subsequently raised in an Amish community in Pennsylvania by his grandparents who posed as Amish after fleeing a mail-fraud indictment in New Jersey. At age twenty-one, he committed his first crime: he robbed a bank by threatening the teller with a pitchfork, which drew headlines as the only known bank robbery by an Amish in the state's history. Chemo then decided to turn to burglary, an unwise choice for a young man who stands six foot nine; he became stuck in the first window he ever jimmied and later spent four months in the county jail. After his release, he decided to try his hand at white-collar crime and eventually became the assistant city manager in a small town where he perfected the art of the shakedown.

But his life would change dramatically thanks to a freak accident during an electrolysis procedure aimed at burning two ingrown hair follicles off the tip of his nose. In the middle of the procedure, the elderly dermatologist suffered a crippling stroke, which caused him to incinerate every pore of Chemo's face. Chemo killed the old doctor and fled, his face now looking like he had glued Rice Krispies to every inch of it. He makes matters even worse when he tries to cover up his scars with Wite-Out. The combination of his scary face and skinny frame (181 pounds spread over a six-foot-nine frame) makes him look like "Fred Munster with bulimia" (200). Rudy Graveline offers him a deal: he'll give him a discount on treatments for his face if he will agree to kill Stranahan.

Hiaasen then adds one more comic detail. After Chemo's hand is bitten off by a barracuda, instead of obtaining a normal prosthesis, he decides to have a Weed Whacker surgically attached to his arm. This proves to be a useful instrument in his various activities, criminal and otherwise. For example, it's particularly helpful in fending off the annoying approach of a Moonie selling a bouquet of carnations. Chemo simply switches on the battery pack under his arm and chops the flowers into confetti.

Mick Stranahan comes closer to being a genuine hero than did either of his predecessors in Hiaasen's first two novels. He exudes a kind of Clint Eastwood laconic cool, the kind of guy who allows his actions to speak more than his words. He is able to sum up his whole life story in simple terms: "I've killed five men, and I've been married five times" (198). Not that he's necessarily proud of either accomplishment, but he has no regrets either. The men he killed—either in Vietnam or on the job—were all trying to kill him. As for the women he married, the reason is simple: "He was constantly falling in love; how else would you explain five marriages, all to cocktail waitresses" (91). As for the five women he divorced? "I loved them all, for a time," he explains. "Then one day I didn't" (210).

Unlike Brian Keyes and R. J. Decker, he's an experienced investigator who needs no help in digging out the truth. Even though Miami-Dade homicide detective Al Garcia makes another appearance, he plays a minor role in the action. It is Stranahan who has to singlehandedly fight off repeated attempts on his life while questioning enough people to expose the truth about Dr. Rudy Graveline.

Thanks to Stranahan, there's more of a thriller quality to *Skin Tight* than there was in either *Tourist Season* and *Double Whammy*. There's little mystery in the novel as it's abundantly clear early on that Rudy Graveline is the person responsible for Vicky Barletta's death. The suspense arises from Graveline's attempts to keep the truth from coming out. Added to the mix is a pair of crooked Miami cops after Stranahan for the suspected murder of one of his former wives (who was actually killed by Chemo when she made the mistake of calling him "Velcro Face"); they too are hired to kill Stranahan.

While Stranahan goes about the business of trying to get the goods on Dr. Graveline, Chemo prepares to mount a second assault on him. But in typical Hiaasen fashion, humor is never entirely out of the picture. Armed with a machine gun strapped over his shoulder and wearing only jockey shorts, Chemo rides a jet ski to Stranahan's stilt house, where he intends to kill him. Stranahan, however, scares him off, causing him to fall into the water, where Lucy, the barracuda Stranahan has been regularly feeding, promptly bites his hand off, necessitating the Weed-Whacker prosthesis.

The character of Dr. Rudy Graveline is a good illustration of how Hiaasen's journalism informs his fiction. "Dangerous Doctors," one of Hiaasen's most acclaimed investigative pieces, was an eye-opening exposé of Florida's problems with incompetent doctors. Not only were there so many, his investigation uncovered evidence of a bigger problem: e. g., how difficult

4. Novels for Adults

it was to get rid of them mainly because the board that heard complaints was composed entirely of fellow doctors who were reluctant to punish one of their own. Graveline is a fictionalized version of this very real problem.

To begin with, he's a fraud. He finished dead last in his medical school class at Harvard, barely squeaked through his residence in radiology, and has no training whatsoever in plastic surgery. How could he become a prominent plastic surgeon whose facility, Whispering Palms Spa (which prominently displays the motto, VANITY IS BEAUTIFUL), employs a staff of eight other surgeons? Easy. No law prevented him from declaring plastic surgery as his specialty: "that was the beauty of the medical profession—once you got a degree, you could try whatever you damn well pleased, from brain surgery to gynecology. Hospitals might do some checking, but never the patients. And failing at one or more specialities (as Rudy had), you could always leave town and try something else" (82).

Then there's the equally serious problem of why no one can stop him. Even though Graveline knows "physicians stick together like shit on a shoe" (112), the state medical board, after examining thirteen malpractice complaints against him, has no choice but to recommend suspension of his license. But Graveline also knows that, "one of the wondrous things about Florida … was the climate of unabashed corruption. There was absolutely no trouble from which money could not extricate you" (112). A gift of a new Volvo station wagon to the underpaid hearing officer in charge of his case results in the restoration of his license and the sealing of all records from the press and the public, "thus honoring the long-held philosophy of Florida's medical establishment that the last persons who need to know about a doctor's incompetence are the patients" (113).

Following a series of botched operations (he severed one patient's ear while attempting to remove a small cyst on it and nearly suctioned another man's gall bladder out of his abdomen during a liposuction procedure), Graveline's incompetence finally caught up with him. He accidentally killed Vicky Barletta during a routine nose job and then recruited his brother, owner of a tree-trimming service, to dispose of her body in his wood chipper. Now he's forced to kill anyone who might expose his crime.

Sensationalist TV newsman Geraldo Rivera was also a subject of one of Hiaasen's columns. In 1986, after watching a two-hour documentary starring Rivera that included live drug busts in several cities, including Miami, Hiaasen wrote a column expressing his disgust at Rivera's show-biz approach to the news that was more "self-serving hokum" than meaningful. But he could only do so much in 700 words. In *Skin Tight*, he can take as much time as he wants to lampoon Rivera and other media yahoos like him.

Reynaldo Flemm is one of Hiaasen's great comic characters; for those who recognize that the character is a thinly disguised version of Geraldo Rivera, it's also one of his most devastating satirical putdowns. Flemm (real name: Ray Fleming) is famous for getting beaten up on camera: "In his professional life he had been beaten by Teamsters, goosed by white supremacists, clubbed by Mafia torpedoes, pistol-whipped by Bandito bikers, and kicked in the groin by the Pro-Life Posse" (351). He's also lazy, vain, and dumb. His producer Christina Marks does all his research, writes his lines, and edits his pieces in such a way as to keep him from looking like the ignorant airhead he really is. Instead of looking for new stories to cover, he's more interested in coming up with new ways to show off how tough he thinks he is. His secret dream is to get shot (not seriously) in the thigh live on national television: "I'm tired of getting beat up," he explains to Christina. "I want to break some new ground" (180).

Vanity and stupidity, however, eventually lead to his downfall. He decides he no longer needs his producer to do his work for him. He'll expose Dr. Rudy Graveline on camera all by himself. Pretending to be a male exotic dancer by the name of Johnny LeTigre, he pays Graveline $15,000 for a nose job and a tummy tuck. He orders his cameraman to wait outside the operating room until he gives him the signal to enter and videotape him forcing Graveline to confess to Vicky Barletta's death. Unfortunately, he was given a general rather than a local anesthetic and in the confusion caused by the cameraman's sudden entrance, Graveline inadvertently vacuums Flemm's aorta out, killing him. In an ironic twist, the body of the man who craved the spotlight is passed off as that of an unidentified pauper and sold to a medical school in Guadeloupe, where surgical students can practice on it.

The humor in *Skin Tight* is darker than that in *Double Whammy*, and many of the deaths are comically gruesome: one victim is run through with a marlin's head; a pair of crooked cops are both garroted in their boat by fishing line Stranahan has strung between trees; a man who is trying to feed an unconscious Stranahan into a wood chipper is shot and falls into the chipper himself. One grisly death is particularly apt: Rudy Graveline is killed when an instrument he uses in nose-job operations is pounded up his nose and into his brain, replicating the way he caused Vicky Barletta's death that began all his troubles.

Hiaasen exploits all kinds of comic possibilities in *Skin Tight*. As part of his plan to nail Dr. Graveline, Stranahan needs a lawyer and a good case of malpractice to bring against him. Rather than simply settling for the ordinary, Hiaasen goes for the humorous alternative. He blackmails his brother-in-law, a sleazy ambulance chaser, into taking a doozy case against Graveline—a man is blinded in one eye when one of the implants Graveline improperly inserted in his wife's breasts explodes while they are making love, hitting him squarely in the eye. Then all three are brought together for one final farcical scene in which the lawyer insists to the woman that for legal purposes he needs to feel her breasts. When her husband comes home unexpectedly and, despite having only one eye, clearly sees what the lawyer is doing, he hurls several jai alai balls at him, knocking him out.

Hiaasen also uses peripheral details, like the Miami Beach punk nightclub named the Gay Bidet where Chemo sometimes works as a greeter, for additional humor. Interspersed throughout the novel are the names of the ridiculous acts that perform there: the Chicken Chokers, whose members wear jockstraps which they wring out in a glass after playing and then guzzle down the contents. The Crotch Rockets; the Fudge Packers, whose four members all play bass guitar; a slut-rock group from London called Cathy and the Catheters; and a vocal quartet known as The Fabulous Foreskins.

Hiaasen concludes the novel with a comic feature he will employ in several of his subsequent books: he adds an epilogue which gives the reader a glimpse into future developments in the lives of his characters. Among them are these gems: Chemo, now serving a seventeen-year prison sentence at the Florida State prison in Raiford, is appropriately put in charge of the winter vegetable garden, where he can put his Weed-Whacker arm to good use; and the producers of Reynaldo Flemm's TV show announce that a $25,000 scholarship in his name will be set up at the Columbia University School of Journalism, from which, ironically, Flemm had twice been expelled.

Florida doesn't play much of a role in *Skin Tight*. The action could easily be set elsewhere, and the main crimes against nature in this novel are the unnecessary operations performed on people by money-grubbing quacks like Rudy Graveline. However, there is one powerful reminder of Florida's sad environmental decline that comes in some late-night musings by Mick Stranahan. As he gazes out over Miami from his home on the water, he "regarded the city as a malignancy and its sickly orange aura as a vast misty bubble of pustular gas" (340). The view to the south—"a throbbing congealment from Coconut Grove to south Miami and beyond"—isn't any better. Nor is what lies west, a ten-story-tall fetid landfill along the shore of Biscayne Bay known as Mount Trashmore.

Stranahan can't decide which is worse, the city skyline or the mountain of garbage. "The turkey buzzards, equally ambivalent, commuted regularly from one site to the other." All this leaves him wondering "what it would be like to wake up and find the city vaporized, the skies clear and silent, the shoreline lush and virginal! He would have loved to live here at the turn of the century, when nature owned the upper hand" (341).

Mick Stranahan is an engaging character and an effective private eye. G. P. Putnam's Sons, the publisher of Hiaasen's first three novels, aware of the commercial advantages of a continuing series, encouraged him to write more Stranahan books. But Hiaasen was reluctant to get tied down to one character. Sonny Mehta, head of Alfred A. Knopf, met with him and assured him if he moved to Knopf he would be free to continue writing the kind of novels he had been writing. He did and has remained with them ever since.

Native Tongue *(1991)*

Florida returns to center stage in *Native Tongue*, another hilarious crime romp wrapped around a satiric assault on some of the state's environmental crimes and cultural excesses. It all begins with the theft of a pair of rare blue-tongued mango voles from the Amazing Kingdom of Thrills theme park in North Key Largo, just south of Miami. Unaware that the voles are the last two surviving members of their species, the two thieves who stole them cavalierly toss them out the window of their truck at passing cars.

Shortly afterwards, Joe Winder, who has just been hired as the theme park's PR writer, gets a phone call asking him to meet Dr. Will Koocher, the park zoologist who tended the rare voles, at midnight on an isolated bridge. Instead of meeting Koocher, he is brutally attacked by a pair of assailants. His life is spared by the timely appearance of a strange man with "a silvery beard of biblical proportions. Mismatched eyes: one as green as mountain pines, the other brown and dead. Above that, a halo of pink flowers" (73). Who else could it be but Skink, the former Florida governor-turned-hermit.

Like Hiaasen's previous protagonists, Joe Winder has a newspaper background; he was an award-winner journalist who lost his job after he got into a fistfight with an editor over an article he wrote that proved that his own father, a developer, had paid off a county commissioner in order to get a zoning variance he needed. He attacked the editor because he refused to publish it, claiming Winder was too emotionally involved in the story. Winder then took a job as a PR writer for Disney World, but lasted there only six months before being fired for having sex with Cinderella's understudy on Mr. Toad's Wild Ride. He now cranks out cheerful twaddle for the Amazing Kingdom of Thrills, a job he describes as a "high-paying bullshit PR job" that takes absolutely nothing out of him, "except his pride" (26).

Events take a weird turn when the body of Dr. Koocher is found in the belly of Orky the Whale, another resident at the amazing Kingdom of Thrills. Suicide or accident? Or perhaps even murder? Winder teams up with his new friend Skink on an investigation that leads to a stunning revelation: the adorable little blue-tongued mango voles named Violet and Vance were fake: no such species ever existed. They were ordinary voles whose tongues were dyed blue. In fact, nearly everything about The Amazing Kingdom of Thrills, including its owner, Francis X. Kingsbury, is a fraud.

Though lauded by the local Chamber of Commerce and honored as the Rotarian Citizen of the Year, Kingsbury is in reality "a two-bit jizzbag on the run from the mob" (251). His real name is Frankie "The Ferret" King who several years earlier was arrested in New York on racketeering charges. After ratting out his co-conspirators, several of whom were members of gangster John Gotti's crime organization, he entered the government's Witness Protection Program. He changed his named to Francis X. Kingsbury and moved to Miami, "the prime relocation site for scores of scuzzy federal snitches (on the theory that South Florida was a place where just about any dirtbag would blend in smoothly with the existing riffraff)" (39). He proved to be a wizard at selling Florida real estate before deciding to become a developer himself. His first project was the Amazing Kingdom of Thrills, designed as South Florida's competition to Orlando's Disney World.

Hiaasen's sour attitude towards Disney is displayed in several of his columns and would be the subject of a book, *Team Rodent: How Disney Devours the World*, published in 1998, where he called the company "an agent of pure wickedness" (18). Aside from the negative consequences of the endless hordes of tourists descending on Florida (garbage, litter, traffic, air pollution), he also criticized Disney for dignifying "blind greed in a state pioneered by undignified greedheads" *(Team 5)*. The Amazing Kingdom of Thrills is even worse. Kingsbury also hates Disney, but for his own selfish reasons. He is obsessed by its success in sucking up tourist dollars and he wants in on the action. He shows his contempt by getting a tattoo on his arm depicting Mickey and Minnie Mouse engaged in sex and by always referring to Mickey Mouse as Mickey Ratface, which is ironic considering his gangland nickname was "The Ferret."

In the 1980s, Disney World earned well-deserved acclaim for its efforts to save the dusky seaside sparrow from extinction. Kingsbury's heavily publicized effort to save the blue-tongued voles from a similar fate was his cynical attempt to outdo Disney World in the feel-good category. It worked, and even the Florida Audubon Society praised the Vole Project as "a shining example of private enterprise using its vast financial resources to save a small but precious resource of nature" (61). Left unsaid is the fact that Kingsbury destroyed 2000 acres of Florida's natural environment on North Key Largo to make way for his park. He also defrauded the U.S. Government out of $200,000 in grant money he received under the Endangered Species Act to save ordinary voles whose tongues were simply dyed blue. Now he will do anything to keep the truth from coming out.

It isn't just the voles that are phony. Everything from Kingsbury's name and the various wigs he wears to the hokey attractions in the park is built on deceit. A typical example is the Wild Bill Hiccup rodeo ride:

> The ride was set up in an indoor corral that had been laboriously fabricated, from the brown-dyed dirt to the balsa fence posts to the polyethylene cowshit that lay in neat regular mounds, free of flies. Twenty-five mechanical bulls (only the horns were real) jumped and bucked on hidden tracks while a phony rodeo announcer described the action through a realistically tinny megaphone [108].

(The ride proved to be costly to Kingsbury, who had to pay a seven-figure settlement to an elderly British tourist who was hospitalized after suffering a 90-degree crimp in his plastic penile implant while riding on it.)

Nothing gets Hiaasen's comic juices flowing better than a spectacle, and he creates a doozy in *Native Tongue*. Each day at the Amazing Kingdom of Thrills ends with a pageant, which gives Hiaasen an opportunity for some over-the-top-humor that embodies a serious point. In an essay on *Native Tongue*, Robert Bowman noted that Hiaasen "critiques the deification of leisure" as well as the way "the tourism industry, representative of Florida culture at large, has historically hinged on the romanticized manipulation of public expectations" (9). The nightly parade of brightly colored floats is designed to tell the story of Florida going back to the time of the Spaniards, though it conveniently overlooks "the plundering, genocide, defoliation and gang rape that typified the peninsula's past." For the "feel-good purposes" of the pageant, the sordid history of Florida is compressed into a series of "amiable and bloodless encounters" (182). One float, titled "Migrants on a Mission," features cheery farm workers singing Jamaican folk songs while breakdancing through the sugar cane fields. Others feature Ponce de Leon wading into the Fountain of Youth with a pair of underage maidens, a tribute to the Killer Hurricane of 1926, during which the wind tears the smock off a settler's wife, and finally the arrival of the legendary Seminole maiden Princess Golden Sun dancing a sexy lambada while dressed in a micro-bikini made of simulated deerskin. All of this prompts Skink to remark, "I never realized cleavage played such an important role in Florida history" (307).

One of Hiaasen's proudest achievements as a journalist was a series of articles he and his fellow investigative team members wrote that resulted in stopping the planned development of the massive Port Bougainville development on North Key Largo. In *Native Tongue* his characters face a similar battle when it is revealed that Francis X. Kingsbury is also the majority owner of a planned resort next to the Amazing Kingdom of Thrills called Falcon Trace. If it isn't stopped, every square inch of oceanfront property will be bulldozed to make way for a golf course and housing development.

In a scene that recalls Hiaasen's own experience as a young boy who watched helplessly as his beloved Everglades playground was bulldozed in the name of "progress," Joe Winder encounters a vision every bit as shocking as he heads to his secret fishing spot. The path through the hardwoods to the mangrove shore has been transformed into empty space: "It looked as if a twenty-megaton bomb had gone off. Bulldozers had piled the dead trees in mountainous tangles at each corner of the property" (97). What happens next leaves him "with a homicidal churning in his belly" (99): he hears the sounds of a high school band playing "America the Beautiful," followed by the local mayor announcing to the gathered dignitaries that this scene of utter devastation will be the future site of the sixteenth hole of the Falcon Trace golf course, the centerpiece of Kingsbury's new resort development.

Initial opposition to the new development started due to the efforts of a seventy-year-old firebrand named Molly McNamara, founder and president of the Mothers of Wilderness, a group of senior citizens concerned about the future of the environment. It was Molly who hired a pair of bumbling burglars to liberate the blue-tongued voles from exploitation by the Amazing Kingdom.

Joe Winder then embarks on his own guerrilla campaign to save the wilderness: he begins by forcing a pair of Falcon Trace workers to use their bulldozers to knock over a billboard promoting the resort and a trailer housing the construction company. Then he sets the bulldozers afire. Later he recruits a friend to launch a rocket-propelled grenade at a cement truck on the property.

He also comes up with a clever scheme to sabotage the park by issuing false press releases about problems he invents. First, there is the hepatitis epidemic among Uncle Ely's Elves. Then there is the infestation of hundreds of poisonous cottonmouth moccasins accompanied by a warning that while the park will remain open, visitors are advised to wear heavy rubber boots if they visit. Winder's phony items force park PR head Charles Chelsea, Winder's former boss, into clever rebuttals of his own, resulting in a comedy of dueling flacks seeking to outdo one another in creative lying.

Skink assumes his usual role of enforcer of environmental justice. Earlier in the novel, we learned about some of his activities since his previous appearance. He tends to his collection of books by favorite authors—Hemingway, Steinbeck, Camus, Salinger, Vonnegut, Gabriel García Márquez (in Spanish), many of them first additions—he keeps in an old Plymouth station wagon with no wheels. He's been testing a new mosquito repellent for the U.S. Marines. He's still shooting at incoming airplanes and rental cars driven by tourists and making theatrically symbolic statements, like tossing a dead baby manatee on the stage during the Miss Florida pageant to remind the public about the dire consequences of waterfront development. However, he saves his most dramatic act for the end of the novel when he burns down the Amazing Kingdom in a fiery apocalypse, prompting Trooper Jim Tile's reminder that his friend is "a man to be admired but not imitated" (297).

With his park in ruins and Falcon Trace now doomed, Kingsbury also suffers two additional setbacks. The winner of a new car for being the five-millionth visitor to the park (another fraud: attendance is nowhere near that number) turns out to be a hitman hired by the Gotti mob to kill Kingsbury for ratting out his friends. The final indignity comes when the Disney Corporation wins a $1.2 million legal judgment against his estate for copyright infringement after his pornographic tattoo of Mickey and Minnie Mouse is spotted on his forearm during his open-casket funeral.

The role of over-the-top weirdo in the novel is played by Pedro Luz, chief of security at the Amazing Kingdom. Like every member of his detail, he's a disgraced ex-cop: he was fired from the Miami Police force for stealing cash and cocaine from drug dealers and then shoving them out of a plane over the Everglades. Now he spends most of his time doing Kingsbury's dirty work (like killing Dr. Koocher and roughing up Molly McNamara), bodybuilding, and gulping steroids. After being hospitalized for injuries suffered when a ferret attacked his ankle, he discovers that an intravenous tube could be put to good use: he spends the rest of the novel sucking down horse steroids directly from a tube attached to a mobile dispenser he wheels around with him wherever he goes.

His new habit causes his skin to break out in acne all over his body and though his legs grow to be as thick as oaks, his penis shrivels to the size of a peanut. But his new-found strength does have some benefits: he uses his head as a battering ram to knock down a locked steel door, and when a car lands on his foot, pinning him to the ground, he simply chews the foot off at the ankle like an animal would.

In the end, he suffers one of Hiaasen's most hilarious fates: while fighting with Skink in front of Dicky the Dolphin's tank, the animal grabs him by the hair and pulls him into the water. Thereupon the frisky sex-starved bottle-nosed dolphin romances Luz to his death by drowning in the same tank where he dumped Will Koocher's body. Lest one might think that Hiaasen has gone too far, he points out in a note to the reader at the beginning of the novel that while all the events in his novel are imaginary, the depiction of aberrant sexual behavior by bottle-nosed dolphins is based on true cases on file with the Florida State marine laboratory.

Hiaasen has great fun with his secondary characters. It comes as no surprise to learn that Molly McNamara is a friend of Skink (and a former volunteer during his gubernatorial campaign). Despite her age, she's not a person to be messed with. For example, though she pays lovable but dim-witted burglars $10,000 to steal the blue-tongued voles, she takes out her displeasure at losing them because of their bungling efforts by shooting one of them in the foot and later the other in the hand after he steals one of his partner's pain pills. In addition, she bites the tip of Pedro Luz's finger off when he attacks her, and when an FBI agent asks her to take a polygraph test, she shoots him in the thigh.

There are numerous other comic delights, including pot-smoking elves, a baboon that picks up a gun and shoots a bad guy, and the misadventures of the three tons of Orky the Whale's remains, which Kingsbury hopes to sell to South Korea or the Sudan as tuna. Even famous *Today* show weatherman Willard Scott makes a cameo appearance when he visits the park to celebrate the occasion of its five-millionth visitor and to do what he's famous for, honoring people who have reached the age of 100 or more. After planting a big smooch on the ear of a 107-year-old-woman (in reality, a thirty-eight-year-old actress hired for the job), he grabs popular park mascot Robbie the Raccoon (actually Joe Winder in disguise) for a live TV interview. "You're certainly a big fella, Robbie," Scott says. "Judging by the size of that tummy, I'd say you've been snooping through a few garbage cans!" To which Robbie shoots back, "Look who's talking, lardass" (283).

Given that *Native Tongue* is fiction rather than real life, nature can emerge the victor. In the epilogue, we learn the good news that the gutted remains of the Amazing Kingdom have been replanted with native trees. And thanks to Molly McNamara, who claims she spotted a pair of rare blue-tongued voles on the Falcon Trace golf report, further development is halted.

Native Tongue is Hiaasen's funniest novel to date, a hilarious cornucopia of comic craziness. (Reviewing it for *The New York Times*, Linda Wolfe aptly described it as a "rowdy, rollicking cartoon strip of a novel.") And yet for all its zaniness, it never ignores its satiric function. The laughs keep coming as do the barbs. Hiaasen continued to garner rave reviews and the novel achieved two important milestones: it was the first to crack the *New York Times* paperback best-seller list; and it earned Hiaasen his first major award, the British Crime Writers' Last Laugh Award as the Funniest Crime Novel of 1992. Only one milestone remained: making it on to the *Times* hardcover best-seller list, which his very next novel would do.

Strip Tease *(1993)*

Oh, what a fun ride it is when a writer with a twisted imagination like Hiaasen's decides to set his novel in a strip club, as he does in *Strip Tease*. First he sets up the crime. Erin Grant is a nude dancer at the Eager Beaver strip club in Fort Lauderdale. One night, a drunken partygoer jumps up on stage and starts hugging her. Another drunken customer leaps to her rescue and pummels the other man with an empty champagne bottle. The incident is witnessed by a third customer, Jerry Killian, who recognizes the man with the bottle as a U.S. Congressman named David Dilbeck. Mild-mannered Killian is head-over-heels in love with Erin Grant and knows that she is battling her ex-husband over custody of their four-year-old daughter Angela. He decides to use the damaging information he has against Dilbeck to force him to get the judge in Erin's case to reverse his decision and award custody of Angela to Erin. Shortly afterwards, his body is found floating in a river in Montana. An autopsy reveals he was murdered.

Hiaasen introduces something new with the character of Erin Grant:

both the perspective of a smart woman and an emotional element missing from his previous books in that her whole focus is not on solving a crime but regaining custody of her daughter. She's a smart woman caught in an unfortunate situation. Her big mistake was marrying Darrell Grant, who turned out to be a pillhead, a convict, and a man whose profession is stealing wheelchairs and then selling them. She lost her job filing intelligence reports for the FBI when her security clearance was revoked after Darrell, from whom she was separated, was charged with a fourth felony. Erin was forced to find a new job where she could earn enough money to pay the mounting legal fees she owes as a result of a fight with her now ex-husband over custody of their daughter Angela.

Darrell convinced a judge that Erin's new job as a topless dancer made her an unfit mother. (The judge is another in Hiaasen's growing gallery of hypocrites. After lecturing Erin on the importance of morality and decency, he becomes a regular customer at the Eager Beaver, accompanied by his Bible which he balances on his knees to hide his hands while he's masturbating to the naked dancers.) Erin's efforts to gain custody of Angela take on a new urgency once she learns that Darrell has been dressing her in her Cookie Monster pajamas and using her as a prop to help him steal wheelchairs from hospitals.

Erin is a woman with principles. She rejects one potential suitor because he complains there's too much talking on "60 Minutes," her favorite TV show. She is the only dancer at the Eager Beaver who refuses to participate in nude oil wrestling, perform table dances, or have sex with customers: "I'll rob Jiffy Marts before I'll turn tricks," she insists (107). She's also intelligent and quick-witted. For example, when she immediately identifies the man in a photo Dilbeck shows her as former Speaker of the House Tip O'Neill, he's impressed. "You *are* something special," he says. To which she replies, "So what do I win ... a dinette set" (310)? And she can take care of herself. When Darrell's brother-in-law gets too sexually aggressive towards her, she knees him in the chin, causing him to bite the tip of his tongue off.

Darrell Grant is a felonious jerk. While working as a hospital orderly, he acquired a taste for narcotics and a professional interest in wheelchairs. Erin, who knew none of this, was won over by his boyish wit and charm. But once their daughter was born, she began to see the real Darrell. Stealing wheelchairs for a living might seem a stretch, but as usual Hiaasen was inspired by a true story, though also as usual he ups the absurdity. He says his aim was to give Erin the worst possible ex-husband he could, and a guy who would help a woman with polio into her van and then run off with her wheelchair certainly fits the bill.

Implausibility isn't normally an issue in Hiaasen's novels where exaggeration is the norm, but there is a giant one in *Strip Tease* involving Miami cop Al Garcia, back for yet another appearance. He and his family are vacationing in Montana when his young son spots a body, later identified as Jerry Killian, floating in the river. (Garcia later determines that Killian was murdered in Florida and his body driven to Montana, where he vacationed and where his death would likely be deemed an accidental drowning while fishing; unlucky for his killers, Montana is the same place Garcia chose for his vacation.) Garcia has absolutely no jurisdiction in the case, but because he wants to punish the creeps who ruined his family's vacation, he decides to look into Killian's murder.

In Hiaasen's hands, the Eager Beaver (formerly the Booby Hatch) is portrayed as a kind of male-only Amazing Kingdom of Thrills, where fantasies are created by the dancers who, like Francis X. Kingsbury and Disney, are in the business of extracting as much money as they can from the paying customers. Having himself visited several strip clubs to interview dancers and observe the customers, Hiaasen came to this conclusion:

> You realize how pathetic the human male is, and what a calculated, predatory scene the bars have set up to exploit their delusions. Only in America would a guy go in and think, I'm in my bowling shirt, and I'm gonna knock the socks off one of these beautiful topless dancers, and she's gonna run off with me. And in about an hour and five minutes he's flat busted, he's spent his entire paycheck on drinks and tips and he's got nothing. And then next week he comes back for more [Rosenbaum 134].

Orly, the Eager Beaver's owner, is a comic version of Kingsbury. Unlike Kingsbury, however, who was a gangster posing as an upright citizen, Orly is the reverse: he pretends to be mob-connected, but the gangster names he drops are ones he gets from reading crime magazines. In reality, his partners aren't Mafia members, just a group of harmless orthopedic surgeons. But like Kingsbury, he's beset by annoying problems. He has to find a new name for his club after a manufacturer of chain saws threatens to sue him for using the name of one of its products. (The Eager Beaver is re-named Tickled Pink, which Erin quips sounds like the name of a gynecologist's yacht.) He loses one of his dancers when the boa constrictor she gets to replace the nine-foot-long Burmese python she normally uses in her act wraps itself so tightly around her leg that she develops a bad case of phlebitis. Among the many things the dancers grouse about is the air conditioning, which Orly sets at a

4. Novels for Adults

low temperature to keep the women's nipples hard. Nipples, he points out to them, "are a mighty important part of this enterprise" (91).

Also like Kingsbury, his biggest headache is his competition, a strip club located just down the road called the Flesh Farm, owned by the Ling brothers. Forced to find an attraction to compete with the friction dancing they offer, he comes up with the idea of topless wrestling in a vat filled with creamed corn. When his dancers complain that such an activity is classless, he suggests they consider wrestling in pasta instead. "What's classier than pasta?" he asks (176).

The strip club's dancers, with names like Urbana Sprawl, Monique Sr., and Monique Jr. (so-called because neither would change her name), contribute to the humor. For example, Monique Sr. performs special dances for the various celebrities she claims she sees in the audience—Alan Greenspan, Bobby Knight, Keith Richards. Urbana Sprawl, famous for the size of her double-wide bosom, complains about having to dance to energetic music like that of ZZ Top: holding one of her titanic breasts in each hand, she explains, "Try jumping around with *these* suckers and you be in traction" (61). On the other hand, the size of her bosom gives her an unfair advantage in creamed-corn wresting matches with the customers: "She specialized in pinning opponents without using her arms" (212).

Hiaasen is also interested in the dynamics of strip-club crowds. In *Native Tongue*, he noted that visitors at the nightly pageant at the Amazing Kingdom cheered "with the blind and witless glee displayed by people who have spent way too much money and are determined to have fun" (307). Male customers who frequent strip clubs are no different, except in the nature of their fantasies. As Erin learned from her five-times-married mother, "an attractive woman could get whatever she wanted, because men were so laughably weak. They would do *anything* for even the distant promise of sex" (24). Experienced dancers knew that, "you could work a guy all night and get every last dollar out of his wallet. You didn't have to blow him or screw him or even act like you might. A girlish smile, a sisterly hug, a few minutes of private conversation ... it was the easiest money in the world, if you could get past being naked "(213).

Shad, the Eager Beaver bouncer, illustrates the occupational hazard of working at a strip club for eleven years: he becomes numbed to the sight of naked women. "I've lost my sense of wonderment," he complains (298). He needs a new career, and hits upon a novel scam as his ticket out: he plants a dead cockroach in a container of yogurt and looks for a lawyer to sue the manufacturer for mental anguish. His plan is scuttled when the lawyer's secretary eats the yogurt by mistake. Then, after reading Franz Kafka's "Metamorphosis," he starts feeling sorry for cockroaches and has to switch to planting a scorpion in a carton of cottage cheese.

David Lane Dilbeck, a nine-term U.S. Congressman (and upstanding deacon in his church), is the main focus of Hiaasen's satire in the novel. Dilbeck suffers from a weakness involving booze and naked women. "All men have weaknesses," he insists, "Mine is of the fleshly nature" (3). One night he falls head-over-heels in love with Erin Grant, to whose defense he gallantly (and drunkenly) rushes in the opening scene of the novel. He later has one of his henchmen steal the lint from her clothes dryer so he can make love to it, and also gets his hands on her pink disposable razor so he can shave his own body with it. He even has a friend buy him one of her shoes. As he explains it, "these little things—they help me get by. It's harmless sport" (207). Al Garcia, however, sees it differently: "I'm trying to imagine what Thomas Paine would think of a congressman who has sex with old shoes and laundry lint" (255).

Hiaasen's hilarious ridiculing of the Congressman has a serious purpose. In a perfect world one might expect better behavior by our elected officials; in the real world, however, that's not always the case, and over the years Hiaasen has used his column to cite numerous examples of outrageous extracurricular behavior by some of Florida's elected officials. (Dilbeck's actions are based on those of J. Herbert Burke, a Republican Congressman from Broward County who was arrested for disorderly conduct in a Florida topless bar in 1978.) Hiaasen isn't the only one with a jaundiced view of politicians: Orly would like to ban them from his club. He says he'd like to put up a sign that reads, "No politicians allowed! Ax murderers and perverts welcome, but no goddamn politicians" (237).

Dilbeck isn't just a doofus politician; he's a politician who has sold his soul to another evil force—Big Sugar, a frequent target in Hiaasen's columns. The industry relies on Dilbeck's vote for the subsidies that have made the sugar farmers rich, and for his willingness to ignore the environmental damage done as a result of the billions of gallons of polluted water they flush into the Everglades. The problem is that Dilbeck has endangered the continued approval of subsidies for his sugar daddies by earning the wrath of his House colleagues: he cast the deciding vote against approving a 22% pay raise for them because he was so drunk at the time of the vote he accidentally pushed the wrong lever. Now his drunken escapades at a strip club have made the situation even worse.

Enter Malcolm J. ("Moldy") Moldowsky, political fixer extraordinaire, who is hired by the sugar lobby to ensure that nothing endangers Dilbeck's re-election. Unfortunately, thanks to the drunken antics of the man he addresses to his face as "shit-for brains," he has his hands full. He also assumes the role of villain the crime novel requires, the bad guy responsible for the murders of the three people who threaten Dilbeck's re-election by attempting to blackmail him with evidence of his drunken antics at the Eager Beaver. To Hiaasen, he also represents a second kind of evil, the political.

It's easy enough to lampoon a puppet of the sugar industry like Dilbeck, but it's much more difficult to satirize an abstract monster like Big Sugar. In his columns, Hiaasen was able to explain the excesses he was railing against, but readers of his novel require more background information, which forces him to include more exposition than usual. He needs to spell out the reasons why he considers the sugar industry to be so evil: e.g., the price the farmers receive for their product is artificially inflated and guaranteed by the U.S. government, allowing "family" farmers like the Rojos to amass a fortune in the neighborhood of 400 million dollars. (The Rojos are based on the Fanjul brothers, whose "family farm" extends over 170,00 acres and whose combined fortune exceeds 500 million dollars); the arrangement shuts out other Caribbean nations from the U.S. market, further damaging their shaky economies; the industry exploits its workers—mainly migrant laborers from Jamaica and the Dominican Republic—by paying them shamelessly low wages for back-breaking work; and it gets all the fresh water it wants for practically nothing, dirties it with tons of phosphates, dumps it back into nature, and then resists all efforts to be forced to pay to clean it up. All of this is made possible by politicians on the take like Dilbeck, who are paid handsomely for their efforts.

The final confrontation between Erin and Dilbeck relies on the same kind of preachiness employed by Skip Wiley in *Tourist Season*. To educate Dilbeck, who is woefully unaware of the consequences of his unwavering support of the sugar industry, Erin brings him at gunpoint to a cane field. She orders him, now stripped to his boxer shorts, to begin cutting the cane with a machete so he can begin to get some sympathy for the laborers who toil in the hot sun every day. When Dilbeck tires after less than a minute, she reminds him that the cane workers have to cut eight tons each day and are paid such low wages that people like the Rojo brother who bought her shoe as a gift for him could easily afford the $1000 he paid for it.

As usual, Hiaasen metes out justice to his bad guys, but the punishments he devises aren't up to his usual standards of comic comeuppance: Malcolm Moldowsky is beaten to death by Darrell Grant with the 9-iron he uses as a splint on his broken arm, and then Grant is ground to a pulp in a sugar mill. Hiaasen's punishments ordinarily fit the crime, but if anyone should meet his end in a sugar mill, it's Moldowsky, the sugar lobby's fixer. And Dilbeck, the man who certainly deserves some sort of harsh punishment, gets away scot free: he is allowed to claim a "heart attack" as the reason why he stops actively campaigning; he wins anyway, though he does resign from Congress the following day.

A far more comically appropriate fate is that enjoyed by Shad, who finally hits it big with one of his insurance scams by winning a $2.3 million judgment from the Rojo brothers after faking injuries when the car he's riding in is bumped in the rear by one of their sugar trucks. Erin also enjoys a fairytale ending: she obtains custody of Angela, gets her FBI job back, and continues dancing at night, this time as Cinderella's stepsister in Disney World's famous Main Street Parade.

Strip Tease received mainly glowing reviews. One of the few naysayers called Hiaasen "the current master of the potboiler" and dismissed his satire and humor as "about as subtle as full-frontal nudity at high noon" (Holahan). More typical was the enthusiastic review by Donald E. Westlake, master of the comic caper novel, who praised Hiaasen for bringing us in fiction "the unpalatable truths that nonfiction is too polite to mention, and doing it hilariously, his harsh judgments and cold-eyed observations wrapped in so many comic bells and whistles that your sides hurt after a while, just from reading. This novel could be dangerous to your ribs." In his review for *Newsweek,* Malcolm Jones, Jr., proposed that Hiaasen "is fast emerging as our most nimble satirist."

Strip Tease was Hiaasen's breakout novel. It was his first novel to reach the *New York Times* hardcover bestseller list and the first to be made into a Hollywood film, though that proved to be a mixed blessing. The 1996 film, written and directed by Andrew Bergman and starring Demi Moore (who received $12.5 million, the highest amount ever paid to an actress in a Hollywood film up to that point) and Burt Reynolds, was a disaster. It earned the Golden Raspberry Award as Worst Picture of the Year; in his book *Politics and Film: The Political Culture of Film in the United States,* Daniel P. Franklin went even further, flatly declaring, "This is the worst film ever made" (203).

While Hiaasen joked that selling a novel to Hollywood is like sending a child to the Charles Manson Day Care Center, he accepted the film's fate with equanimity. He understood the difficult challenge the filmmakers faced in capturing the comic tone of the narrative voice he used in his novel. When asked if he's mad about what Hollywood did to the book, he replies that they didn't do anything to it; it's still right there on the shelf. One lousy film adaptation will likely have little effect on his reputation as a writer. "If that's the worst thing that ever happened to you," he says, "you've had a pretty damn good career" (Bowman "Carl").

Stormy Weather *(1995)*

Though he has often joked that there's nothing wrong with South Florida that a good Force-Five hurricane couldn't fix, Hiaasen knows that a hurricane is deadly serious business. When one hits Florida, as it often does, it kills innocent people and leaves utter devastation in its wake. One can't get angry at Mother Nature for simply doing what comes naturally. One can, however, get very angry at what humans do and, more importantly, don't do that makes the suffering so much worse.

Hurricane Andrew, one of the most destructive hurricanes in U.S. history, made a direct hit on South Florida with 165 mph winds in August 1992. The resulting devastation was unprecedented: in Miami-Dade County alone, 25,000 homes were destroyed and another 100,000 severely damaged. In addition to causing damage exceeding $26 billion, the storm left sixty-five people dead. It was a natural disaster, however, that was made much worse by human error, as Hiaasen pointed out in a series of columns he wrote following the tragic event.

His first column on the hurricane, written just days after the monster storm hit, took the form of an address to God that begins: "OK, God, you got our attention" (*Kick* 273). He went on to praise the heroic efforts of many people. "If you were testing courage and compassion," he wrote, "you won't find more of it anywhere. Heroes walk every street, or what's left of the streets." But then he noted that if Florida was being tested on "how we've cared for this astonishingly fragile peninsula," it failed. Cramming four million people along a 1300-mile vulnerable coastline is complete lunacy; failing to ensure safe housing there is criminal.

Humans can't change the course of a hurricane, but Hiaasen insists we can "damn sure build houses with walls that don't disintegrate and roofs that don't peel like rotted bananas" (*Kick* 274). He's not angry at God for sending another hurricane as a warning; in fact, he once suggested that, "it's nice to see that nature still rises up and occasionally kicks you in the nuts. It's kind of good when that happens; it teaches us all a little humility" (Middlemas 95). What does get him angry are those responsible for making it much worse than it needed to be, those who should have been listening but who "were too busy counting their campaign contributions from big developers. Now as always, the suffering is heaped on the most helpless—those whose only sin was buying into the Florida dream" (*Kick* 274).

According to Hiaasen, far too much of the hurricane's destruction was avoidable because it was simply a result of the cozy relationship between shoddy builders, corrupt inspectors who rubber-stamped their work, and developers who sold the product. (Low-cost but well-built houses constructed by Habitat for Humanity, for example, largely survived the storm intact.) The survivability of houses could be improved by stronger building codes and more determined prosecution of those who do shoddy work as well as those who approve it. Until that happens, the only way to distinguish the many honest and conscientious builders who use proper materials and methods from those who don't is simply to wait for the next hurricane.

In a number of columns written long before Hurricane Andrew ever hit, Hiaasen singled out corrupt building inspectors for special abuse. He began one column like this: "Once again it's that merry season of the year when contractors all around Dade County are racking their brains and wondering: What do I give the building inspector this Christmas" (*Kick* 269). Another takes the form of an imaginary journal kept by a building inspector:

> 12:30 P. M. Tried to inspect the New World Old Cutler Financial Plaza In-the-Bay, but traffic was lousy and it started to drizzle. Just so happened I could see the structure perfectly from Hooters, where I'd stopped for a late lunch. So I used my binoculars to count the floors: forty-two, right on the button! As I was phoning in my inspection, somebody broke into my car and left a deed to a three-bedroom condo in Cozumel. Not only that, they were considerate enough to put it in a third-party offshore trust [*Kick* 272]!

Then there's this, from another building inspector's diary of his first days on the job:

> A sad day at work, as one of the other inspectors was injured in a freak accident. Seems he was struck in the chest by a huge wad of $50 bills as he was leaving a construction site, and had to be airlifted to the hospital. My boss says this is the third time something like this has happened this year—boy, I didn't know this job was going to be so dangerous [*Paradise* 127]!

4. Novels for Adults

Hiaasen structures *Stormy Weather* (which is dedicated to Donna, Camille, Hugo and Andrew, the names of four major hurricanes that have hit the U.S.) around three pairs of characters. The first involves Edie Marsh, an attractive woman with predatory eyes who spent six months in Palm Beach trying to sleep with a Kennedy. If she managed to find one to seduce, she planned to threaten to go to the police with a graphic tale of rape and torture that would force the Kennedy family to pay handsomely to make the problem go away. Unfortunately, the only Kennedy she ever happened to meet was a perfect gentleman, so she decides to move to Miami just in time for the hurricane.

There she partners up with an ex-con with a crooked jaw named Snapper to take advantage of the storm. They find a house that's been blown apart where Edie can pretend to have been injured by flying debris from the home next door, whose owner they can threaten to sue. Unfortunately for them, that man is a bigger con artist than they are: he sold dozens of trailer homes he described to potential customers as being certified as storm-proof by the U.S. government. He lied; they weren't, and were all blown away. But he has a new idea he proposes to Edie and Snapper.

Any day now he expects to get the insurance settlement for his destroyed home. The problem is it is co-owned by his wife, who three months earlier ran off with a local professor. He offers Edie $10,000 to pose as his absent wife and the same amount to Snapper to be his bodyguard until the money is paid and he can get out of town. But as in a Donald E. Westlake comic caper novel, things quickly begin to go wrong.

The second couple, Max and Bonnie Lamb, are honeymooning at Disney World. But when Max, a junior account executive at a New York advertising firm, hears news reports about a hurricane bearing down on Miami, he persuades his new bride to head there. It turns out he's not interested in offering aid to the victims but in videotaping the devastation. The more he appears to be enjoying the scenes of destruction and human suffering, the more Bonnie suspects her mother may have been right when she whispered in her ear on her wedding day that her new husband was an asshole.

Events take an unexpected turn when Max disappears after chasing after an escaped rhesus monkey that ran off with his video camera. This sets up a Hollywood "meet-cute" scene when Edie happens to encounter a handsome man who is searching for one of the monkeys that escaped, along with an assortment of other exotic animals, from the wildlife-import business he inherited from his uncle. Augustine Herrera lives a directionless life thanks to a generous insurance settlement from a plane crash he survived. He spends his ample free time practicing his favorite hobby, juggling human skulls, while waiting "for a woman to come along and fix him" (25). Might that woman be Bonnie Lamb? Their growing mutual attraction and the "will-she-or-won't-she" suspense over whether she'll ditch her missing husband for the handsome stranger provides the romantic interest in the novel.

The first member of the third pairing is our old friend Skink, perhaps the only man in Florida who enjoys the hurricane: he has himself lashed to the Card Sound Bridge so he can experience the full force of the storm. When he later spots Max Lamb shooting his videos, he takes him prisoner for "desecrating the habitat" (54). "A hurricane is a holy thing," he tells him, "but you treated it as an amusement." So he snaps an electrified shock collar around his neck and begins schooling him on the real Florida and its history, shocking him whenever he gives a wrong answer.

Now that Hiaasen has his primary players in place, he begins intertwining their stories and adding additional characters, one of whom represents the main crime he's interested in exposing. A corrupt building inspector named Avila is so good at what he does (or more precisely doesn't do) that he is able to inspect eighty houses a day without benefit of a ladder. He seldom even leaves his truck except for the regular two-hour lunch break he takes at a nudie bar. Avila speeds past construction sites so fast "that contractors frequently had to jog after his truck in order to deliver their illicit gratuities" (114).

One ironic result of his dereliction of duty as a building inspector is that the storm creates a new job for him as a roofer, though the only part of that job he's interested in is grabbing the customer's cash deposit and then disappearing. "Thanks to the hurricane, there's a hundred fifty thousand houses in Dade County need new roofs," he gloats. "Only a damn fool couldn't make money off these poor bastards" (96). But he is eventually tracked down by Ira Jackson, who earlier killed the salesman who sold his mother the flimsy trailer she died in by crucifying him to a jumbo satellite dish. As Jackson prepares to nail Avila to a tree, an escaped lion from Augustine's wildlife farm appears out of nowhere and gobbles him up.

Hiaasen says he wanted a larger cast of characters than usual in order to capture the chaos that follows in the wake of a major hurricane. This, however, puts added stress on his ability to juggle so many stories. (Even Augustine, proud owner of nineteen skulls, can barely manage to keep five in the air.) At times, the narrative becomes bogged down and never attains the compulsive readability his previous novels displayed. *Stormy Weather* also lacks the kind of outrageous villains he normally uses who keep the reader wondering, "What crazy thing will he do next?" Snapper is simply a mean thug with a deformed jaw.

Hiaasen does, however, do an excellent job of dramatizing the power of the storm and the human suffering left in its wake. With a reporter's sharp eye for vivid details, he paints an alarming picture of the hurricane's aftermath that begins with evidence of the storm's awesome power: a school bus impaled by a forty-foot pine; a motorboat resting in a living room; a mangled bicycle wrapped around a palm tree; a car on the roof of a gas station; dead cows on the highway. Then there's the upheaval among Florida's animal population: herds of disoriented cows and horses wandering through the suburbs; frogs on the walls of a home; mosquitoes hatching in a bathroom sink.

Above all there is the human toll: an elderly woman is killed by a flying barbecue; 200,000 people are without shelter, forced to live in makeshift tent cities or huddled in the one room in their house with a roof, cooking on a small Sterno stove on the bedroom dresser; a ten-year-old boy sits in front of his battered home with a rifle in his hands, ready to shoot at looters. And while the storm brought out the best in many, others fell victim to darker impulses:

> Thousands of hurricane victims had stampeded to purchase chain saws for clearing debris, and now the dangerous power tools were being used to vent rage. A gentleman with a Black & Decker attempted to truncate a stubborn insurance adjuster in Homestead. An old woman in Florida City used a lightweight Sears to silence a neighbor's garrulous pet cockatoo. And in Sweetwater, two teenaged gang members successfully detached each other's arms (one left, one right) in a brief but spectacular duel of stolen Homelites [69].

The storm also had an unexpected effect on the sex-trade industry; according to one hooker, the hurricane turned all her regulars into "decent, faithful, God-fearing family men" (237).

Animals play an important role in underscoring how the balance of nature has been altered by the storm. For one thing, there are all those wild animals now roaming through the landscape. In addition to the camera-stealing monkey and the hungry lion who feasts on Ira Jackson, we hear about a fourteen-foot-python resting comfortably in the salad bar of a fast-food restaurant and a Cape Buffalo loitering in the produce section of a ruined supermarket. But as Hiaasen reminds the reader, "an escaped cobra had as much natural right to a life in Florida as did all those retired garment workers from Queens" (38). (A pair of annoying miniature dachshunds named Donald and Marla, presumably named after Donald Trump and Marla Maples, his wife at the time, keep popping up throughout the novel but mainly serve a minor comic purpose.)

Animals also play a comic role in administering justice to Avila, a devotee of *santeria*, the Afro-Cuban religion whose followers perform animal sacrifice to appease the gods. Avila's choices of sacrificial offerings to Chango, his personal deity, prove to be disastrous. An uncooperative billy goat gores him in the groin. A South American coatmundi takes offense at being readied for sacrifice and kicks over a candle in Avila's garage, setting the lawn mower on fire. It eventually ends up settled in Avila's mother-in-law's orange coiffure. When Avila turns his fire extinguisher on the animal, he accidentally sprays some in his mother-in-law's eyes, sending her running away screaming. In the novel's epilogue, we learn that under a new name Avila has resumed his career as a building inspector in another part of the state. He still practices *santeria*, but this time, a rabid rabbit he attempts to sacrifice bites him on the thigh, resulting in his death shortly afterwards.

Human suffering is too painful to make fun of, so the comedy in *Stormy Weather* is consequently muted, with much of the satire aimed at peripheral issues: e.g., advertising. Max Lamb's job is coming up with catchy jingles to sell products, which leads to this sarcastic putdown by Skink: "Five thousand years ago we're doodling on the walls of caves. Today we're writing odes to fruit-flavored douche" (126); and TV evangelists like Pat Robertson, whose pitch for contributions is avidly watched by several members of The Church of High Pentecostal Rumination who have traveled to hurricane-stricken Florida in search of new converts: "The Ruminators didn't share Robertson's paranoid worldview, but they admired his life-or-death style of fund-raising and hoped to pick up some pointers" (179).

Hiaasen also chooses not to make Snapper, his main bad guy, a comic character; the only humor associated with him is the hilarious back story Hiaasen creates for him. Born Lester Maddox Parsons, Snapper was named after the Georgia governor who became nationally famous for chasing black customers out of his restaurant with an ax handle. He grew up in a Ku Klux Klan family that was asked to leave after his drunken father accidentally set the Klan leader on fire instead of the cross he was supposed to light. He earned his nickname after a game warden rearranged his jaw with the butt of a shotgun, leaving it thirty-six degrees out of alignment. Skink later makes matters worse by attaching The Club, an anti-theft device designed for automobiles, to his face, but the comic potential of his grotesquely altered appearance is limited.

Before turning to his next novel, Hiaasen wrote one-thirteenth of one. He, along with twelve other South Florida authors including Dave Barry, Edna Buchanan, and Elmore Leonard, were each asked to write a separate chapter which would be published weekly in *Tropic*, the *Miami Herald*'s Sunday magazine. The completed effort, titled *Naked Came the Manatee* (a deliberate echo of *Naked Came the Stranger*, the 1969 best-selling literary hoax written by twenty-four journalists under the name Penelope Ashe), was published in 1996.

Hiaasen was given the dubious honor of tying everything together in the final chapter, which he did in his typically absurdist way. Not only does he give Booger, the manatee Dave Barry introduced in the first installment, a happy ending by having "thirteen hundred pounds of saucy sea cow nooky" (201) paddle into his lonely life, he explains the presence of the three heads of Fidel Castro that earlier contributors had stuck him with. He even devises a hilarious scene in which Fidel Castro, hiding out in disguise on Miami Beach, is first mugged by someone whose tattoo identifies him as one of the prisoners among the Marielito boat people he sent to Florida in 1980. Then a small boy runs off with his toupee. Declaring that Miami is too damn scary, he hightails it back home to Havana.

Lucky You *(1997)*

Sometimes the targets of a satirist's pen—racist rednecks, clueless bosses, and tourist scams—are sitting ducks, easy to make fun of. That doesn't stop Hiaasen, who after the toned-down humor of *Stormy Weather* lets loose and creates enough colorful goofballs and outrageously hilarious situations to turn *Lucky You* into one of his funniest novels.

JoLayne Lucks, an African-American woman, lives up to her name by winning the Florida Lotto. As usual, she played the same six numbers—17-19-22-24-27-30—each one representing her age when she had "jettisoned a burdensome man" (3). Now she can smile at how those six discarded men "had finally amounted to something" (4). It turns out, however, that there is one other winning ticket being held by a pair of clueless good ole boys named Bodean Geezer and Chub. Bode, the "brains" of the duo, isn't satisfied with half the jackpot—$14 million—and figures it's just another government plot to keep two white boys like them from winning the whole thing. If he can get his hands on the other ticket, he can collect the entire $28 million, the amount he believes he needs to finance the white supremacist militia he dreams of starting. He and Chub head north to the tiny rural town of Grange near Tampa where the other winning ticket was sold. They obtain the name of the other winner and set out to steal her ticket.

JoLayne, a former nurse, now works at a veterinary clinic in Grange. After learning that Simmons Wood, a forty-four-acre parcel of wooded land where she likes to walk, is going to be sold for development into a mall, she begins rescuing as many small turtles or cooters as she can before the bulldozers arrive. (She ends up with forty-five.) Winning the lottery will now make it possible for her to purchase the land and preserve it as a nature refuge. But then her ticket is stolen when she is viciously attacked by Bode and Chub, who are relieved to learn she's black and therefore OK to beat up. They grab the ticket, but in the scuffle JoLayne leaves the two of them looking "like gator puke" (46) after she slices Chub's left eyelid in half and chews off a large chunk of Bode's eyebrow before the pair are able to escape with her ticket. There is an added urgency in retrieving her ticket: she has only seven days to counter an offer from the Central Midwest Brotherhood of Grouters, Spacklers and Drywallers International's pension fund, which is acting in cahoots with a Chicago crime family to skim as much money from the project as possible before abandoning the site, leaving behind an ugly ruin.

Racism isn't funny, but as Archie Bunker demonstrated, racists can be when they are made the butt of the joke. The ridiculing begins with this introduction: "Bode Gazzer was five feet six and had never forgiven his parents for it. He wore three-inch snakeskin shitkickers and walked with a swagger that suggested not brawn so much as hemorrhoidal tribulation. Chub was a beer-gutted six two, moist-eyed, ponytailed and unshaven. He carried a loaded gun at all times and was Bode Gazzer's best and only friend" (4). The two form a bond based on a contempt for "government, taxes, homosexuals, immigrants, minorities, gun laws, assertive women and honest work"(5).

Bode has turned being a perennial loser into a philosophy of life. He has spent his entire life "perfecting the art of assigning blame. His personal credo—*Everything bad that happens is someone else's fault*—could, with imagination, be stretched to fit any circumstance" (16). He can find a ready excuse for every failure, every shortcoming. This soon devolves into a full-blown case of hard-core bigotry where people of different races, religions, and ethnicities can always be cited as the cause of his problems.

Chub (real name: Onus Dean Gillespie) is another loser who turned virulently anti-government when the IRS seized his van for failure to pay taxes. He eventually moved to Miami where he began making and selling fake handicapped stickers for cars. This led to his meeting Bode, who informed him he was performing a patriotic service by reducing the number of blue handicapped parking spaces that would be needed by the blue-helmeted U. N. Troops when they invaded the U.S. Chub is eager to join up with Bode's new militia, the White Rebel Brotherhood. However, after learning that there's a popular rock group with same name that includes several black members, Bode is forced to change the name to the White Clarion Aryans.

Tom Krome is a feature writer for *The Register,* a South Florida newspaper. His boss, a man named Sinclair with the empty title of Assistant Deputy Managing Editor of Features and Style, lives in fear that one day the older and more experienced Krome will humiliate him in front of the entire newspaper staff, so he sends him out of town on assignment as much as he possibly can. A phone call from his brother-in-law telling him about a fellow resident of Grange with the name of Lucks who has just won the lottery gives Sinclair a good excuse to send Krome out of town again to write a feature on the winner. Krome is disdainful of most of his boss's lame-brained ideas and his love of alliterative headlines (e.g., LADY LUCK WINS THE LOTTO), but he agrees to travel to Grange to interview the winner. Almost immediately he falls under the spell of the delightfully bright and witty JoLayne Lucks. When Sinclair refuses to grant him more time to investigate the story after her ticket is stolen, Krome quits his job, freeing him to help JoLayne get her ticket back.

Hiaasen now begins introducing multiple complications, most of which enhance the humor. For example, there are the two other women in Tom Krome's life. One is his wife, Mary Andrea Finley Krome, whom he has been trying to divorce for four years. She's a stubborn woman and "the last true Catholic" in a family she claims hasn't had a divorce in 500 years. An actress often on the road, she's adept at eluding anyone trying to serve her with divorce papers. Her professional career gives Hiaasen an opportunity to have some fun with the road-show productions she appears in, especially a musical version of *Silence of the Lambs,* which ends with the cast and chorus singing lines like these:

> Oh, Hannibal the Cannibal,
> How deliciously malicious you are [106]!

Katy, the other woman in Krome's life, is married to a jealous judge who, despite his own history of marital affairs, is less than forgiving when it comes to his wife's infidelity. He has his law clerk first shoot out all the windows in Krome's house and then later has him burn the place down. Unfortunately for him, he dies in the blaze, but because his dental records closely resemble Krome's, Krome is mistakenly declared dead, which leads to this absurdly humorous exchange:

> "Bad news?"
> "Sort of," Tom Krome said. "Apparently I'm dead." When he turned around, he appeared more bemused than upset. "It's going to be on the front page of *The Register* tomorrow."
> "Dead." JoLayne pursed her lips. "You sure fooled me."
> "Fried to a cinder in my own home. Must be true, if it's in the newspaper."
> Jo Layne felt entitled to wonder if she really knew enough about this Tom fellow, nice and steady as he might seem. A burning house was something to consider.
> She said, "Lord, what are you going to do?"
> "Stay dead for a while," Krome replied. "That's what my lawyer says" [158].

You can't have the Three Stooges with just two bubbas, so Hiaasen drags in a third, a nineteen-year-old clerk at the Grab N'Go in Grange where JoLayne purchased her winning lottery ticket. Shiner, a young man who doesn't have an "easy time putting two and two together" (55), possesses the sort of "submissive dimness that foretold a long sad future in minimum-security institutions" (112). Bode and Chub have an easy time converting him to their cause, opening his gullible eyes to the realization that his "sorry-ass excuse for a life" isn't really his fault after all, but simply the result of a "vast conspiracy against the ordinary working white man" (51).

Shiner quits his job, shaves his head (exposing an unsightly scar from the time he feel asleep on the hot engine block of the car he was attempting to tune), and gets a tattoo of the initials of the White Rebel Brotherhood (only to later earn that the militia's name is now the White Clarion Aryans). Then he heads to Miami to proudly present Bode and Chub with the security tape from the Grab N' Go, the only evidence proving that JoLayne was the person who had purchased the winning lottery ticket there. It takes a dim bulb like Shriner, who thinks the Nazi symbol is called a "swatch ticker," to fall for Bode's lame contention that seat belts are part of the government's plot to ensure that millions of Americans would be belted in when the NATO helicopters begin landing on the highways.

4. Novels for Adults

Hiaasen takes obvious delight in ridiculing his redneck buffoons, whether they are mindlessly firing their semi-automatics into bushes they fear might contain NATO troops invading the U.S. from the Bahamas, fleeing the approach of the Black Tide, whoever or whatever that is, or simply slipping and sliding on a spilled sack of groceries. Things become even goofier after Slider kidnaps a Hooters waitress named Amber whom Chub has fallen in love with. Among other things, we are treated to the ridiculous sight of Chub with a bike patch over one eye, a pair of Amber's orange Hooters shorts on his head, and a rotting crab claw clamped tightly to his hand after a tussle with the crab over his lotto ticket which had fallen into the water.

In the end, Hiaasen dispatches his loathsome racists in distinctly unglamorous ways. Bode bleeds to death when the sharp barb on a stingray's tail pierces his femoral artery. (For no discernible reason, Bode's final wish as he's dying is to brush his teeth with WD-40 oil, although in a note Hiaasen advises his readers that there is no approved dental use for the product.) Now stranded alone on an isolated island, Chub watches in horror as the buzzards devour his partner's body. Eventually he succumbs to the same fate: all that remains of the ponytailed white supremacist are some scattered bones and a pair of skimpy orange Hooters shorts attached to the pole he used in a futile attempt to flag down help from the skies.

The heartiest laughs in the novel are provided by the good folks of Grange, many of whom are engaged in the age-old Florida business of fleecing the tourists. They of course can't compete with multi-million-dollar behemoths like Disney World, SeaWorld, or Universal Orlando, but their quaint little Mom-and-Pop roadside attractions have made Grange the home of the phony religious scam. (Grange's real-life counterpart is the small Florida town of Cassadaga, where an abundance of folks with crystal balls has given the place the title of Psychic Capital of the World.) Much like the Amazing Kingdom of Thrills and the Eager Beaver strip club, these clever operations aim at giving their customers what they want, in this case fabulous "miracles." Among the notable attractions are a four-foot-tall fiberglass statue of the Madonna that weeps perfumed tears; a man with the stigmata, bleeding wounds in his hands (and later in his feet after he talks an employee at the muffler shop to dill holes there); and a road stain in the shape of Jesus's face, which Shriner's mother, attired in a white bridal gown, attends to devotedly.

One scene in particular illustrates how Hiaasen, once he's arranged his players, can squeeze every last laugh out of a comic situation. When the Madonna's weeping mechanism fails to function properly one day, its owner

Demencio comes up with another idea so as not to disappoint the visiting pilgrims: he paints the faces of Jesus's apostles on twelve of JoLayne's cooters he has been caring for in her absence. This proves to be such a hit that he then digs a trench around the fiberglass statue for the turtles and fills it with "holy" water, cups of which he sells to the pilgrims.

Meanwhile, Krome's editor Sinclair has come to Grange to visit his sister who lives there. When he happens to stumble upon the apostolic turtles, he has a spiritual experience. He's so overwhelmed he begins visiting daily and starts speaking in tongues (actually gibberish versions of his favorite alliterative headlines). Demencio decides you can't have too much of a good thing, so he paints Biblical faces on the backs of JoLayne's remaining thirty-three cooters and has them join their apostolic brethren. This sends Sinclair into heavenly bliss as he sits Buddha-like in the moat of "holy" water feeding lettuce to the forty-five turtles scrambling all over his body, all the while crooning, "*Muugghhh meechy makk-a-mamma*" (translation: MUGGER MEETS MATCH AGAINST MARTIAL-ARTS MOM) (203).

Lucky You ends on a happy note. Amber convinces Shiner that the right thing to do with the lottery ticket the two of them end up with is to return it to JoLayne, which he does. She also encourages him to get a job as a busboy at Hooters where, she assures him, all the waitresses are as nice as she is. Shiner's mother gets a new tourist attraction after the state highway department paves over her Jesus stain: Jesus's face is miraculously transferred to an omelette she displays in a Tupperware pie holder. JoLayne is now able to purchase Simmons Wood, where she and Krome return the cooters to their natural home. She tells Krome that turtles can live for twenty or more years, and suggests that the two of them can look forward to a future where they can sit and watch the turtles, now all grown up, sunning themselves on a log.

The humor in *Lucky You* is more light-hearted than in Hiaasen's previous novels, and there is more warmth in his portrayal of the characters he's making fun of. Instead of indicting the scam artists of Grange for greedy commercialism and hypocrisy, he's more amused than outraged at what they are doing. Nobody's getting rich off their enterprises, as the owners make only small sums from donations and the sale of soft drinks, T-shirts, and angel food snacks. Nor are they necessarily cynical about what they do. They adhere to the principle that, "tourists were tourists and there wasn't much difference, when you got down to the core mentality of it, between Mickey Mouse and a fiberglass Madonna" (12). As Demencio, the owner of the weeping Madonna, says, "I'd rather peddle religion that a phony goddamn rodent" (12). He knows he's running a scam, but he also understands that the devout souls who wait patiently in the hot Florida sun deserve more than just a drop of salty water from his weeping Madonna, so he adds perfume to the water: "This was supposed to be Jesus' mother, for heaven's sake. Her tears *ought* to smell special" (11).

Behind all the laughs, however, there is a dark message in *Lucky You*. The novel was written shortly after the bombing of the Federal building in Oklahoma City in 1995 by anti-government terrorist Timothy McVeigh that killed 168 of his fellow Americans. Many of the items found in Bode's apartment—posters of David Koresh and David Duke, empty ammo clips, stacks of gun magazines, a Confederate flag, a Nazi armband, a humorous cartoon about the Holocaust, a how-to pamphlet on fertilizer bombs—serve as a chilling reminder that it wouldn't take much to turn him into a person who might blow up a government building like McVeigh did or mow down worshippers at prayer in an African-American church as Dylann Roof would do in Charleston in 2015. *Lucky You* serves as a sober warning that in real life, as daily news reports too often remind us, racism, anger, frustration, and paranoia can be a horrifyingly deadly combination.

After the miserable failure of the film version of *Strip Tease*, Hiaasen was understandably reluctant to see another adaptation of one of his novels. However, a staged reading in his home of a theatrical version of *Lucky You* put together by London director Francis Matthews and University of South Florida theater professor Denis Calandra changed his mind. In 2006, the production, with music and songs by American Loudon Wainwright III, had its premiere at the Waterfront Playhouse in Key West. Two years later it was featured at Scotland's famed Edinburgh Festival Fringe. While some reviewers applauded the farcical energy of the production, others, especially those familiar with the novel, felt that the production, like the screen version of *Strip Tease*, suffered from the lack of Hiaasen's sardonic narrative voice.

Sick Puppy *(2000)*

Sick Puppy begins with an incident of comic vengeance. A young man named Twilly Spree watches in disgust as a man ahead of him driving a Range Rover tosses a couple of empty Burger King cartons out the window. Twilly pulls over to pick up the trash and then follows the Range Rover home. He later returns to the man's house and watches as he and his wife leave in her

BMW convertible. He follows them to a restaurant and while they are inside dining, he pays a garbage truck driver $3000 for the loan of his truck and then dumps its load of four tons of garbage into the open Beemer.

An unemployed twenty-six-year-old college dropout with a "brief but spectacular history of psychological problems" (11), Twilly is a volatile combination of serious anger-management issues and a five-million-dollar inheritance. The source of his anger, like Hiaasen's, can be traced to a childhood experience involving the environment. His father was a real-estate salesman specializing in oceanfront property, so the family often moved to new locations. When Twilly was fourteen, he returned to Marco Island, a place where he fondly remembers collecting tropical seashells along the dune-fringed beaches when he briefly lived there as a child. What he now sees shocks him:

> He comprehended for the first time what his old man did for a living. The island had sprouted skyline: a concrete picket of towering hotels and high-rise condominiums. Waterfront, of course.... He hoped he was seeing a mirage, a trick of the fog and clouds but when he glanced up, the hotels and condos were still there, looming larger than before. As the sun began to rise, the buildings cast tombstone shadows across the sand. Soon Twilly found himself standing in a vast block of shade—shade, on an open beach under a bright clear sky! He sunk to his knees and punched the hard-packed sand with both fists until his knuckles were skinned [24].

What's a person to do? Carl Hiaasen is fortunate in having a productive outlet for his anger in being able to write about it in his columns and novels. Twilly's more like *Tourist Season*'s Skip Wiley (his name even echoes Wiley's) in that he's not very good at channeling his anger in positive ways. For example, when a woman on the beach tells him to stop his tantrum because he's frightening her children, he chomps down on her foot and bites off a painted toenail. When he learns that his uncle's bank is loaning fourteen million dollars to a rock-mining company that's digging craters in the Amazon River basin, he blows the bank up. When he spots a Florida State legislator who blocked clean-water reforms while accepting illicit campaign donations from a cattle ranch that was flushing raw sewage into an estuary, he follows him into a rest room, lectures him for forty minutes on the immorality of water pollution, and then pisses all over his shoes: "There, that's what your pals on the ranch are doing to Black Drum Bay," he tells him. "How do you like it" (27)?

Palmer Stoat, the litterbug, is a jerk, which Hiaasen makes clear right from the beginning of the novel where he shows him shooting an aging African black rhinoceros from a distance of thirteen yards at a Florida private game preserve. Even his minor habits are irritating; he slurps and slobbers his food when he eats; he takes photographs of himself during sex with his wife; he loves to quote the lyrics of rock songs, but he invariably gets them wrong (e.g., "Come on baby, light my candle"). Twilly will have his hands full trying to educate this cretin. Despite putting a note on the windshield of his Range Rover that reads, "Quit trashing the planet, fuckwad" (47) and filling it up with 3000 dung beetles, Stoat fails to get the message. The very next day Twilly sees him toss a Kentucky Fried Chicken box out the window.

The duel between Twilly and the thoughtless litterbug reaches a new level when Twilly decides to kidnap Stoat's dog, a black Lab named Boodle, in order to teach him a lesson. But when Twilly sneaks back into Stoat's home to retrieve some medication the dog needs, he is surprised by the unexpected presence of Stoat's beautiful wife Desie. She insists that Twilly take her to Boodle so she can check on his health. When he explains to her that he was simply trying to cure Stoat of his littering, she tells him he's aiming too low. Her husband, she informs him, is a powerful state lobbyist and political fixer who is currently brokering a deal involving a land developer and the governor that will transform a small island in the Gulf called Toad Island into Shearwater Island, a seaside community with a pair of championship golf courses. Now it isn't littering that Twilly wants to stop, it's the destruction of Toad Island, and Desie offers to help him.

Like *Strip Tease*'s Malcolm Moldowsky, Stoat is a soulless conniver without any principles beyond making money (Hiaasen describes him as "about the worst human being I've ever put in one of my books" (Crooks): "No cause was too abhorrent for Stout—he'd work for anybody and anything, if the price was right" (125). His cynicism about the politicians he deals with reflects Hiaasen's own well-known attitude towards them:

> As a lobbyist, [Stoat] had long ago concluded there was no difference in how Democrats and Republicans conducted the business of government. The game stayed the same: It was always about favors and friends, and who controlled the dough. Party labels were merely a way to keep track of the teams; issues were mostly smoke and vaudeville. Nobody believed in anything except hanging on to power, whatever it took.... Stoat himself was registered independent, but he hadn't stepped inside a voting booth in fourteen years. He couldn't take the concept seriously; he knew too much [58].

Twilly decides to hold Boodle for ransom in order to force Stoat to scuttle the planned development of Shearwater Island. He also changes the dog's name to McGuinn, after Roger McGuinn, guitarist and founding member of the Byrds (who would later thank Hiaasen for the honor after meeting him for the first time at a book signing). All Stoat has to do is stop construction of a new $28 million bridge to the island. (Hiaasen likes that number: it was also the amount of the Lotto jackpot in *Lucky You.*)

Hiaasen paints an eye-opening behind-the-scenes portrait of political power at work, as Stoat pulls all the necessary strings to get the bridge funding cancelled; once he gets his dog back, he'll simply arrange for the governor to restore the funding. This requires him to promise Willie Vasquez, the vice chairman of the House Appropriations Committee who calls himself the Rainbow Brother, that he'll get a community center in his district in return for his support. To keep Robert Clapley, the development's owner, happy, he promises to take him hunting at the private wildlife park where he shot his rhino. He also promises to throw in some powdered rhinoceros horn, a reputed aphrodisiac. Along with governor Dick Artemus, they can all be persuaded to do whatever it takes to get what they want, but they have no illusions about their partners in the deal: To Stoat, Vasquez Washington is just "another greedy little maggot on the make" (38) and Artemus is "an obsequious glad-handing maggot" (122). To Clapley, Stoat is nothing but a "fuck-weasel" (117) and a "turd fondler" (118).

There's a good chance that a land developer in a Hiaasen novel is either a crook or a phony or perhaps even a person with kinky sexual tastes. Robert Clapley is all three. The source of his fortune is drugs; his previous project, a seventeen-story apartment complex in Miami, was financed entirely with the profits from the marijuana and cocaine he dealt. This time, however, he gets legitimate financing for Shearwater from Swiss investors, but that doesn't mean he's shed his gangster ways. When the Shearwater project is threatened by a field biologist, he orders his hitman to kill him.

His twisted sexuality goes back to his childhood, when he became fascinated by his sister's Barbie dolls. After meeting a pair of gorgeous Eastern European call girls, whom he nicknames Barbie One and Barbie Two, he comes up with the bright idea of forcing them to undergo a series of plastic surgeries designed to transform them into real-life identical Barbie doll twins. His plan, a perverse, self-serving effort to reshape natural beauty for his own personal benefit, is essentially a small-scale version of what he intends to do to Toad Island. However, the plan has to be put on hold when the Barbies refuse to submit to any further surgery until he gets them some more of the powdered rhino horn with the "magical" properties he had obtained from Stoat.

Governor Dick Artemus, a multimillionaire owner of seven Toyota dealerships, became governor mainly because he was "three inches taller and ten-times better looking than any of the Democrats" (100). With a "preternatural talent for bullshitting" (285), he could "talk the buzzards off a shit wagon" (128). In Hiaasen's view, however, he isn't thoroughly evil, just a typical politician who knows how to play the game. In fact, he even does do one good thing: he's responsible for bringing Skink into the action halfway through the novel. He's learned that Skink has a brother named Doyle, who returned from Vietnam with severe psychological problems. As governor, Skink was able to find a safe refuge for him in a lighthouse that has been closed to the public for years. Artemus threatens to demolish the lighthouse and kick Doyle out onto the streets unless Skink agrees to help him find Twilly before he performs some nutty headline-grabbing stunt that might jeopardize the Shearwater project.

It doesn't take long before the two eco-terrorists meet and join forces, with Skink becoming a mentor to the younger version of himself. At one point, he advises Twilly that, "there's probably no peace for people like you and me in this world. Somebody's got to be angry or nothing gets fixed. That's what we were put here for, to stay pissed off" (304). When Twilly asks if Artemus is worth killing, Skink explains to him that it would be a waste of ammo: "They got assembly lines that crank out assholes like him. He wouldn't even be missed" (319). Instead, he has a better idea: after a meeting with Artemus in the Governor's mansion, he shows his contempt for him by pulling his pants down and scratching the word SHAME into his bare butt with a buzzard beak that's tied to the end of his braided hair.

One of the few characters in the novel with a functioning conscience is Dr. Stephen Brinkman, a field biologist hired to determine whether there are any animals on the endangered species list living on Toad Island that might torpedo the planned development. Brinkman finds none, though he does observe a large population of tiny quarter-sized oak toads. Watching the bulldozers begin burying the toads by the thousands makes him feel complicit in their destruction. The list of animals he systematically catalogued living on the island, he now realizes, is nothing but a death list of all the creatures that will be destroyed in the name of "progress." However, before he can stop the bulldozing, he is shot and killed by Clapley's hit man. Hiaasen's characters often end up dying in gruesome ways they richly deserve. Brinkman doesn't deserve to die, but there is a something tragically appropriate in being bulldozed into the ground like all those innocent toads he couldn't save.

His killer, known only as Mr. Gash, is a thug from Clapley's drug-dealing days. His oddball appearance—he dresses in a houndstooth checked suit and his hair is moussed and dyed so that it looks like he has a blond porcupine stapled to his head—makes him look like a clown, but he's one of the sickest puppies in the novel: he gets his kicks by stuffing live baby rats in people's mouths to force them to do his bidding; and his favorite sexual practice involves dangling from an iguana-skin harness above a threesome of naked women sprawled on a custom-made gigantic bed.

Most disturbing of all is his obsession with taped 911 calls that record the final horrifying moments in a person's life. Exhilarated by the sound of fear in the human voice, he sets his compilation tapes (*The World's Most Bloodcurdling Emergency Calls, Snipers in the Workplace*) to the sound of classical music—Mahler for domestic disputes; Tchaikovsky for cardiac arrests; Shostakovich for house fires—which he plays over and over for his amusement. Hiaasen devises the absolutely perfect fate for him. In the process of rescuing Twilly, whom Gash has shot and wounded, Skink shoots Gash in the mouth, severing his tongue. Skink then leaves him pinned beneath a bulldozer. His final words are captured on this desperate 911 call, which is featured in the latest volume of *The World's Most Bloodcurdling Emergency Calls.*

CALLER: Hep meh! Peezh!
DISPATCHER: Do you have an emergency?
CALLER: Yeah, I gah a emoozhezhee! I gah a fugghy boo-gozer oh meh azzhhh!
DISPATCHER: "Boo-gozer"? Sir, I'm sorry, but you'll have to speak more clearly. This is Levy County Fire Rescue, do you have an emergency to report?
CALLER: Yeah! Hep! Mah baggh is boge! Ah bing zzhaa eng mah fay! I ngee hep!
DISPATCHER: Sir, do you speak English?
CALLER: Eh izzh Engizh! Mah ung gaw zzha off! Whif ah gung!
DISPATCHER: Hang on, Mr. Boogozer, I'm transferring you to someone who can take the information...
CALLER: Ngooohh! Hep! Peezh!
DISPATCHER TWO: Diga. ¿Dónde estás?
CALLER: Aaaaaagghh!!!
DISPATCHER TWO: ¿Tienes un emergencia?
CALLER: Oh fugghh. I gaw die [284].

Like many of the locations in Hiaasen's novels, the Wilderness Veldt Plantation in central Florida where Stoat bagged his rhino is yet another per-

4. Novels for Adults

version of the natural world. By substituting the fake for the real, it becomes a place, like strip clubs and theme parks, where money buys fantasies. The owner of the private game reserve purchases castoff exotic animals like old toothless lions and three-legged wildebeests from petting zoos and charges rich men outlandish amounts so they can delude themselves into thinking they are stalking big game in Africa. Shooting defenseless animals for sport is evil enough, but paying $30,000 for the privilege as Stoat did or slaughtering rhinos for the reputed aphrodisiac effects of their horns is even worse.

Twilly's idea of justice is simple: shoot the whole bunch behind the effort to destroy Toad Island. Skink, however, counsels patience, having faith that Nature eventually settles all scores. In a scene that reads like a comic twist on Ernest Hemingway's famous "The Short Happy Life of Francis Macomber," Hiaasen comes up with perhaps his most satisfying example of nature's revenge. The agents of retribution are Stoat's own dog and a senile rhino. McGuinn playfully bites the tail of the lethargic rhino Clapley intends to shoot, sending it running off in terror. As it lumbers toward Clapley and Stoat, both fire at the frightened beast, but miss. Clapley, rather than getting more of the rhino horn he came for, is instead impaled on the horn of the charging animal. Stoat is then trampled to death under the "wild" beast's hooves. With their deaths, Toad Island is saved. The island is purchased by Twilly, who re-names it Amy Island in honor of his mother and deeds every parcel of land for preservation.

The novel ends with Twilly, now with Skink riding alongside him as a passenger, speeding at 110 mph after a car full of people tossing beer bottles, a plastic cup, and a lighted cigarette out the window of their car. Hiaasen leaves it up to the reader to imagine the demented punishment the two deeply disturbed men will come up with.

Although it's normally easy to distinguish the good guys from the bad ones in his novels, Hiaasen raises some interesting moral questions in *Sick Puppy*. For example, to what degree are we able to consider Twilly Spree a hero? We can certainly appreciate Skink's contention that there's nothing shameful about anger, that sometimes "it's the only sane and logical moral reaction" (305). We can also cheer on Twilly's efforts to stop both Stoat's littering and the destruction of Toad Island. But how can we overlook the fact that he blew up a bank, forced a plane to make an emergency landing after he shot up one of its wings, and fractured the cheekbone of one guy and dislocated the jaw of his companion after he spotted them throwing beer cans at a pelican? Most disturbing of all, he's also responsible for the death of a man whom he saw dumping barrels of toxic waste into a river: After retrieving the hazardous material, he used a rain gutter to pour almost 200 gallons of it into the man's home while he slept. When the man awoke, he lit a cigarette, which turned his house into a fireball, killing him.

To argue that Twilly's heart is in the right place isn't enough to excuse his criminal behavior. A pair of quotes from the novel draw attention to the thorny question about how far one is justified in going in pursuit of a moral end. Skink is a fan of British novelist Graham Greene and carries of copy of Greene's *The Comedians* with him throughout the book. (The novel is also one of Hiaasen's favorites: he ranks it fourth on a list of his ten favorite books (Zane 76)). Greene had a strong interest in moral themes and flawed characters who struggle, not always successfully, to do the right thing. Skink at one point says he'd like to think Greene "would have found me interesting ... or at least moral" (290). On the other hand, Jim Tile, in light of Skink's many serious crimes—arson, wanton destruction of property, even homicide—cautions Twilly that although Skink is a dear friend of his, "he's not necessarily a role model" (302).

Hiaasen further complicates the moral picture with the character of Karl Krimmler, the chief engineer on the Shearwater project, who hates nature: "In nature Krimmler saw neither art nor mystery, only bureaucratic obstacles. A flight of swallowtail butterflies or the chirp of a squirrel could send him into a black funk that lasted for days" (29). Elsewhere we are told that, "Nothing gladdened his soul so much as the sharp crack of an oak tree toppling under a steel blade. Nothing fogged him in gloom so much as the sight of earth-moving machinery sitting idle" (194).

So far, so good: he appears to be just another soulless cretin with zero appreciation of nature's bounty. But then we learn that like Twilly, he too was profoundly affected by a childhood incident: at age six, he was bitten on the scrotum by a wild chipmunk. While his injury was minor, he was traumatized to such a degree that he became phobic about the outdoors and all its inhabitants. Does this excuse his crimes against nature? Does being shocked by seeing what is happening to nature, as Twilly was, carry more moral weight than being scarred for life emotionally by one of its critters, as Krimmler was? Are we meant to see both characters as victims whose morally questionable behavior is somehow justified?

The relationship between Twilly and Desie Stoat is also problematic. It's easy to see why Twilly would be attracted to her, since he has "a habit of falling in love with any woman who was nice enough to sleep with him" (45).

But it's much harder to understand her attraction to him. Sure, her husband has few redeeming qualities aside from his money, but it's still difficult to see why she would immediately fall for Twilly, whom an ex-girlfriend's father once called a "homicidal madman" (46), even if his heart is pure and he can quote rock lyrics accurately. What kind of life can she expect to have with a man she describes as having "no ambition beyond wreaking havoc, and no imaginable future that doesn't include felony prison time" (227). Even her husband is astute enough to figure out what she's doing: "You want to be Bonnie Parker, is that it? Or maybe Patty Hearst? You want to end up a newspaper headline" (212).

With so many sick puppies in the novel, it's refreshing to note that there is at least one healthy one, and that one is the only real dog in the story. Hiaasen must have enjoyed his experience of writing from a manatee's point of view in *Naked Came the Manatee*, because in *Sick Puppy* he treats the reader to several hilarious scenes from McGuinn's doggy perspective. (Hiaasen, a self-proclaimed sucker for labs, was likely inspired by one of his own.) McGuinn's brain may be "no bigger than a stick of Dentyne" (366), but no human in the novel enjoys life more than he does. For some, living a dog's life means an unhappy existence. Not so for McGuinn:

> That's the thing about being a Labrador retriever—you were born for fun. Seldom was your loopy, free-wheeling mind cluttered by contemplation, and never at all by somber worry; every day was a romp. What else could there possibly be to life? Eating was a thrill. Pissing was a treat. Shitting was a joy. And licking your own balls? Bliss. And everywhere you went were gullible humans who patted and hugged and fussed over you [190].

Like all Labradors, McGuinn "frequently was puzzled by human behavior," but unlike writers like Hiaasen, he happily "spent almost no time trying to figure it out" (191).

Basket Case *(2002)*

Hiaasen likes to try something different in each of his novels, partly for the benefit of his readers but also to stretch his writing muscles. *Basket Case* is unique in that it's his first novel written in first-person narration. It's also his only novel that's primarily a murder mystery with the identity of the killer not revealed until the very end. The result is a book that is shorter, leaner, more realistic and less carnivalesque than his previous work.

Jack Tagger is a forty-six-year-old obituary writer for the *Union-Register*. Formerly an award-winning investigative reporter for the paper, he was demoted to the obituary page after publicly criticizing the paper's new owner and told his byline would never appear in the paper again. When he spots a death notice for James Bradley Stomarti, better known as Jimmy Stoma of the rock band Jimmy and the Slut Puppies, who died at the age of thirty-nine while scuba diving in the Bahamas, he argues with his editor Emma Cole that Stoma deserves a lengthy obit. But when he subsequently learns several suspicious things—that Jimmy was working on a comeback album at the time of his death, that no autopsy was performed before he was cremated, and that a former bandmate who was with him when he died is later murdered—he begins to suspect that Stoma may not have died accidentally. The former investigative reporter is now not only on the scent of a good story, he's also possibly on the trail of a killer.

Jimmy Stoma once had a well-deserved reputation for bad-boy behavior fueled by drugs and alcohol; among his many arrests was one for performing wearing nothing but a Day-Glo condom and a rubber Halloween mask in the likeness of the Rev. Pat Robertson. The Slut Puppies sold over six million albums (their biggest hit was titled *A Painful Burning Discharge*) and won a Grammy, but Jimmy eventually left the group and dropped out of sight. In recent years he got clean and sober and became a fitness enthusiast and avid outdoorsman.

Stoma was talented, but the same can't be said of many of the other so-called artists in the business, beginning with his wife Cleo. Her talent is showmanship, not music. She made her first splash at age fifteen by singing ABBA songs in a topless rock band. Her one hit song, "Me," was launched with a music video directed by Oliver Stone in which it appeared she briefly flashed her pubes. She uses the occasion of Jimmy's funeral to sing "Me" and to plug her newest song she claims Jimmy was producing for her at the time of his death. But when Tagger obtains a hard drive containing the songs Jimmy had been secretly working on for four years, he recognizes the new song Cleo sang and begins to suspect she might have had motive enough to kill her husband to get that song for herself.

Stoma's musical career gives Hiaasen an opportunity to write several song lyrics, the most notable of which is "Basket Case." Although he wrote only two lines of the song for the novel ("My baby is a basket case/A bipolar mama in leather and lace"), his publisher asked him to finish the song so they could use it to promote the book. With the help of musician friend Warren Zevon, with whom he had previously collaborated on a pair of songs, the two completed "Basket Case." which was later included on Zevon's 2002 CD,

4. Novels for Adults

My Ride's Here. Other Jimmy Stoma lyrics Hiaasen wrote allowed him to have some fun doing what he does best, i.e., playing with words. In "Cindy's Oyster," a snarky song Jimmy wrote about his wife, we get three different versions of a lyric that evolves over time.

Tagger's demotion to writing obituaries has affected him both professionally and personally. "At one time, I was a serious reporter doing what passed for serious journalism," he says sourly. "Now I write exclusively about the unliving" (14). Worse, he has to answer to an editor, Emma Cole, who is younger and far less experienced than he is. She has, in his view, a "sorority-sister soul" and little talent for the job. As far as he's concerned, her main mission is to ensure that he remain where he is, writing obituaries with no hope of any kind of professional redemption.

Spending every day writing about the newly dead has also left him with a severe case of morbidity. The deaths of John Kennedy, George Orwell, and Elvis Presley at age forty-six weigh heavily on a man of that same age whose professional life has hit a dead end. (It turns out he's mistaken about Elvis, who actually died at forty-two. According to Hiaasen, "That's probably because he used the same cheap almanac that I did, which had it wrong, and was too lazy to double-check. By the time I caught my mistake it was too late to change it in the novel, so now it becomes Jack's screwup, another of his morbid fixations. Such are the fringe benefits of writing fiction" (CH website).) The narrative is filled with Tagger's obsessive references to famous figures like Oscar Wilde, John Lennon, Edgar Allan Poe, Jack London, F. Scott Fitzgerald, and Franz Kafka who were all younger than he is when they died. "If death could snatch such heavy hitters as Elvis and JFK," he realizes, "a nobody like me is easy pickings" (33).

Because the novel is narrated in present tense, we see events unfold as they happen. This allows the reader to witness changes in Tagger's attitude as they actually occur. It starts when he first begins noticing Emma's brightly painted toenails. It's a small thing, but it indicates to him that there's a spunkiness about his boss, a side to her that "rollicks carefree and fanciful" (133) he never noticed before. When she jolts him with an unexpected punch to the nose after he crawls under the table to get another peek at her painted nails, he begins recalibrating his view of her. He's surprised by what he comes to realize: "God help me," he says, "I've got a crush on my editor—the woman whom I vowed to outwit, demoralize and drive out of the newspaper business. My mission has been derailed by raw straightforward lust, and I couldn't be happier" (231).

It takes a close brush with death to snap him out of his morbid anxieties. In a dramatic scene reminiscent of some of the exciting episodes at sea in the thrillers Hiaasen wrote with Bill Montalbano, Tagger finds himself in the middle of Lake Okeechobee during a powerful storm late at night. He's there to trade the hard drive he has obtained with Jimmy Stoma's unreleased music on it for Emma, who has been kidnapped by Cleo's bodyguard Jerry. During the tense standoff, Jerry points his gun at Tagger, which for the first time in his life brings him face to face with real death. After the exchange, Jerry's airboat suddenly turns and begins racing towards him. As it's about to crash into his much smaller boat, Tagger shoots at the driver. He misses but distracts him enough to cause the airboat to overturn, killing both passengers. Tagger suddenly finds his neurotic preoccupation with his own early demise giving way to "a new, more flexible attitude toward the concept of dying" (280).

His transformation continues after he receives a package in the mail from his mother on his forty-seventh birthday. Despite his repeated pleas over the years, she has refused to tell him anything about the death of his father, who left when he was only three, including when and how he died. In the package is a birthday card and, to his great surprise, his father's obituary. He now learns that his father was a drunken goofball, a Key West street entertainer best known for juggling a quartet of cockatoos who could recite passages from Shakespeare, Chekhov, and Tennessee Williams. He died at age forty-six after falling out of a tree. Also enclosed is this note from his mother: "Happy 47th, Jack! (See? You made it!)." Later, while walking through a cemetery, Jack makes no effort to avert his eyes from the grave markers or the dates of the departed's birth and death. "If the years should add up to forty-seven, so what. Happy Birthday to me" (301).

Authors of long-running series narrated in first person know that success requires a narrator whom both the reader and the author find interesting. Spending an entire novel in the head of one character is a challenge for the novelist, especially one used to the freedom of an omniscient point of view. Hiaasen admits he wrote the first five chapters both ways before deciding he liked the first-person version better and stuck with it.

The switch from first to third-person voice resulted in a different comic tone and voice in *Basket Case*. The third-person omniscient point of view allowed Hiaasen to shift freely from character to character and to describe actions that a first-person narrator like Tagger would have no way of knowing about. In addition, he narrated in a distinctive satiric voice that is a major

4. Novels for Adults

source of humor in every novel. Tagger has to narrate his story in a voice consistent with the person he is shown to be, and all the humor must come from that voice or from the characters he meets and the actions he observes. As a result, the comic volume is lowered and the tone less outrageous.

This of course doesn't mean that *Basket Case* is humorless. Far from it. Hiaasen's novels are routinely filled with outrageous freaks and oddballs, although in *Basket Case* the number of such characters is much smaller since they must all come from Tagger's circle of friends or people he might reasonably encounter. One of them is Carla Candilla, the seventeen-year-old daughter of his favorite ex-girlfriend, and a savvy veteran of the local club scene who's his only pipeline to modern youth culture. The conversations between the irreverent teenager and the man she affectionately refers to as "daddy dearest," "old timer," and "gnarly old fart" are a comic delight.

Janet Thrush, Jimmy Stoma's sister, is a woman with an unusual profession: equipped with a video camera set up in her living room, a web site, and a 900 number, she makes her living dressed in various costumes—e.g., a meter maid or a Swat-team member—and then stripping down to her underwear to satisfy her customers' sexual fantasies. She also has a lively sense of humor, as illustrated in this description of her job:

> "Four bucks a minute, Jack, that's what these gomers pay me to give 'em a 'parking ticket.'"
> "In your bra and panties."
> "Yeah, but still..."
> "It's good money," I agree.
> "This guy Larry"—Janet, cutting her eyes toward the living room—"he likes me to write him up for double-parking his timber rig in front of a massage parlor. That's his secret fantasy, I guess. He's calling all the way from Fairbanks, Alaska. Now, ask me do I care if he's whacking off in Fairbanks, Alaska, while he's staring at me in my underpanties on his PC? For four bucks a minute he can tie his cock in a knot and clobber a moose with it, far as I'm concerned."
> "Don't give him any ideas" [66].

A visit to a nightclub called Jizz also provides a good example of description that while written in Tagger's voice still manages to evoke the Hiaasen sense of the ridiculous, though necessarily a bit more modulated than usual:

> The club is lit with fruity-colored strobes that dice up the cigarette haze like a psychedelic SaladShooter. A Nordic-looking DJ in unlikely rasta garb is in command of the synthesized dance music, thumping as tediously as a cardiac monitor. Everywhere are fashion-conscious couples practicing for the South Beach scene; the guys still look like off-duty valets, and the women still look like cashiers at Blockbuster [155].

The kind of outlandish behavior common in Hiaasen's previous fiction would be out of place in *Basket Case*, though he does include one scene that is a lower-key variation of one he used in *Skin Tight*. After Carla's mother left Jack, she gave him a gift of a baby Savannah monitor lizard he named Colonel Tom, after Colonel Tom Parker, Elvis Presley's famous manager. Thanks to a steady diet of beer and pastries, the lizard grows to a length of three feet. Unfortunately, the rich diet also proves fatal. Tagger stores the dead lizard, now folded into the shape of an ampersand, in his freezer until he can give it a proper burial. One night, when he hears someone breaking into his apartment, he grabs the only weapon he can find—the frozen remains of Colonel Tom—and uses it to fight off the intruder. Later he learns that the man—Cleo's bodyguard who was searching for Jimmy Stoma's missing hard drive—lost an eye in his encounter with Colonel Tom.

Hiaasen has been a newspaperman long enough to have witnessed some dramatic changes in the profession. Many of them, like the shocking transformation that turned his beloved Everglades playground into shopping malls when he was a boy, left him profoundly angry. Even before the rise of digital media began to pose a grave new threat to the very survival of newspapers, Hiaasen observed destructive changes taking place that, like those that devastated Florida's natural environment, were the consequence of human greed. The main villain in *Basket Case* is polo-playing Race Maggad III, CEO of Maggad-Feist ("maggot feast"), owner of twenty-seven daily newspapers, including the *Union-Register*.

Maggad, whom Tagger scornfully dismisses as a "vapid yuppie puke" and a "money-grubbing Yupster twit" (115), embodies the evil of corporate ownership which values profit over product. Satisfying company shareholders is more important to him than providing readers the news. To Hiaasen, this is nothing less than a form of "spiritual corruption—an abandonment of principle." In his view, newspapers have "an unwritten contract to take care of the planet. There's a moral obligation to be upheld" (Reardon).

Newspapers obviously need to make a profit to survive, but demanding a twenty-five percent profit margin as Maggad does (and as Tony Knight, head of Knight-Ridder, owner of Hiaasen's own newspaper the *Miami Herald*, also did) is nothing but pure greed, a margin, Tanner says, that would be the envy of most heroin pushers. "You damn sure can't have *good* journalism when you're milking the cow for twenty-five percent" (309), he insists. Cutting essential staff is short-sighted and counter-productive. Spending twelve million dollars to move corporate headquarters from Milwaukee to San Diego so that Maggad's expensive Porsches won't suffer salt damage—money Tagger argues could have been used to hire 250 more editors and reporters—is obscene. Each swing of the corporate ax results in a reduction in the space for news and even more "dumbed-down crapola, fluff and gimmicks and graphics" (115).

Tagger often waxes nostalgic about the good old days when newsrooms "reeked of coffee and cigarettes and stale pizza. You'd hear the wire machines chattering and the police scanners gabbling and the pasteup guys snorting at dirty jokes" (82). It was a heady time for young journalists like Tagger (and Carl Hiaasen) who firmly believed that a newspaper should be "the conscience of the community" and that "news isn't just the filler between advertisements. It's the spine of the business" (96).

Things are much different now. Though he once dreamed of "kicking butt on the front page" like Bob Woodward and Sy Hersh (145), Tagger's now reduced to writing obituaries. And thanks to owners like Maggad for whom profits trump news, newspapers are forced to "buy the loyalty of readers with giveaways and grocery coupons, not content" (83). Fortunately, there are still enough "prickly, disrespecting, shit-stirring bastards" (205) like himself who are willing to continue to fight for the highest ideals of journalism. "Nobody with a living brain cell goes into the newspaper business for the money," notes Tagger. "They're in it because digging up the truth is interesting and consequential work.... Done well, journalism brings to light chicanery, oppression and injustice, though such concerns seldom weigh heavily on those who own the newspapers" (249).

In the end, the good guys win. Janet Thrush couldn't bear the thought of her brother being cremated, so she confesses she switched the tag that would have sent Jimmy's body to the crematorium to another body in the funeral home. This now makes it possible for his body to be exhumed and an autopsy performed. Tests determine that he was drugged just before beginning his dive, which eventually leads to his wife's conviction for his murder. Several of Jimmy and the Slut Puppies's old songs are re-released and become hits. And thanks to clever planning by the previous owner of the *Union-Register* before he died, ownership is returned to his family and his widow begins re-hiring staff. Emma gets promoted and Tagger plans to return to the paper, this time as a member of its new investigation team.

In Jack Tanner, Hiaasen created a character interesting enough that he could easily have continued to write additional mysteries featuring him. Instead, he chose to go in a surprising new direction: his next novel, *Hoot*, was his first written for young readers. Television did take a serious interest in Jack Tanner when it was announced in 2013 that Rob Reiner had signed to produce and direct a series based on the character for SpikeTV, but to date nothing has yet materialized.

Skinny Dip *(2004)*

Skinny Dip opens with a sober statement of facts: "At the stroke of eleven on a cool April night, a woman named Joey Perrone went overboard from a luxury deck of the cruise liner M. V. *Sun Duchess*" (3). But as Joey plunges toward the dark ocean, the tone suddenly changes as the narrative shifts to her point of view: "I married an asshole, she thought, knifing headfirst into the waves." (The novel's title, which refers to the fact that Joey's clothes were ripped off when she hit the water, was suggested by Hiaasen's longtime friend Warren Zevon, who died as the book was nearing completion. It is dedicated to his memory.)

Unlike Hiaasen's previous novel, which employed the structure of a murder mystery, *Skinny Dip* is a story about a failed murder, and there's no mystery about the culprit. Joey and her husband Chaz, on a cruise to celebrate their second wedding anniversary, were taking a late night stroll on the deck when he suddenly bent down, grabbed her ankles, and flipped her backwards over the railing. Fortunately, she's a powerful swimmer (she was co-captain of her swim team at UCLA) who is able to make her way toward the Florida coastline. As she battles fatigue to stay afloat, she also struggles to understand why her husband would want her dead. It couldn't be her money: she had ensured that her entire $13 million inheritance would go to a wildlife fund in the event of her death. Nothing on the list of possible reasons she comes up with—she sometimes dozed off during hockey games, even during playoffs; she could whip him in tennis whenever she felt like it; she belonged to a weekly book club—seems to be a strong enough motive for murder.

The story takes a fortuitous turn for Joey when she manages to grab onto a sixty-pound bale of Jamaican marijuana floating in the ocean beside her. Later she is found stark naked and unconscious by a man in a boat. His name is Mick Stranahan, whom Hiaasen's readers will remember as the retired investigator for the Florida Attorney's Office who solved the mystery in *Skin Tight*. Stranahan takes the damsel in distress to his house on a small nearby island, where she explains what her husband has done. She persuades him

4. Novels for Adults

not to call the police. Instead, she enlists his aid in a scheme to get revenge on her "worthless horndog" of a husband.

Chaz Perrone believed he had planned the perfect crime down to the smallest detail (he even planted a copy of Flaubert's *Madame Bovary*, a novel about an unhappy wife who commits suicide, beside Joey's side of the bed to lead police to suspect she may have jumped to her death). But during a conversation with Broward County detective Karl Rolvaag, he makes a crucial error when he mentions that the Gulf Stream flows from north to south. How could a marine biologist like Chaz Perrone make such a stupid mistake? Simple. He's a dolt. Rolvaag now has a good reason to begin looking more deeply into the death of Joey Perrone.

As a young man attracted by the promise of wealth, Chaz Perrone decided to become a doctor, though the idea of interacting with sick people repelled him. Poor grades, however, ended any hope he had of getting into medical school. Later, armed with "Ken-doll good looks, his priapic affability, and a bachelor's degree in a subject he loathed—biology" (41), the only job he could get was hosing down kennels at the Humane Society. He tried to purchase a mail-order M. A. from a diploma mill, only to learn after he mailed off a certified check for $999 that the school had been shut down. He concluded he'd have get a real degree, but again was disappointed, this time to be told he'd have to spend time in the outdoors if he wanted a degree in field biology. Having to study coastal sea lice was distasteful to someone like himself with an "antipathy toward the great outdoors and all denizens great and small" (42).

Nevertheless, against all odds, he obtained his degree and landed a job with a cosmetics manufacturer as what serious biologists refer to as a "biostitute," i.e., one who falsely attests that his company's products contain only negligible amounts of toxins and carcinogens. Whenever he finds evidence of tumors in the mice he tests, he simply tosses the damaging evidence away. Later, thanks to the connections of Red Hammernut, multimillionaire owner of 13,000 acres of Florida vegetable farms and a big donor to powerful politicians, Chaz gets a position with the South Florida Water Management District. His job is to report the amount of phosphorus Hammernut's farms are pouring into the Everglades. In reality, his job simply entails recording low numbers so no one will know that Hammernut Farms is flushing more pollutants into the Everglades than the state's largest cattle ranch and sugarcane grower combined. After Joey happens to see him at home writing some random numbers on a chart, he suspects she might know what he's doing. We now know the motive behind her murder.

Joey takes revenge to a new level of inventiveness. Nothing for her as simple as dumping garbage or dung beetles into a car, as Twilly Spree did in *Sick Puppy*. She prefers the psychological approach. She begins by secretly slipping into her home to replace items like a dress and lipstick that Chaz had thrown out or stealing his favorite George Thorogood CDs. On one visit she cuts her face out of a wedding photograph of her and Chaz and slips it under his pillow. The plan works. Chaz not only becomes confused, he becomes impotent with girlfriend Ricca. Not even a replacement copy of Thorogood's "Bad to the Bone" can rally "Chaz's bone to its usual badness" (99).

A farcical scene ensues when Joey is forced to hide underneath the bed when Chaz unexpectedly returns home while she's there. To deal with his new impotence problem, Chaz has scored some extra-powerful erectile-dysfunction drugs from a friend. By the time his partner for the evening, a New Age reflexologist named Medea, arrives, he's raring to go. The entire scene is described from Joey's point of view underneath the bed. Though she can only see feet, she describes the sounds and smells of the action above her in vivid detail.

It begins with the familiar sounds of Chaz's pre-sex ritual: "the brisk uncapping of his stick deodorant, the soft rotary whine of the nose-hair clippers, the rhythmic plucking of floss through molars, the plangent yodel of his gargling" (159). Then comes the pungent aroma of the scented candles and incense sticks. When the bed springs start squeaking, Joey worries for her safety and is struck by the irony that Chaz might still kill her, this time by crushing her to death if the bed should collapse under the weight of all that noisy copulating above her. But then Medea's discordant humming and Chaz's loud heaving suddenly stop when poor Chaz gets a whiff of Joey's familiar perfume and is unable to continue.

Meanwhile, Mick Stranahan pretends to be a blackmailer who claims to have witnessed Chaz dump his wife overboard. He also pressures his sleazy lawyer brother-in-law to create a phony will that leaves Joey's entire $13 million inheritance to Chaz, giving him an obvious motive for her murder.

Chaz obviously needs help, which comes in the person of Earl Edward O'Toole, better known as Tool, another in Hiaasen's gallery of memorable bad guys. He possesses all the requisite features: size (six three, 280 pounds), striking appearance (head shaped like a cinder block, upper body densely matted with thick dark hair), thuggish qualifications (muscle and a lack of conscience), a menacing look ("he could scare hot piss out of an igloo" (123)), and an unusual hobby (he collects highway-fatality markers and plants them

4. Novels for Adults

in his yard like a mini-Arlington National Cemetery; as he explains it, "They look real nice in the ground, plus you don't gotta prune 'em like you do trees and shrubs" (179)).

His wooly appearance has also led to a problem with drugs: he was shot by a poacher who mistook him for a bear, leaving him with a bullet painfully lodged in his butt crack. To alleviate his suffering, he has become addicted to fentanyl, which he obtains by stealing patches of the drug from the backs of sedated cancer patients in nursing homes. In order to attach the patches, he has to shave sections of his back which leaves it looking like a checkerboard.

Red Hammernut hires Tool, who formerly worked for him as a field boss, to keep a watchful eye on Chaz Perrone, who is being questioned by Rolvaag and blackmailed by Stranahan. He needs to ensure that Chaz's role in falsifying water samples on his farms is never revealed, or his whole operation would be shut down. Hiaasen, however, adds two features to Tool's character that elevate him far above the standard stereotype of the hired thug: he speaks some of the funniest lines in the book and is offered the opportunity for redemption.

One of the funniest scenes in the novel comes during a conversation Rolvaag has with him about Joey's disappearance. Rolvaag bends over to read the inscription on one of the highway markers Tool is pounding into the ground that memorializes a forty-five-year-old man who was killed by a drunk driver:

"Friend of yours?" Rolvaag asked.
"My dog," said Earl Edward O'Toole, avoiding eye contact.
"That's quite a name for a dog. Randolph Claude Gunther."
"We called him 'Rex' for short."
"I never heard of one living forty-five years," the detective remarked. "Parrots can. Tortoises can. But I'm not so sure about dogs."
Earl Edward O'Toole took another hard swing with the hammer. "Well, he come from good stock" [178].

As the conversation continues, Tool comes up with increasingly ridiculous answers to Rolvaag's questions. After Tool tells him that Rex died in a plane crash, Rolvaag asks why the memorial reads, "Please Don't Drink and Drive." The pilot was drunk, explains Tool. What about all the other crosses lying on the ground? "Rex's puppies," Tool replies, "They was all on the same plane."

But it is Tool's redemption that is the most surprising thing about him.

His usual method of getting fentanyl patches is to enter a nursing home dressed in hospital whites and look for sleeping patients he can steal them from. But his latest attempt is foiled when the patient, a scrappy eighty-one-year-old dying woman named Maureen, elbows him between the eyes when he tries to peel a patch off her back. Then she invites him to sit down, and they end up talking more about his pain than hers. When he gets up to leave, she asks if he would pop in again some time. He does, and an unlikely friendship develops.

She takes a motherly interest in the hairy thug and offers him some sage advice: "It's never too late for choosing a new direction" (241), she tells him. "Life goes by so darn fast, every wasted moment is a crime … and every crime is a wasted moment" (241). Her words soon have a positive effect on Tool. He begins bringing her food (fried alligator and Key lime pie), orders the nursing staff to pay better attention to her, and when her IV runs out of pain medication, pulls the last remaining patch off his back and gives it to her. Observing a Jamaican nurse's kindness towards Maureen gets him thinking about how he used to mistreat the Jamaican farm workers and steal from them when he worked as a crew boss on one Hammernut's farms. He also begins to question his willingness to do whatever Hammernut asks: "A week ago Tool would've said yes to any fool job, no matter how bad, as long as it paid in cash. But then he'd met Maureen" (297).

Chaz Perrone is the last person in the world who should be working in a place like the Everglades. To begin with, "nothing about nature awed, soothed or humbled him—not the solitude or the mystic vastness or the primordial ebb and flow. To Chaz, it was all hot, buggy, funking-smelling and treacherous. He would have been so much happier on the driving range at Eagle Trace" (75). He's also deathly afraid of alligators, and the mere thought of an attack causes him to yowl "like a hemorrhoidal bobcat" (76) while he noisily hacks his way through the "steaming shithole" (77). On the other hand, if you don't care a hoot about the Everglades, you're the ideal person for the job Red Hammernut wants done.

The battle to save the Everglades before it's too late has long been a subject dear to Hiaasen's heart and a recurring item in his newspaper columns. The Everglades has been slowly dying for many years, the victim of pollution, drought, and overdevelopment. Florida state agencies possessed the power to at least stop the pollution, but lacked the will to do so until a Federal lawsuit charged the State Department of Environmental Regulation with failure to do its duty. This prompted both political parties in a rare spirit of

4. Novels for Adults

bipartisanship to join together in a long-overdue effort to save the Everglades. In the late 1990s, the U.S. Congress and the Florida Legislature allotted $8 billion to finally begin to clean up the polluted waters.

Hiaasen's ire in *Skinny Dip* is not directed at Florida's past failures to save the Everglades. Real progress has been made. His attack is aimed at those like Hammernut who know how to game the system. In this regard Hammernut closely resembles Dr. Rudy Graveline of *Skin Tight* who knew how to buy his way out of punishment for his history of medical malpractice. All Hammernut has to do is make hefty contributions to the right politicians and then pull a few strings to get his man Chaz a job with the state agency monitoring water quality. Then he gets him assigned to his own property. All Chaz has to do is simply write down shockingly low numbers of pollutants in water the color of root beer he pretends to test, thus allowing Hammernut to continue using the Everglades as his private cesspool. Hammernut ends up saving himself millions of dollars in the process, and is even given an award by the local Sierra Club for his amazingly successful clean-up efforts.

Thanks to Joey's revenge plan, Stranahan's blackmail scheme, and Rolvaag's Lt. Columbo-style persistence, Chaz is turned into an emotional and physical wreck. Like Macbeth, he's haunted by the appearance of what he believes is Joey's ghost who has come back from the dead to ask him why he killed her. The little blue pills he's been taking for his impotence leave him with a painful erection that won't go away. After mistakenly concluding that his girlfriend Ricca is the blackmailer's partner, he attempts (unsuccessfully, as usual) to murder her. And then after realizing that Hammernut now wants Tool to kill him, he shoots him too, also unsuccessfully. When all three of his intended murder victims eventually turn up very much alive, all the poor fellow can do is moan, "How can it be so hard to kill somebody" (320).

The ending of *Skinny Dip* is something of letdown compared to Hiaasen's earlier novels. The good folks are rewarded as usual: Joey moves in with Stranahan on his small island; Rolvaag finally gets to retire and return to his home state of Minnesota; Tool ends up with the $500,000 in blackmail money Hammernut agreed to pay Chaz for not exposing his scam, finds a veterinarian who is able to remove the bullet from his butt, and, after liberating Maureen from the nursing home, takes her to Canada where together they can watch the return of the migrating pelicans from Florida.

As for punishments, Hammernut gets what he deserves: Tool impales him on one of his roadside fatality crosses after Hammernut makes the mistake of slapping him in the head and calling him a "doped-up dickhead of a gorilla" (333). But Hiaasen seems unsure what to do with Chaz. Initially he had Tool and Hammernut shrink-wrap him from head to toe, but he managed to gnaw a hole in the plastic large enough to allow him to breathe. Then Hammernut orders Tool to shoot him, but the new, reformed Tool deliberately misses, allowing him to escape death once more. In the end he's simply marched into the swamp by a strange man he's never met before who calls himself Captain. Hiaasen's readers know him better as Skink.

Skink serves in the novel solely as a convenient device, what the ancient Greek dramatists called a *deus ex machina*, literally a "god from the machine" who was lowered on stage to resolve a plot complication. He makes only two brief appearances in the novel: in the first, he miraculously happens upon Ricca in the nick of time to rescue her after she had been shot and left for dead by Chaz; in the second, he materializes out of nowhere to be the administrator of Chaz's punishment. Hiaasen used Skink in a similar manner at the end of *Sick Puppy* where he left it up to the reader to imagine what punishment Skink and his new friend Twilly Spree might come up with for a carload of litterers they are chasing after. But readers of *Skinny Dip* have a right to expect more.

No one deserves one of Hiaasen's trademark punishments more than Chaz: the man attempted to kill three innocent people, and his deliberate malfeasance as a water inspector threatens the very survival of the Everglades he was paid to protect. Leaving him in the middle of a swamp with only a canteen of water and a reminder of Tennyson's famous line, "Nature, red in tooth and claw" (355), doesn't seem quite good enough. In addition, those readers whose introduction to Hiaasen happens to be *Skinny Dip* will have no idea who the strange man named Skink is or why he's doing what he does to the young man with him.

Despite the unresolved ending, which caused the reviewer for *Publishers Weekly* to wonder if the final pages of the novel were missing and another to complain that it made the book feel "like a cruise aboard a well-appointed boat that leaks. The ride is comfortable and fun until the underlying structure sinks" (Linskey), *Skinny Dip* is among the most entertaining of Hiaasen's novels. Chaz and Tool, two of Hiaasen's most inspired comic creations, provide plenty of laughs and memorable lines. Some of the funniest are those related to Chaz's insatiable randiness: "He spent more time in condoms than in the stacks"(41); "He's got so many bimbos, you'd need radio collars to track them all"(83); "I wouldn't trust that guy with my bowling ball" (73).

Hiaasen was understandably thrilled when Mike Nichols and Elaine

May, whose comedy albums were among those he listened to with his dad when he was a young boy, signed on to make the film version of *Skinny Dip*. May would write the screenplay and Nichols would direct (a perfect choice as he also directed the film version of Joseph Heller's *Catch-22*). Unfortunately, Nichols got sidetracked doing *Charlie Wilson's War* with Tom Hanks. That turned out to be his final feature film, and *Skinny Dip* never made it to the big screen.

Nature Girl *(2006)*

Though not among his best novels, *Nature Girl* does demonstrate Hiaasen's wizardry as a puppet master. As usual, he begins by introducing a cast of misfits and oddballs, ranging from the damaged and disappointed to the deluded and doltish. The fun begins once he starts them dancing to the merry tune he creates for them.

Honey Santana lives with her twelve-year-old son Fry in a trailer park in tiny Everglades City, Florida (pop. 513). To describe Honey as tightly wound would be an understatement. Ever since the birth of Fry, she has suffered from a tendency to overreact to ordinary situations. Fry spent the first two weeks of life in the hospital struggling to breathe, which left Honey susceptible to uncontrollable spells of apprehension and dread, especially when it came to the safety and well-being of her son.

She has also begun hearing musical static from a "boom box in her brain pan" (91) that plays odd combinations of music like "Smoke in the Water" and "Rainy Days and Mondays" or Nat King Cole singing a duet with Marilyn Manson. (Her malady resembles that of Skink, who in *Skinny Dip* also heard odd duets in his head, e.g., David Lee Roth and Sophie Tucker or Bobbie Gentry and Placido Domingo.) In addition she has developed a "rabid intolerance of callousness and folly" which has doomed her to demand "more decency and consideration from her fellow humans than they demanded of themselves" (29). She is on high alert for transgressions against normal human decency and decides her mission in life is to try "to fix the entire human race, one flaming asshole at a time" (207).

Honey was married to Perry Skinner, Fry's father, for seventeen years until he asked her for a divorce after she had "simply worn him out with her bewildering projects and antic crusades" (43). He's a caring father to his son and is still in love with Honey. He keeps a watchful eye out for her, and contributes financially whenever she needs assistance. He also plays a behind-the-scenes role in punishing her boss after he gropes her.

Louis Piejack owns the fish market where Honey worked until she abruptly quit one day when the lecherous goat grabbed one of her breasts. Her immediate response was to whack him in the testicles with a wooden crab mallet. Ex-husband Skinner arranges a follow-up punishment by hiring a trio of guys to jam Piejack's offending hand into a stone-crab trap, which results in three of his fingers being pinched off by the crabs. Thanks to some surgical bungling in the process of re-attaching his fingers, his pinkie finger is accidentally sewed to the stump of his thumb and his thumb is attached to his index finger. When Honey later makes the mistake of dropping by to offer her sympathy, he mistakes her concern for a romantic come-on and begins stalking her.

Fry, mature beyond his years, assumes responsibility for his mother's well-being. For example, he shuts off her computer access after she once fired off ninety-seven e-mail messages in one day to the White House complaining about its support for oil drilling in Alaska, which drew the interest of the Secret Service. He even monitors her driving to ensure that she keeps her eyes on the road whenever she gets excited. However, her mood swings take a toll on the boy; he's a track star who usually wins handily except for those times when something his mother does worries him. Then he finishes dead last.

Half-breed Seminole Sammy Tigertail is the nephew of Tommy Tigertail, who was a member of Skip Wiley's *Las Noches de Diciembre* terrorist group in *Tourist Season*. Sammy spent the first fourteen years of his life living with his white father in suburban Broward County where his name was Chad McQueen. Immediately after his father's sudden death, his stepmother shipped him off to the reservation where he became known as Sammy Tigertail. The blue-eyed young man is proud to learn he's a descendant of the great Seminole leader Thlocklo Tustenuggee, also known as Tiger Tail. On the other hand, he's disappointed that the Seminoles, who never surrendered to the white man, are now embraced by the lily-white business establishment and courted by Florida politicians eager for the support of their new corporate empire based on casinos and bingo parlors. Where does he fit in?

The rest of the main characters live a thousand miles away in Ft. Worth, Texas. Boyd Shreave works for a telemarketing outfit called Relentless, Inc. where he phones people (often at the dinner hour) and tries to sell them real-estate property in northern Florida. Despite years of experience hawking everything from corrective footwear and farm equipment to herbal baldness remedies and exotic pet supplies, the truth is he's a lousy salesman: "Almost nobody wanted to buy anything from Boyd Shreave. They just wanted him to go away" (9). The only reason he got the job with Relentless is that he has a smooth, affable telephone voice. The only reason he stays is the gorgeous woman working in the cubicle next to him.

Six-foot-tall ash-blonde Eugenie Fonda once enjoyed a brief brush with fame thanks to a fling she had with a tree trimmer who she later learned murdered his wife while she was involved with him. A book about the whole affair became an instant bestseller, earning Eugenie a half-million dollar windfall. Unfortunately, she invested it all in Enron, which went belly up, leaving her broke and in need of a job, which led to her taking one on the phone bank at Relentless and to an affair with Boyd Shreave. For her, the affair is nothing more than an idle distraction, the "natural backwash of being stuck together in the most boring, brain-numbing job on the planet" (20).

One person perversely interested in the intimate details of Boyd's affair with Eugenie is his wife Lily, wealthy owner of a chain of pizza restaurants. She hires a local private eye named Dealey to get the goods on her cheating husband. He comes through with convincing evidence, including a video of the pair of lovers engaged in intercourse. But Lily wants more. She wants evidence of actual penetration, and she's willing to pay Dealey $10,000 in cash to get it.

Now that Hiaasen has introduced his players, he has to find a way to get them all together on Dismal Key, a tiny (and real) uninhabited island in the Ten Thousand Lakes region of the Everglades. The first to arrive is Sammy Tigertail. After he inadvertently kills his first opponent during his debut as an alligator wrestler and then a passenger on his very first day as an airboat pilot drops dead of a sudden heart attack, he concludes he needs to escape civilization. Armed only with a Gibson Super 400 guitar that once belonged to Mark Knopfler of Dire Straits that he obtains from the Seminole Tribe's Hard Rock cafe, he heads into the wilderness to learn how to play it and to search for a new sense of who he is.

Before reaching Dismal Key, however, he chances upon a young coed named Gillian St. Croix who's bored with college life and with her dull boyfriend. When Sammy identifies himself as a Seminole, she points to her Florida State sweatshirt and proudly exclaims that she's one too. (The Florida State football team is known as the Seminoles.) Sammy may be in search of peace and solitude, but Gillian is simply "waiting for something phenomenally stupendous to happen to me" (130) and sees Sammy as her ticket to adventure. "I want to be your hostage," she announces (70). Against his better judgment, Sammy agrees to take the cute coed with him.

Getting the characters from Texas to Dismal Key is more complicated. It starts with a phone call that interrupts Honey's dinner with Fry. The caller identifies himself as Boyd Eisenhower (Boyd Shreave was advised to adopt the name of a president to sound more trustworthy) who begins to try to sell her some riverfront property in northern Florida. Being interrupted in the middle of dinner on the same day she was groped by her boss is too much. "Is this what she raised you to be, your mother?" she asks Boyd. "A professional pest" (12)? Stung by the reference to his mother, who once called him "a lazy sack of muleshit" (75), he fires back, "Go screw yourself, you dried-up old skank" (12).

To get back at Boyd, Honey turns the tables on him. She phones him and pretends to be selling, what else, Florida real estate. She offers him an attractive deal: in return for listening to a sales pitch, he'll receive two free plane tickets to Florida, accommodations at a four-star resort, and an ecotour by kayak through the Ten Thousand Islands. Having just been fired from his job at Relentless for being rude to Honey and eager to get away from his wife, Boyd persuades Eugenie to accompany him to Florida. Once Honey gets him in her clutches, she plans to take him to Dismal Key to lecture him on the decline of manners and civility in modern society. "If a common bottom feeder such as Boyd Shreave could be reformed, Honey reasoned, the future would be incrementally brighter for all mankind, including Fry" (207).

Private eye Dealey simply follows lovebirds Boyd and Eugenie to Florida. It seems unlikely that he would ever be able to get a video of actual penetration, but when Lily Shreave ups the offer to $25,000 in cash, he's more than willing to give it a shot. There are worse ways of wasting a few days than spending them in the Florida sunshine.

He begins stalking Boyd and Eugenie, who are temporarily staying in Honey's trailer prior to their trip to Dismal Key. He's hoping for an opportunity to catch them in the act. Instead, he encounters Louis Piejack, who's also stalking Honey. "Honey Santana is all mine," he warns Dealey, "I was here first" (135). When Piejack notices the video camera Dealey is carrying, he uses the sawed-off shotgun he's carrying to force him to come with him as he follows Honey. Since his damaged fingers won't allow him to operate the video camera himself, he hopes Dealey can shoot some sexy videos for his own private enjoyment. Meanwhile, Fry becomes concerned after he spots Piejack cruising in front of his mother's tailer and persuades his father to follow her when she leaves for Dismal Key.

4. Novels for Adults

Populating a deserted island with strangers who are stranded together has proven to be very popular with writers: notable examples include *The Tempest, Robinson Crusoe, Treasure Island, Swiss Family Robinson, Lord of the Flies, Gilligan's Island,* and *Survivor*. (One wonders whether Hiaasen might have even toyed with the idea of titling his book *Gillian's Island* after one of its inhabitants.) Dismal Key gives Hiaasen a convenient location where romance, comedy, education, and even suspense can take place.

The second half of *Nature Girl* turns into a comic farce with *Deliverance*-type overtones of violence and terror. Unfortunately there's not much of a story here, just a frenetic series of encounters with characters colliding into one another. Some of the comic misadventures are humorous: e.g., Boyd accidentally shoots himself in the groin with a taser gun; Piejack develops a painful infection after his skin is punctured with sharp needles when he falls into a cactus patch, and the bandages on his damaged hand are colonized by fire ants; then Fry, who has come to Dismal Key with his father, vomits all over his shoes.

Other instances of violence are anything but funny. Dealey is accidentally shot in the shoulder by Sammy Tigertail. Piejack's "wooing" of his beloved "lil' Honey Pie" is funny until it isn't as he grows increasingly violent and aggressive. He fractures Honey's jaw with a large branch and shoots her ex-husband Skinner in the hip. The threat of further violence ends when Skinner splinters Piejack's skull with a single blow to the head from Mark Knopfler's Gibson that he borrowed from Sammy Tigertail.

In the end, Honey fails in her mission to enlighten Boyd, though not due to lack of trying: "The man was unreachable; a dry hole. For such a lunkhead there could be no awakening, no rebirth of wonderment" (225). But the effort is not wasted: her encounter with real danger cures her fear of imagined ones, and the jolt that fractured her jaw also silences the music in her head. At the end of the novel, Skinner moves in with her and Fry while he recuperates from his injury, and the couple appears to be well on the way to making his stay permanent.

Eugenie returns to Texas, quits her job at Relentless, and accepts Dealey's offer to join his private-detective business. Instead of the penetration video Lily Shreave hoped for, she has to settle for a short video Eugenie shot of chameleons mating set to Ravel's *Bolero*. She likes it so much, however, that she agrees to pay $10,000 for it. Gillian gets a story she can tell her grandchildren about being kidnapped by a handsome Indian and held hostage on a mangrove island in the Everglades. But she's not done with Sammy, who has decided to stay behind on Dismal Key: she hires a helicopter to track him down, and it appears he will likely allow her to find him.

Boyd Shreave is a total loser. Here's a man with a rich wife and a gorgeous girlfriend, but he's such a dullard that both of them dump him. Honey tries her best to jolt him out of his dullness, but he blows that opportunity too. He also bungles the chance to be the messiah that several members of the First Resurrectionist Maritime Assembly for God who have gathered on Dismal Key are anxiously awaiting. When Boyd wades ashore wearing a glowing lamp on his head and bearing the stigmata on his hands (which were actually bloodied in a fall from a tree), he is hailed by the loopy faithful as their long-awaited savior. Unfortunately, as soon as he opens his mouth, he reveals himself to be "just another loudmouthed schmuck" (293) and he's left behind when the Resurrectionists leave. In the end, he simply decides to stay in Florida and—what else?—sell real estate.

In *Nature Girl* Hiaasen also adds some new wrinkles to his usual formula. For the first time he includes a young character, no doubt inspired by his experience in creating similar characters for the young adult novels he had begun writing. Erin Grant in *Strip Tease* did have a six-year-old daughter, but she was used primarily as the motivation behind her decision to become a strip-club dancer. By contrast, Fry is a fully developed character who is forced to assume adult responsibilities because of his parents' split and his mother's sometimes erratic behavior, which he manages with love and a sense of humor.

The novel also features more female characters than usual, and in Honey Santana Hiaasen has created one of his strongest to date. In an essay on gender politics in Hiaasen's fiction, Alan Gibbs argued that many of his previous female characters (notably JoLayne Lucks and Joey Perrone) found their efforts to control the revenge plot against their antagonists eventually being taken over by the male protagonists, thus denying them ultimate authority. In Honey's case, however, "there is no question of any male character assuming control over the plot" (83). "Of all Hiaasen's female characters," he concludes, "Honey remains the one who most successfully retains a capacity for independent and self-motivated action" (84). She also became one of Hiaasen's own favorites: "She was one of those characters I grew to like and admire the more I worked on the book" (Rife "BOOKS").

On the other hand, the novel also omits (or at least downplays) such usual features as criminal activities, environmental issues, and serious satire. Despite the presence of a private detective, *Nature Girl* is not a crime novel. Louis Piejack becomes increasingly dangerous and must be eliminated, but he is far from the kind of career criminal Hiaasen usually depicts. Telemarketing is an annoyance, not a crime, and in the grand scheme of good vs. evil, it's no big deal.

Also missing, in a way, is Florida, which plays a minor role in the proceedings. Many of the main characters don't even live in the state and when they travel from Texas to Florida, it's not to scam the locals, as is often the case when outsiders arrive. Dismal Key does allow Hiaasen to emphasize the natural beauty of a location like the Ten Thousand Islands, especially when Honey forces Boyd to climb with her to the top of a poinciana tree so he can witness the magnificence around them as the sun rises: "The vista from atop the poinciana was timeless and serene—a long string of egrets crossing the distant 'glades; a squadron of white pelicans circling a nearby bay; a pair of ospreys hovering kite-like above a tidal creek, It was a perfect picture and a perfect silence" (225). But the effort is wasted on Boyd, whose soullessness renders him impervious to the gift Honey has taken so much trouble to offer him:

> Not being the spiritual sort, Boyd Shreave saw no divine hand in the unbroken wilderness that lay before him; no grand design in the jungled labyrinth of creeks and islets. Such unspoiled vistas inspired in Shreave not a nanosecond of introspection; when it came to raw nature, he remained staunchly incurious and devoid of awe. He would much rather have been back in Fort Worth, watching *American Idol*, swilling beer and gorging himself on microwave burritos [281].

Though incapable of appreciating the beauty of the place, Boyd represents no real threat to its survival. Dismal Key isn't being eyed for development nor are its waters being poisoned by polluters. It's simply an isolated setting that offers a convenient background for the action of the novel.

Taken on its own terms, *Nature Girl* can, like *Gilligan's Island*, simply be enjoyed as a light-hearted escape from worrying about more serious issues. Its humor serves no greater purpose than pure enjoyment. The novel may not live up to the very high standards set by Hiaasen's previous books, but as one reviewer remarked, even "an ordinary, almost automatic Carl Hiaasen novel is about 10,000 times better than no Hiaasen novel at all" (See).

Star Island *(2010)*

Star Island is about celebrity bad behavior and our insatiable hunger for news about it. While the subject of celebrities may appear to be slighter than some of the meatier issues Hiaasen has previously satirized, it's important to distinguish between talentless celebrities and celebrity culture. The Kardashians may be silly and not worth bothering about, but America's fascination with people like them is a much more serious issue, one worthy of Hiaasen's satirical attention.

Hiaasen dates our current obsession with celebrities to the infamous 50-mile low-speed freeway chase in 1994 involving O. J. Simpson and the L.A. police that was covered live on national television. A "sorry freak show," he called it in a column at the time, one that "couldn't have happened in any other country" ("The O. J." 123). What bothered him most was the effect such a fascination with the famous was having on his own profession of journalism. He noted with alarm later that year that more reporters were camped outside O. J.'s home than accompanied former President Jimmy Carter on his trip to North Korea: "If that's disgraceful," he wrote, "so is the fact that our audience is infinitely more interested in celebrity homicides than nuclear site inspections" ("The O. J." 124).

This trend became even more pronounced a decade later with the 2005 trial of Michael Jackson on child molestation charges, which was covered by 2200 journalists who, Hiaasen noted, could have been digging up more serious stories elsewhere. "The smelly stuff that was once left to the capable vultures at the *Star* and the *Enquirer*," he wrote in a 2007 column, "is now front-page fodder in your hometown paper and the lead story on the six o'clock news" (*Dance* 302).

The situation has only gotten much worse today in the age of the Kardashians. (There is a direct connection between them and O. J. Simpson: Robert Kardashian, father of the brood, was a friend of Simpson's and also one of the defense attorneys at his trial for the murder of his wife.) Simpson and Michael Jackson were at least authentic celebrities, individuals who became famous for real accomplishments in athletics and popular music. We now live in the age of talentless singers—"You could fill a dump truck with all the hot young singers who can't yodel their way out of a grocery sack," says Hiaasen ("Author")—and nobodies who are famous simply for being famous.

Americans are the world's most ravenous consumers of what Hiaasen calls "a celebrity journalism that features nitwits and naifs over Nobel laureates" (*Dance* 303). The press deserves its share of blame in the rise of celebrity culture, but it's also true that overhyped celebrities would "evaporate like a moose burp" (*Dance* 305) if the public quit paying attention. Sadly, Hiaasen is no doubt correct when he says, "I'll bet more Americans can name all the

4. Novels for Adults

Kardashians than can name the president of Afghanistan" ("Author"). The hardest part of the research he had to do for *Star Island*, he admits, was reading all those tabloid rags and watching celebrity TV shows to familiarize himself with these instant celebrities. What he learned was disheartening: "In my lifetime, I've never seen so much dissemination of information about people who are so ultimately inconsequential" (Moore).

Star Island features a talentless twenty-two-year-old pop singer named Cherry Pye (real name Cheryl Gail Bunterman), an amalgam of such notorious train wrecks as Britney Spears, Lindsay Lohan, and Amy Winehouse (though without her talent). She became a star at age fifteen with a sexy song titled, "Touch Me Like You Mean It," though in reality she has a voice that sounds like "a sackful of starving kittens" (266). She's a totally manufactured celebrity, thanks in large part to modern technology that is able to make her sound "like a Baptist choir girl" (200). (Hiaasen jokes that he could take his Labrador to a studio in the morning and, thanks to Auto-tune and ProTools, "by the evening I'd have a CD that made him sound like Pavarotti" (Ferguson).) Cherry is equally famous for a self-destructive lifestyle devoted to sex, drugs, and alcohol. Of all the young stars crashing and burning in the public eye, she appears "most likely to beat the others to the grave" (32).

It's hard to like such a vain, spoiled, petulant, self-indulgent, shallow, and empty-headed young woman. She's also whiny—in preparation for her upcoming tour, her lack of a singing voice requires her to learn to lip-synch her own songs, but even this is difficult to master: "there's, like, eighteen songs to learn," she grouses, "and they're all different" (41). And she makes stupendously stupid decisions—she overdoses on a concoction of alcohol, hydrocodone, birdseed, and stool softener, which produces aftereffects far more uncomfortable than a simple hangover.

In the end, however, you have to feel sorry for the poor girl. She's not evil, just a helpless victim who is being exploited by her parents, her concert promoter, and the culture than has built her up and is now eagerly watching her crash and burn. Unlike so many of Hiaasen's characters, she's hurting no one but herself. She's just not smart enough to save herself from the kind of excessive behavior that money and fame often promote.

Cherry's father Ned has no illusions about his daughter's talent, fully aware she "couldn't yodel her way out of a broom closet" (200). He's also smart enough to realize she isn't just going through a phase. It's clear to him that his daughter has a genuine and indiscriminate taste for drugs and alcohol and is simply "shallow as a symbol. Having worked in a Hummer showroom, he considered himself an authority on the species" (201). He's willing to leave his daughter's welfare in the hands of his wife while he's content to continue counting the money she earns for the family.

Cherry's mother Janet is a master of denial. She blames her daughter's many visits to the hospital on "gastric issues" rather than drug overdoses and prefers to think of her frequent stints in rehab as visits to "dietary camp." In this passage, Hiaasen savagely skewers stage mothers like Janet Bunterman who knowingly fail to apply the brakes to stop the inevitable train wreck in time:

> It would have been understandable for a mother at that moment to stare at her spoiled, hapless offspring and doubt herself, or at least feel hobbled with remorse. Yet, long ago, Janet Bunterman had willingly accepted the role of her daughter's primary enabler, exploiter and apologist, reasoning that such duties were better handled within the family. The fact that the whole pathetic clan was financially reliant on Cherry was the galvanizing force behind her mother's devotion, although Janet Bunterman preferred a more novel rationalization. Even though Cherry didn't write her own lyrics and the vocals were shamelessly overdubbed, her music still brought happiness to millions of loyal young fans. It was them for whom Janet Bunterman imagined herself sacrificing so tirelessly [168].

Others who profit off Cherry include her twin publicists, Lucy and Lila Lark, who specialize in out-of-control celebrities, many of whom end up dead or in prison, and record producer/concert promoter Maury Lykes, who has an eye for fresh young prospects and a criminal fondness for underage girls. Everybody has a financial stake in preventing her from doing anything that might jeopardize the sales of her new CD (entitled *Skantily Klad*) and upcoming concert tour.

Enter Ann DeLusia, an aspiring twenty-four-year-old actress with a striking physical resemblance to Cherry Pye. Janet Bunterman hires her as a stunt double for her troubled daughter (although she never tells Cherry about Ann's existence). Ann's job is to act as a decoy who can appear in various public places whenever Cherry is too wasted or secretly off on another visit to rehab to do so herself. Ann takes the gig because it pays more than she's been making doing commercials. She's also intrigued by the prospect of seeing what living like a celebrity is like. However, to maintain the masquerade she is forced to get a temporary tattoo to match the one Cherry has on her neck of Axl Rose of Guns N' Roses perched on a centaur. One character describes it as "the ugliest ink I've ever seen on a woman who wasn't screwing a motorcycle gang" (122).

The other key part of the engine that drives our celebrity culture is the media, which is represented in *Star Island* by a member of the paparazzi, an

4. Novels for Adults

overweight, hygiene-challenged photographer named Bang Abbott. (The term paparazzi comes from Paparazzo, the name of a freelance photographer in Federico Fellini's classic 1960 film *La Dolce Vita*. Fellini said he chose the name because it suggested to him a buzzing insect, hovering, darting, stinging. Hiaasen prefers another term; he calls them the "maggot mob.") Abbott previously was a staff photographer for the *St. Petersburg Times*, where he won a Pulitzer Prize for a photo he took of a Canadian tourist being mangled by a lemon shark. Unfortunately, he lost his job when it was later revealed that he had lured the shark to shore with some fish guts. Now he applies his skills to a new trade—photographing celebrities in embarrassing or compromising situations.

He has no illusions about his job nor does he lose any sleep over the ethics of his profession. As far as he is concerned, "trafficking in the vulgarities of fame" is a "legitimate industry" (163). But he also knows that paparazzi like himself aren't solely responsible for creating our celebrity culture. "We're just feedin' the beast," he insists. "Soon as nobody cares about Hollywood anymore, we're all out of business" (163). Sure, he has to endure some indignities (Queen Latifah floors him with her handbag, Woody Harrelson spits at him, Charlie Sheen pisses in his ear, and a nun even gives him the finger), but it's a small price to pay because as long as American newsstands remain "celebrity crapfests" (317), he can make a very good living. (He was once paid $17,000 for an embarrassing photo of Jessica Simpson.)

Bang becomes obsessed with Cherry, especially after she has sex with him on a private plane bringing the two of them from California to Florida. But after she steals his camera containing compromising photos he snapped of her while she was passed out on the plane, he kidnaps her at gunpoint. Only later does he realize he made a big mistake and has kidnapped Ann DeLusia instead. So he decides to hold her for ransom to get what he really wants: a day alone with Cherry and his camera.

Things turn loopy in typical Hiaasen fashion when he brings back two of his most popular characters. The first is the old guy who rescues Ann after her car skids off the road and crashes when she tries to avoid hitting him while he's bending over to pick up some roadkill. That man, of course, is Skink, a familiar sight with his bald head and shower cap, though the braids that sprout from the sides of his head are now strung with red and green shotgun shells. He hasn't lost his taste for revenge against those whom he considers most deserving of it. Before letting Ann go, he enlists her help in his latest project.

Skink has Ann flag down a bus carrying a developer named Jackie Sebago and a group of investors in a huge condominium complex he's building on North Key Largo. After haranguing the group for forty-five minutes, Skink singles out Sebago for special punishment for having illegally cut down twenty acres of red mangroves to provide a better view of the Atlantic from his townhouses. He ties him to a poisonwood tree and then dresses him in a diaper into which he places a spiny sea urchin, which results in a severe rash and multiple painful punctures to Sebago's scrotum. Then he sets Ann free, but not before giving her a phone number to call if she's ever in trouble. She will later have a good reason to use that number when Bang Abbott kidnaps her.

Meanwhile, Skink continues his campaign of revenge. Some of his actions are comically appropriate: he defecates in a washing machine in the home of his former lieutenant governor, a man who turned out to be just as crooked as all the other politicians he railed against. But setting fire to a woman's suitcase and kidnapping her dog just because he overheard her mention that her dead husband once reeled in a hammerhead shark and then beat it to death with a baseball is needlessly cruel and vindictive.

The other character Hiaasen brings back is Chemo, who played a prominent role in *Skin Tight*. Hiaasen received a note from Elmore Leonard after that novel appeared telling him how much he liked Chemo and thanking him for not killing him off. As Hiaasen began thinking about *Star Island,* he remembered that Chemo, who had been sentenced to a seventeen-year prison term, would now be free and available for an encore performance. When Cherry Pye's bodyguard quits his job, who better than the menacing Chemo to be his replacement. Upon his release from prison, Chemo had joined an army of his fellow convicted felons in the mortgage-peddling racket, but when the real-estate bubble burst he became again available for private-security work.

Chemo still sports the Weed Whacker that was attached to his arm in *Skin Tight* and puts it to good use in *Star Island*: he shreds a seagull that tries to use his new salmon-colored hairpiece for nesting material; later he takes a large chunk out of Bang Abbott's flabby ass, an appropriate punishment for the man responsible for the lemon shark attack that caused a similar injury to an unsuspecting Canadian tourist. He also adds a new weapon to his arsenal, a cattle prod which he uses for educational purposes. Thanks to a Carmelite nun who corresponded with him when he was in prison and who sent him a book on basic grammar, Chemo has become a stickler for proper language usage. He may be unable to cure Cherry of her reckless behavior, but he can clean up the way she talks: every time she utters words like "awesome," "sweet," "sick," "totally," and "dude," he jolts her with the cattle prod.

Celebrity worship is but a symptom of a larger problem in our culture, i.e., the rise of the fake and phony, and *Star Island* contains several prime examples of this. Cherry's publicists, Lucy and Lila Lark, were born fraternal twins but longed to be identical. They managed to locate a Brazilian plastic surgeon who could help them achieve their dream by rearranging their noses, cheeks, teeth, breasts, tummies, buttocks, and thighs. Their faces have been botoxed so much that they have lost the ability to frown (an important expression in their profession) and their own mother can no longer tell them apart.

Miami Beach itself, which Skink dismisses as "entirely unnatural" and "an obscene facade" (246), is another good example of fabrication. Originally a mangrove swamp, the island was largely created by sand dredged up from the ocean floor. Every few years, thousands of tons of more sand have to be added to keep up the facade. The South Beach area of Miami Beach, famous for being a "sun-soaked runway for preening grotesques and needy narcissists" (245), provides the perfect setting for much of the action of the novel for it embodies the pretension, self-absorption, and empty-headedness that defines celebrity culture in America. (Hiaasen's antipathy for South Beach is well documented: "I would much rather be surrounded by water moccasins," he once declared, "than to be standing on Ocean Drive and have the cast of *Jersey Shore* appear. I would much rather have a water moccasin attached to some personal part of my body than to have to deal with someone named Snookie" ("Carl WGBH").)

The South Beach clubs for the glitterati all have preposterous names like Abscess, Opium, Cameo, Ortho, and Pubes. In order to stand out from the others, each one tries to develop a unique theme, which only heightens the absurdity even more. For example, at Ortho, which is owned by a group of Colorado bone surgeons, patrons are required to wear snap-on replicas of casts. Pubes is even more ridiculous. The bartenders and wait staff all wear V-cut vinyl pants that expose tufts of their pubic hair and the dance floor features 900-square feet of synthetic bush.

In a stroke of comic genius, Hiaasen sends both Skink and Chemo, the two most unlikely visitors imaginable, to South Beach. Each dresses appropriately to fit into the freak parade around them, which leads to an eye-opening spectacle: Skink, a Calusa ceremonial mask etched on his face with lipstick, is dressed in a tailored pinstriped Ermenegildo Zegna suit with a matching eye patch; Chemo, sporting red Sarah Palin–like glasses, wears corduroys, vintage Beatle boots, a tan beret, and a leather jacket that conceals his weed whacker.

Except for Jackie Sebago, who is killed by a hitman hired by a disgruntled investor in his condominium project, the novel ends happily for most of the characters. Cherry Pye survives, though her career doesn't. At last report, she's appearing in a reality TV show called *Almost Sober*, the initial episode of which is devoted to her efforts to get her unsightly tattoo removed. Bang Abbott survives a sniper attack ordered by one of his sources whom he failed to pay the $200 he agreed to for a tip about a celebrity. Like Tool in *Skinny Dip*, he too is left with a bullet painfully lodged up his butt, which convinces him to switch to a safer job photographing toddlers, prom couples, and small pets. Ann DeLusia refuses to cash in on her new-found fame as a celebrity double. She even turns down film offers from Judd Apatow and the Coen Brothers so she can appear in a new movie by famed Spanish director Pedro Almodóvar. Chemo, thanks to an upturn in the real-estate market, is able to return to his former job in the mortgage-peddling racket.

While many of our stars and celebrities are certainly superficial and satirizing them is as easy as shooting fish in a barrel, our obsession with them and with celebrity worship in general is a far more sobering and serious matter. "We're hopelessly, hungrily hooked on squalid spectacle," Hiaasen once observed. "We crave the inane and irrelevant. It's our national dope; a legal way to stay stoned" (*Dance* 330).

In 1973, British journalist Alistair Cooke published a book entitled *Alistair Cooke's America* that was based upon his decades of observation about life in this country. In his conclusion, he listed several parallels he saw between the causes for the fall of the Roman Empire described by Edward Gibbon 200 years earlier in his classic *History of the Decline and Fall of the Roman Empire* and what he was witnessing in contemporary America. Among them were these: 1) a love of show and luxury; 2) an obsession with sex; 3) freakishness in the arts masquerading as originality; 4) enthusiasm pretending to be creativeness; 5) a developing moral numbness to vulgarity, violence, and the assault on the simplest human decencies (387). One can only imagine what his reaction might be if he were still alive today.

And what about the future? "We have seen the future," Hiaasen once wrote, "and it's in the gutter" (*Dance* 302).

Bad Monkey *(2013)*

Bad Monkey opens with a gruesome discovery: "On the hottest day of July, trolling in dead-water calm near Key West, a tourist named James Mayberry reeled up a human arm. His wife flew to the bow of the boat and tossed her breakfast burritos" (3). What follows comes closest of all of Hiaasen's novels to being a conventional detective story with several murders, an ex-cop's search for clues to the killer, and plenty of suspense and thrills. But there is nothing conventional about the story once Hiaasen begins telling it. This one also includes a severed arm that keeps turning up in surprising places (at the end of a fishing line, stashed among the Popsicles in a freezer, stolen from a grave and later found stuffed in a Callaway golf bag), a Medicare scam, a voodoo queen, a hurricane, and a monkey with a foul disposition that once starred with Johnny Depp in *Pirates of the Caribbean*.

Andrew Yancy formerly worked for the Miami Police Department but was pressured to resign after he blew the whistle on the illegal activities of a fellow cop who was fraudulently pocketing reward money from Crime Stoppers. He's now on suspension from his current job with the Monroe County Sheriff's Department in the Florida Keys thanks to a misplaced sense of chivalry. After overhearing his girlfriend Bonnie Witt's husband call her a tramp, he assaulted the man in broad daylight; in full view of 300 cruise-ship passengers, he shoved the portable vacuum cleaner he was using to clean his car up the man's rectum. When Bonnie asks why he chose to do that instead of simply punching her husband in the nose, Yancy replies, "You always said he had a bee up his ass. I was only trying to help" (17).

While on suspension, he's asked by the sheriff to deliver the severed arm that was reeled in by the visiting tourist to the medical examiner in Miami. The sheriff wants to avoid any bad publicity that might scare tourists away from the Keys and hopes that in Miami, the "floating-human-body-parts capitol of America" (7), the arm might match up with other body parts already there. At the morgue Yancy meets Dr. Rosa Campesino, the attractive Cuban-American medical examiner, who determines that the arm doesn't match any remains currently in the morgue. So Yancy puts it back in his portable cooler and returns home, where he stores it in his freezer.

Meanwhile, his girlfriend's husband agrees to drop charges against Yancy on the condition that he stay away from his wife and resign from his job, which he does. Luckily for him, however, he's offered another position in the country government; unfortunately, it's as a restaurant inspector. Many jobs bring with them certain occupational hazards. In *Basket Case*, for example, Jack Tagger discovered that writing obituaries left him with a severe case of anxiety about his own mortality. Yancy experiences anxieties of a different kind once he begins working on roach patrol.

Bloody crime scenes never made Yancy queasy, but the mere glimpse of "a desiccated rat carcass in a vat of stale muffins left him poleaxed with revulsion" (42). One continuing source of humor involves his frequent visits to Stoney's Crab Palace, which he routinely cites for violations, despite the owner's best efforts to bribe him not to do so. On his very first visit, this is what he finds: "seventeen serious health violations, including mouse droppings, rat droppings, chicken droppings, a tick nursery, open vats of decomposing shrimp, lobsters dating back to the first Bush presidency, and, on a tray of baked oysters, a soggy condom" (30).

One of the more odious tasks he has to perform is collecting all the cockroaches he finds in a restaurant kitchen and then compiling separate counts of the dead and live ones. He soon starts imagining seeing creepy insects everywhere. The thought of contaminated food scares him so much (especially when he learns that his predecessor on the job died after contracting Hepatitis A from eating contaminated food) that he limits his diet to Popsicles and energy bars. His clothes become increasingly baggy as the pounds melt away. How much longer can he survive on this job?

The severed arm in Yancy's freezer is eventually identified by Eve Stripling as belonging to her husband Nick, who went missing while fishing. He must have fallen into the sea and his arm bitten off by a hungry shark. But when Dr. Campesino notices that a distinctive pale rectangular outline on the arm is identical to that of a Wyler Genève Tourbillon wrist watch that sells for $145,000, it appears that Stripling might have been murdered and the watch stolen. It also begins to look like the grieving widow is the prime suspect in his death. Even though Yancy no longer has a badge or any official authority, he decides to investigate. Now calling himself Inspector Yancy (he likes the Scotland-Yardish ring to the title), he hopes that if he can prove that Eve Stripling murdered her husband, he might be able to get his old job back.

The arm also plays a minor role in his love life. When girlfriend Bonnie Witt accidentally finds it in Yancy's freezer, she's horrified and wonders what kind of man she's been involved with. She subsequently breaks up with him, which makes him available for new female companionship. Enter Rosa Campesino. She had earlier declined Yancy's lunch invitation, but after a resumption of their professional relationship, she offers to cook him a meal, which leads to more than that. They soon become lovers as well as a crack crime-solving duo.

From this point on, *Bad Monkey* might have continued as a standard detective novel with Yancy and Rosa combining forces to uncover clues leading to the solution of the mystery. But that's not Hiaasen's method. He suddenly shifts the action to Andros Island in the Bahamas to tell a seemingly unrelated story about a sixty-four-year-old local man named Neville Stafford who is desperately trying to stop an American developer named Christopher and his wife from building an upscale resort on his family's beachfront property. His half-sister legally sold the land to Christopher against his wishes, so he has no recourse. As a desperate last resort he hires a local woman known as the Dragon Queen to place a voodoo curse on the developer.

While this detour from the main action gives Hiaasen an opportunity to introduce the kind of colorful characters he loves (including the monkey in the title), it will soon align with Yancy's criminal investigation. Meanwhile, the reader is invited to enjoy the goofball activities on Andros Island. The cigar-smoking, rum-swilling Dragon Queen is reputed to be a rapacious man-eater: three of her previous boyfriends all died under suspicious circumstances. Neville seeks her out to give her the sleeve he obtained from one of Christopher's shirts so she can cast a spell on its owner, but nothing happens. He returns to make an appeal for even stronger magic, but this time the Dragon Queen demands his sexual services as payment. The prospect of sex with the crazy woman repels Neville. Instead, he agrees to give her Driggs, a diaper-wearing, white-faced capuchin monkey he won in a game of dominoes, which she mistakenly thinks is a pink little boy.

Like many of Hiaasen's characters, Driggs has an absurdly funny back story. He comes from a family of entertainers: his father worked on *Friends* and a cousin appeared in the movie *Ace Ventura: Pet Detective*. Unfortunately, Driggs's prickly disposition, short attention span, and "an adolescent preoccupation with his own genitalia" (230) have doomed his career. His job as "Rally Monkey" for the Los Angeles Angels came to an abrupt halt after a "scrotum-grooming reverie" was broadcast live on the stadium's Jumbotron. He eventually ended up in the Bahamas where he landed a job on *Pirates of the Caribbean* that was being filmed there, but was soon fired after he was caught masturbating on wigs in the costume trailer.

(Hiaasen, who has described Driggs as the Lindsay Lohan of monkeys, was able to draw upon his own unfortunate experience with an ill-behaved primate. At age eleven or twelve he and his sister, without informing their parents, saved up until they had the $16.95 needed to purchase a monkey by mail. When the animal arrived by delivery truck, it was mightily pissed-off. Hiaasen's four-year-old brother Rob asked if he could pet the animal. Sure, said young Carl. The monkey then proceeded to bite and gnaw at the poor kid for some time. Shortly afterwards, the nasty monkey was gone (Davies).

His show business career now in tatters, Driggs is reduced to begging for handouts from tourists. Those who refuse his demands are likely to be treated to a punch to the genitals, a twist to a nipple, or a load of feces thrown at them. The quality of his life improves once he comes under the Dragon Queen's supervision: most days he can be found perched on her motorized scooter wearing a doll's tiny tiara and smoking a meerschaum pipe.

The two stories converge when the evidence trail Yancy has been following leads him to Andros Island. He has determined that Eve Stripling and her boyfriend were responsible for the murder of Nicholas Stripling, as well as those of two other individuals connected to the case. Her partner, a mysterious man always dressed in a yellow poncho, turns out to be Christopher Grunion, the man who bought Neville's property. More surprises follow. When Rosa visits the resort posing as a potential condo buyer, Grunion, who has learned her true identity, pulls a gun and refuses to let her leave. Hiaasen then drops a bombshell: Grunion didn't kill Nicholas Stripling; he *is* Nicholas Stripling.

It turns out that the federal authorities were hot on Stripling's tail for Medicare fraud. He was selling motorized scooters to phantom customers, defrauding the government to the tune of $11 million. Fearing that he was about to be arrested, he took drastic action: he convinced a doctor who was a partner with him in the Medicare scam to saw off his arm, which was then conveniently planted where it would later be "found" by a fisherman. His "death" would put an end to the investigation into his criminal activities.

At this point in the story a hurricane hits Andros Island, throwing everything, including the plot, into disarray and confusion. We subsequently learn that Eve Stripling drugged her husband and then dumped his body off the new boat he just bought. All that remains after the sharks finish feasting on him are, ironically, his severed right arm and the expensive Tourbillon watch, which Driggs ends up wearing around his neck. We are also informed that shortly after dumping her husband overboard, Eve Stripling accidentally crashed her speeding boat into a coral reef, killing herself. Thus ends the mystery, as well as the planned resort on Neville's property.

4. Novels for Adults

Solving the mystery of the severed arm isn't the only vexing problem Yancy has to grapple with in *Bad Monkey*. There's the matter of what to do about the house being built next to his waterfront bungalow on Big Pine Key. One of his greatest pleasures is viewing the spectacular sunsets over the Gulf of Mexico while watching tiny white-tailed Key deer nearby nibbling on the red mangroves. But developer Evan Shook has blocked the sunsets and scared away all the deer with the 7000 square-foot house he is building next door to Yancy. Thanks to payoffs to the right people, the house, the tallest on the island, will tower nine feet higher than the building code allows. ("It's the Keys, man," Yancy is reminded. "The code is for suckers" (6)). The worst part of the whole deal is that Shook isn't even building his own dream house; he's constructing the vulgar monstrosity on spec, hoping to make a killing on the deal.

Yancy launches a clever campaign of guerrilla warfare against Shook. He starts by sneaking items into the man's house—a dead raccoon; a giant hive filled with stinging honeybees; a Santeria shrine containing a dead rooster, a saucer of cat blood, and a rat skull—all aimed at scaring off prospective buyers. He even turns a dog bite into a weapon; after being bitten on the butt by a Rottweiler while snooping around Stripling's house, he displays the nasty wound to potential buyers and tells them he was attacked by a pack of vicious wild dogs that are terrorizing the neighborhood. Yet despite all his efforts, Shook still manages to find a gullible couple who agree to purchase the property. What can Yancy do now?

The solution to his problem comes from an unlikely, but very funny, source. Bonnie Witt, the ex-girlfriend whose husband Yancy attacked with the vacuum cleaner, makes a surprise return to Big Pine Key. Just before breaking up with Yancy, she confessed to him that her real name is Plover Chase and that she is a fugitive from justice. Some fifteen years earlier, she was a Tulsa schoolteacher who was convicted of extorting sex from a fifteen-year-old student of hers in exchange for an A grade on his report card. On the day of her sentencing, she jumped bail and fled to Florida, where she has lived under an assumed name all these years. Now she suddenly reappears in the company of the young student she was convicted of having sex with.

Cody Parish, an "oversexed slacker" with thinning hair and a big gut, is a comic case of arrested development. Though now thirty, he still refers to his former teacher as Ms. Chase, though when he learns that she now uses the name Bonnie, he starts calling himself Clyde. He has come up with a plan to write a diary about life on the run with the outlaw Ms. Chase, which he hopes to sell to Hollywood. The following drivel he writes in his diary after Bonnie dumps him ensures that will never happen:

> My whole world was crashing down. How could she take my heart in her hands and choke it like a baby bunny rabbit?
>
> Maybe she just went batshit crazy which can happen when the monthly hormones take over. I've seen it before, and watch out!
>
> I'd take her back in a heartbeat, and no man would blame me. I'd go through the fires of Hell and follow her anywhere, except back to Tulsa because I am seriously done with the Olive Garden [267–68].

In a misguided effort to win Yancy back, Bonnie burns Shook's megamansion to the ground. That solves one problem for Yancy, but creates another. He gets his sunset views back, but because he was once romantically involved with a wanted criminal and now an arsonist who some suspect might have torched Shook's house at his urging, he can't be reinstated to his former job right away, despite his crime-solving heroics. For the time being, Yancy has to remain on roach patrol and take what comfort he can in the belief that "all that stood between him and his detective badge was a few thousand cockroaches" (316).

Readers looking for satire in *Bad Monkey* may be disappointed. There are passing references to such familiar Hiaasen targets as corrupt building inspectors, land developers with no consideration as to the consequences of their actions, Medicare fraud—all subjects he has treated at greater length in other novels. And when the action starts to flag over the final 100 pages of the novel, a hurricane can only do just so much to pump up the excitement.

On the other hand, readers won't be disappointed in Hiaasen's characters, especially the unforgettable Andros Island trio of Neville, Driggs, and the Dragon Queen. Andrew Yancy and Rosa Campesino are engaging individuals who form a crack investigative team as well as become romantic partners whose saucy repartee makes the sparks fly. The brainy, witty, and sexually adventuresome Rosa is always ready with a fresh quip: e.g., when the hurricane blows the roof off the house at the exact moment she and Yancy reach orgasm, she blurts out the perfect response—"*That* is what I'm talkin' about, Mister!" (241). Even the dimwitted characters come up with some unintentionally funny lines: "Nobody said he was Alvin Einstein" (80); "This ain't Nazi Russia!" (125); "Like the book says, you can't go homeward angel" (268). And then there's Driggs, who proves you don't have to utter a single word to be uproariously funny.

4. Novels for Adults

Razor Girl *(2016)*

Razor Girl starts out innocently enough with a minor traffic accident. On his way to Key West to meet with his client Buck Nance, star of America's top-rated TV reality show *Bayou Brethren*, about four bearded Cajun brothers who raise roosters, Hollywood talent manager Lane Coolman's car is hit from behind by a careless driver named Merry (as in Merry Christmas) Mansfield (like the 1950s blond bombshell who, ironically, died in a car crash). This being Florida, however, such things are seldom normal. When Coolman exits his car to speak to the driver, he is surprised to see what caused the accident: Merry was in the middle of shaving her bikini area when she hit his car. Why is she shaving herself, he asks:

"I got a date," she explained.
"You couldn't take care of that at home?"
"No way! My husband would get so pissed" (4).

She confesses to Coolman that she's an escort and explains she was grooming herself on her way to meet a client. Her damaged car has to be towed away, so Coolman offers to drive the gorgeous red-haired woman the rest of the way to Key West.

But things are not quite what they appear to be. Merry is no escort, nor is she an artifact appraiser with an expertise in eighteenth-century Spanish maritime she also claims to be. What she really is is "an independent contractor in the collection process." What that means is she is hired to crash into cars driven by people who are dodging a debt. She and her partner then kidnap the victim and deliver him to the person who hired them. The bikini-shaving part is her signature move. (She got the idea from the same newspaper account that inspired Hiaasen to use the real-life accident for his own purposes. While the actual event involved a woman who accidentally ran into a car of tourists while she was grooming herself while driving, Merry uses the shaving gambit in the service of her accident scam. It works so well because all her victims are men.) But when Merry delivers Coolman to her waiting accomplice, they discover they've grabbed the wrong man. Coolman just happened to be driving a car similar to that of the person they were hired to kidnap, a man named Martin Trebeaux.

Meanwhile, Coolman's client Buck Nance is making a public appearance at a local bar in Key West, where he begins with some comic anecdotes and then a couple of jokes, one homophobic, the other racist. He quickly learns that Key West is the wrong place to tell jokes like that, and he is forced to flee the restaurant when a wild melee breaks out. Fearful for his life, he decides he needs a disguise. The first thing he does is slip though the back door of a restaurant kitchen to shave off his characteristic flowing beard, the remnants of which he stuffs into a vat of quinoa. When the restaurant owner discovers the hairy mess, he calls the local food inspector. Readers of *Bad Monkey* will be happy to learn that defrocked cop Andrew Yancy is still stuck in his job on roach patrol.

Happily, Yancy is given another opportunity to solve a crime and perhaps get his old job back when a tourist dies after an encounter with a man who appears to be the missing Buck Nance. While riding the Conch Train in Key West, Abdul-Halim Shamoon was accosted by a racist man who harangued him for being Muslim. Abdul-Halim then either jumped or was pushed from the moving train, causing him to fall onto a ceramic seahorse he had just purchased. Tragically, a piece broke off and pierced his aorta, killing him. Witnesses said the assailant was wearing a panama hat and had a tattoo across his back that read, "Hail, Captain Cock," Buck Nance's famous nickname. Is the missing TV star also a murderer? Yancy wants to find out.

In truth, not much investigation is needed. It is quickly determined that the assailant of the Muslim was a big fan of Buck Nance named Benny "the Blister" Krill, who comes up with the crazy idea of kidnapping Nance and Coolman to force them to give him a role on *Bayou Brethren* as Buck's long-lost twin brother Spiro. Sounds absurd, doesn't it? But that's what *Razor Girl* is, another of Hiaasen's outrageously absurd comedies thanks again to the colorful cast of characters he has assembled.

Razor Girl is notable for being the first time Hiaasen has used the same protagonist in back-to-back novels. Yancy is an engaging character whose efforts to escape roach patrol and get his old job back plus his experience as a crime solver provide good story lines that Hiaasen can play comic variations on in his new novel. The first of these involves the hazards of being a restaurant inspector. Yancy is forced to continue making regular visits to the notorious Stoney's Crab Palace, where he sees nothing to change his opinion that the place is "like a petri dish with menus. When they say 'catch of the day,' they mean infection" (174).

But now he has something other than the fear of getting sick from all the contaminated food he finds in restaurants to worry about: giant Gambian pouched rats. The rats, the largest in the world, weighing as much as nine pounds, are an invasive species that has found its way to Key West. Even before he actually sees one, Yancy begins having nightmares about "the buck-toothed bastards" charging at him "like bull rhinos" (125). His first face-to-face encounter with one of the ugly critters "the size of a Corvette" convinces him he needs some quiet time "to steady his nerves and reassess his fast-dwindling role in the universe" (127).

The other problem involves the mega-house next to Yancy's home. When ex-girlfriend Bonnie burnt the place down at the end of *Bad Monkey*, Yancy thought his problem was solved. Unfortunately for him, the land was purchased by a multimillionaire lawyer named Brock Richardson who intends to build his own monster home. (When Yancy asks Richardson's fiancée Deb why he needs to build such an enormous house, she replies, "Nobody in Florida with Brock's kind of money builds a one-story house. I can't believe you'd say that" (84)).

Yancy is forced to mount another stealth campaign against the new owner. His cleverest ruse involves planting a tooth on the property and then hiring a high school drama teacher to pose as an anthropologist. He informs Richardson that development of the property must cease indefinitely until it can be determined if the tooth is evidence of an ancient Calusa burial ground. If it is, of course, a house can't be built there. The other ace in the hole Yancy holds is a $200,000 engagement ring that slipped off Deb's finger. She's been frantically searching for it, but Yancy doesn't tell her that he's found it. Instead, he stashes it in a dish of fish dip in his refrigerator and waits to see how he might be able to use it as leverage to save his sunset views.

Two other men with problems of their own meet by chance in a bar and begin exchanging stories. Martin Trebeaux, the man Merry Mansfield was supposed to run her car into when she mistakenly hit Coolman's car, has a problem involving sand. Everyone in Florida desires oceanfront property. However, because of rising sea levels and the damaging effects of frequent hurricanes, Florida's beaches are washing away and must constantly be replenished. Using a fleet of marine barges he purchased with money he received from falsified BP oil-spill claims, Trebeaux started a dredging company named Sedimental Journeys that restores Florida beaches. Renourishing the beaches is a reliable money-making proposition for the simple reason that every grain of sand that is dumped eventually gets washed away and has to be replaced.

Unfortunately, there's only so much sand that can be safely dredged from the offshore ocean floor, so Trebeaux has to find another source. Sand barged in from the Bahamas works until the government there cancels his agreement. Trebeaux then decides to use fake sand—a mixture of crushed limestone, asphalt fragments, and broken glass—that not surprisingly leaves beach lovers with lacerated feet and shredded fingers. Unfortunately for him, the Royal Pyrenees Hotel and Resort, where he contracted to provide sand, is owned by the Mafia. Dominick "Big Noogie" Aeola, the capo in charge for the Calzone crime family, summons Trebeaux to an emergency meeting. When he fails to show up, Big Noogie hires Merry Mansfield to kidnap him. After mistakenly crashing into the wrong man (Coolman), she locates her assigned victim, rear-ends his car and hands him over to Big Noogie. Big Noogie demands new sand and Trebeaux doesn't have a source of any; instead he lies and promises he has a deal with Fidel Castro for a fresh supply, though he's never even set foot in Cuba.

Attorney Brock Richardson has raked in millions of dollars from liability suits against the makers of Pitrolux, a deodorant armpit gel that also boosts testosterone that is being marketed to "middle-aged men with slack penises and gagging body odor" (95). It turns out that the product really does have disastrous side effects, which Richardson discovers after using it on himself. Yes, Pitrolux gives him powerful erections, but it also causes penis-shaped growths to suddenly pop up under his armpits.

When Trebeaux says he developed a rash after taking Pitrolux, Richardson offers to add his name to the list of clients in his class action suit against the company. When Richardson mentions his troubles with his next-door neighbor, including the fact that Yancy has his missing $200,000 ring, Trebeaux offers the assistance of his Mafia friend (who has now taken over his company). Big Noogie will know how to deal with an annoyance like Yancy, especially when there is the possibility of getting his hands on that $200,000 ring. Sure enough, a pair of Big Noogie's goons soon show up at Yancy's house to threaten him and grab the ring hidden in his refrigerator.

Yancy has one other problem. Rosa Campesino is so burnt out after performing too many autopsies and then working to save lives as an emergency-room doctor that she decides to move to Norway for a while. Yancy sees the handwriting on the wall and figures she's about to dump him; it doesn't help matters any that whenever she calls Yancy's house, a different woman answers, either Deb who happened to be visiting or Merry Mansfield, who has invited herself in as a guest for a while.

Most men would be happy to have a problem visitor like Merry. At first, she appears to be a dimwit who shaves herself while driving. Then she comes across as a duplicitous schemer. But she's much more complicated and far more interesting than those first impressions. Like most of Hiaasen's female characters, she's one step ahead of the male characters at all times. ("Men are so freakin' predictable" (332), she declares in what might serve as her motto.) She, on the other hand, is anything but predictable; one of her many charms is the way she keeps everybody off balance.

The smart and saucy red-headed beauty is a delightfully entertaining liar with a spicy wit and a raunchy sense of humor. She is one of those Hiaasen characters whose role in the novel expanded the more he wrote about her thanks to her energy and ability to keep surprising the reader (and himself). She began primarily as a simple instrument to get the plot moving. But this changes when she unexpectedly turns up at Yancy's door one day and brazenly invites herself in, explaining to Yancy that she has no place else to go:

"This is a phenomenally bad idea."
"Where's your spare bedroom, sugar?"
"It's uninhabitable at the moment."
"You've got a couch, right? Don't pretend you're not going to let me in, because we both know you will" [119].

Yancy knows he shouldn't become involved with Merry in any way. For one thing, she's a criminal and he's already paid the price for his previous involvement with a woman who was a fugitive from justice and an arsonist. But what man could resist the charms of this flirtatious redhead who reminds him of Susan Sarandon, whom he's had a crush on since seeing *Thelma and Louise*.

The two of them soon end up as both investigative and sexual partners. When Benny Krill slices Yancy's stomach when he tries to question him, Merry's there to rush him to the hospital. Later she nurses him at home, and even chauffeurs him around as the two of them try to solve the mystery of the missing redneck star. In the end, she saves the day after Krill has forced Yancy into his car at gunpoint by doing what she does best—crashing her car into his.

Merry jazzes up every scene she's in. She's a captivating liar who can convince you she went to a boarding school in Switzerland and was also a backup Snow White at Disneyland. Which statement is true? Who knows? Unlike Hiaasen's typical bad guys who lie to cover their shady dealings, Merry lies as part of her performance art designed to keep everyone off balance. She takes special delight in confusing Yancy. "You don't know what to do with me, do you?" she says to him. "I love that" (206)!

She also brings a charmingly ribald edge to her banter with Yancy. For example, when he asks why she invited herself into his house, her answer is deliberately provocative: "Not to have wild upside-down-in-the-mirror sex, if that's what you're thinking" (121). When he tries to get her to tell him her real name, she replies, "Merry Mansfield," then adds suggestively, "And even if it wasn't, you're still going to ask me for crazy hot sex" (135). Though she agrees to nurse him after he's been stabbed in the stomach, she warns him there'll be no "rehab nookie." "There's nineteen sutures in my gut," he reminds her. "That won't stop you from trying," she counters. "It's only a matter of time. You could be in a body cast and I'd still make you pop a tent" (168). She further tantalizes him by warning him not to think about the two of them in the shower together, all slick and soapy: "Not that I'd ever let that happen, but just try not to think about it" (153). Good luck with that!

By the end of the novel, appropriate justice is meted out, much of it administered by Big Noogie. Martin Trebeaux makes the fatal mistake of inviting Big Noogie's girlfriend to join him on his trip to Cuba, where he hopes to persuade the Castro brothers to sell him some of the island's beautiful sand. Big Noogie has him bumped off and his body buried—where else?—on a beach underneath all that luxurious Cuban sand. Though Yancy once again fails to get his old job back with the sheriff's department, thanks to Big Noogie his sunsets are no longer threatened. As a favor to Yancy for finding his missing dog, Big Noogie forces Richardson to sell his property to Yancy for $2500. Merry Mansfield is happy to lend him the money and perhaps remain there with him.

The primary satirical target in *Razor Girl* is the *Bayou Brethren* reality show. Like so many other things in Hiaasen's fiction, it's a total fraud. *Chomp*, one of his young-adult novels, features a TV reality show about an intrepid wilderness adventurer that is totally scripted and requires the American actor who stars in it to learn a fake Australian accent. *Razor Girl* expands the focus beyond simple TV fakery to explore the dangerous effects such shows can have on their gullible viewers.

The redneck heroes of the show, Buck Nance and his brothers Clee Roy, Buddy, and Junior are in reality the Romberg brothers from Whitefish Bay, Wisconsin, who got their start in show business as an accordion band called Grand Funk Romberg. They originally grew their trademark long-flowing beards for the portion of their act where they played a medley of ZZ Top hits on their accordions. After getting a gig in Arkansas, they changed their name to Buck Nance and the Brawlers. A producer looking to cash in on the popularity of *Duck Dynasty* was impressed by their bearded appearance and began the task of transforming them into the redneck Nance Brothers. They first had to have their shiny teeth darkened and chipped, learn to speak Cajun,

4. Novels for Adults

and get schooled in how to dip tobacco, shoot guns, and ride motorcycles. (Hiaasen admits to complete puzzlement over the popularity of such redneck shows: "Being a white guy from the South, I find it amazing that so many TV viewers are enchanted by beards, bad dentistry and moonshine accents" (Liang).)

Although the show purportedly takes place in a Louisiana bayou, it's actually filmed on a set built in the Florida panhandle where the producers also constructed a church, the First Chickapaw Tabernacle of Hope and Holiness, where Buck serves as deacon. Here he preaches racist sermons to an audience of community-theater actors and drama students who are required to sign confidentiality agreements. The only thing that isn't fake about the "reality" show is its popularity with TV viewers.

The producers of *Bayou Brethren* strategically aimed the show at two distinct audiences: those cynically amused by the boorish culture of the Nance clan and those who identify with it. There is, they understand, "a precarious tightwire" between "harmless rednecks and odious white trash" (160). Unfortunately, Benny Krill, who considers himself the *Bayou Brethren*'s number one fan, happened to be in the audience at the bar when Buck Nance told his racist jokes. Benny's especially fond of Buck's anti–Muslim rants that are cut from the TV show but find their way to *YouTube*. (In one such rant, Buck makes sure he covers all the bases by ending with this message: "Oh, and all these things I'm warnin' you about? Same goes for the homosexual crowd and the Negroes" (105).) Convinced that he and Buck "were on the same righteous page, ideologically" (160), Benny sets out to track down the missing Buck himself.

Hiaasen's satire is two-pronged. On the one hand, like the satire in *Star Island*, it reveals his alarm at the ascendancy of the fake and phony in American culture; but this time he goes further and singles out TV reality shows for helping to erase the line between the real and the fake. Even more disturbing is the role such shows can play in encouraging the kind of hatred that leads to violence against the "other" in our country. Buck gradually becomes horrified at seeing the effect he has on such an impressionable idiot like Benny Krill and comes to understand that words, especially hateful ones, do have consequences.

Hiaasen gives Buck an opportunity for redemption rather than punishment. Spending time with Benny shakes his "confidence in the superiority of the white male" (197), and he begins to accept some responsibility for inciting the man to hateful actions: "It was one thing to market a television program to attract low-class shit-kickers," he realizes. "it was another thing to *create* them. Buck surmised the pirated outtakes of his sermons were an inflammatory factor, and he felt fairly shitty about whatever Blister did to the Muslim on the Conch Trail. It was no better than murder" (239).

In the end, Buck becomes an authentic hero when he stops a trigger-happy Benny Krill from committing any more violence by snapping his neck like one of the chickens he raises on his TV show. Though offered double his usual salary to return to *Bayou Brethren,* he decides to leave television. He also turns down $2 million to write about his experiences in Key West. Instead, he returns to Wisconsin to open a music shop where he hopes to introduce young people to the joys of the accordion.

Hiaasen wrote *Razor Girl* before the 2016 Republican Convention where a member of the *Duck Dynasty* TV show addressed the audience. He admits he wishes he had thought of that for his novel, but then quickly realized he couldn't put it in his book because no one would have believed it. Also, in light of the current culture in our country, with so many voices speaking the kind of coded racist language that serves to embolden some to violent actions against those they consider "other," Hiaasen says if he were writing the book today, he would be tougher on Buck than he was.

Hiaasen's usual method of allowing his characters to determine the story sometimes produces mixed results. Just as every joke isn't equally funny, not every Hiaasen novel achieves the same success. *Razor Girl* masterfully combines all the elements—characters, situations, setting, dialogue, comedy, and satire—into an exhilarating ride. His control over the narrative never falters and his sense of humor has never been sharper. Gleefully obscene, riotously funny, and as satirically topical as his latest column, *Razor Girl* shows Hiaasen at the top of his game.

5

Novels for Young Readers

Hoot *(2002)*

It's tempting to conclude that writing children's books must be easy, based on the number of celebrities who have written one. (A representative list would include Madonna, Jerry Seinfeld, Bruce Springsteen, Bill Cosby, Steve Martin, Jim Carrey, Keith Richards, Kelly Clarkson, Jamie Lee Curtis, and Jay Leno.) In some cases, these books are little more than a brand-enhancing merchandising ploy. A more serious list might include celebrated novelists who have also written for young readers: James Joyce, Salman Rushdie, John Updike, Margaret Atwood, and perhaps most notable of all, Ian Fleming, the creator of James Bond, who wrote the children's classic *Chitty-Chitty-Bang-Bang* (1964).

Inspired perhaps by J. K. Rowling's Harry Potter series, several contemporary novelists—among them Michael Chabon, Isabelle Allende, Sherman Alexie, John Grisham, and James Patterson—have branched out into writing full-length novels aimed at readers ten years old and up. (Rowling herself reversed the process, moving from the Harry Potter books to a series of crime novels for adults featuring a detective named Cormoran Strike.) But no one has had more success in making the transition than Carl Hiaasen.

At the suggestion of an editor, Hiaasen decided to try his hand at writing one. Never having written anything for kids before, he prepared by reading a few books in the genre set in Florida (among them *Holes* by Louis Sachar and *Tangerine* by Edward Bloor) to get a sense of how adults are portrayed in such books. One of the most helpful pieces of advice he got was not to write down to his audience, so he tried to remember how he looked at things when he was a kid (he jokes that his wife pointed out that slipping back into adolescence wasn't that big a reach for him). A novel based on his childhood experience involving the destruction of the wilderness area he grew up playing in would allow him to focus on his favorite environmental theme. If he could keep the same smart-ass attitude and the same themes as his adult novels and still make kids laugh, he felt he might be able to pull it off. The result was *Hoot,* the first of five novels for young readers that would soon bring him a whole new audience.

Hiaasen writes what those in the trade call middle-school novels (for readers ten and up) or young adult fiction (for readers twelve and up). These are largely marketing terms, and writers of such books often have a readership that extends beyond both categories. Hiaasen, for example, says he has gotten letters from readers as young as six and as old as seventy-five. But obviously authors who switch from an adult audience to a younger one have to make certain accommodations. Since he would be focusing on youthful characters, there would be no problem avoiding adult activities like sex and extreme violence. There would also have to be no raunchy dialogue or foul language. A sentence like this—"He used very bad words to curse his rotten luck" (*Hoot* 132)—is all he would need to say. He could employ his usual narrative technique of telling multiple stories, but limit the number to simplify the plot. Finally to separate his audiences, he would use one-word titles for his young-adult books rather than the two-word titles his adult novels carry.

Hoot opens with Roy Eberhardt's face being mushed against the window of the school bus taking him to Trace Middle School. Roy is new to the school, having just moved (reluctantly) with his family from Montana to the small town of Coconut Cove, Florida. As the new kid, he has become the prime target of local bully Dana Matherson, who has chosen poor Roy as his latest punching bag. But while Roy's face is pressed against the window, he sees a very curious sight: a young barefooted boy runs toward the bus but keeps right on going past it. Who is this strange kid and where is he going?

Meanwhile, there's another mystery at a nearby vacant lot which is being readied for the construction of the latest Mother Paula's All-American Pancake House. Project manager Curly Brannitt explains to patrolman David Delinko that someone is vandalizing the property: first, all the survey stakes were pulled out and the holes filled in; then alligators were dumped into the portable toilets. When Delinko returns before dawn the following day in hopes of catching the culprit, he nods off in his patrol car. Awakened by a phone call, he's shocked to learn that it's mid-morning since the windows of his car are still dark. Getting out, he sees that someone has spray-painted all the windows black. What's going on here?

Fascinated by the running-boy's behavior, Roy begins watching for him every day. One day he reappears, running as fast as before. This time Roy jumps off the bus in hot pursuit. He follows him across a golf course and into the woods but eventually loses the trail. Despite being warned to mind his own business by a female schoolmate with blond curly hair and red-framed glasses named Beatrice Leep, he later finds the boy, who won't reveal his real name. He says he's called Mullet Fingers because of his ability to catch the slippery fish with his bare hands. Feeling sorry for the barefoot boy, Roy decides to bring him a pair of his old sneakers, but is stopped once again by the threatening Beatrice. She tells him she will give them to Mullet Fingers who, she now reveals to him, is her stepbrother.

Beatrice is one tough cookie. Hiaasen said he based her on a girl he knew in elementary school who terrorized him more than any guy he knew. But in *Hoot* she employs her toughness in more protective ways. For example, when a star linebacker once snuck up behind her and smacked her on the bottom, she chased him down and broke his collarbone in three places. When Dana Matherson drags Roy into a janitor's closet and begins pummeling him, she rescues him, then strips Dana to his underwear and ties him to the school flagpole. Fortunately, she likes Roy and soon becomes his trusted friend and confidante.

After her parents divorced, Beatrice chose to live with her father, a former NBA star with the comically appropriate name of Leon "Lurch" Leep. He recently married a woman named Lorna who has a son about Beatrice's own age. The boy and his mother have a strained relationship; on the day of her wedding to Beatrice's father, he ran away. Lorna later shipped him off to military school, but he ran away from there too. Now he has secretly made his way back to Coconut Cove, but only Beatrice knows where he is: living in an abandoned ice-cream truck in a junkyard filled with wrecked automobiles near the site of the new Mother Paula's All-American Pancake House.

In some ways, Mullet Fingers is a young version of Hiaasen's most famous creation, Skink. Like him, he lives in an abandoned vehicle in the woods, though he doesn't share Skink's fondness for roadkill. And he too is something of an environmental terrorist. He's the one who is trying to sabotage the construction of the new pancake house. Skink would certainly applaud his reason for doing so: the site is home to several burrowing owls who make their nests underground. Once construction begins, they will all be bulldozed over. Mullet Fingers is doing whatever he can to stop that tragedy from happening.

When Roy sees the tiny burrowing owls for the first time, he understands what his new friend is trying to do. As he explains it to his parents, the issue is clear: "How would you and Mom like it," he asks his father, "if a bunch of strangers showed up one day with bulldozers to flatten this house? And all they had to say was 'Don't worry, Mr. and Mrs. Eberhardt, it's no big deal. Just pack up and move to another place.' How would you feel about that" (156)? But what he can do about it is another matter.

In Hiaasen's adult fiction, there aren't many characters with a conscience. The bad guys never think twice about the morality of their evil deeds. But in *Hoot* we have a young kid who does. Roy knows what's right, but wonders whether he can choose methods that are wrong? His mother offers the best counsel she can: "Honey, sometimes you're going to be faced with situations where the line isn't clear between what's right and what's wrong. Your heart will tell you to do one thing, and your brain will tell you to do something different. In the end, all that's left is to look at both sides and go with your best judgment" (160).

Roy and Mullet Fingers can also be seen as younger versions of the two main characters in Hiaasen's first novel, *Tourist Season*. In that book, Skip Wiley is a terrorist who commits serious crimes including kidnapping and murder in an effort to scare tourists away from Florida in order to halt the overdevelopment of his state. Brian Keyes, his friend and former newspaper colleague, agrees with Wiley's aims but rejects his violent tactics. In that novel, however, we don't get to see what led Wiley to decide to take the violent path. Did he ever agonize before deciding to use immoral and illegal methods? In *Hoot*, by contrast, Hiaasen allows his young readers to participate in Roy's struggle with his conscience over whether he should cross the line as well as share his fears that his new friend might take actions that will cause him to get arrested.

Hoot is the most autobiographical of Hiaasen's novels. It is, he says, like a page ripped from his own childhood. One of the defining moments of that childhood occurred when he and his boyhood friends saw the wilderness where they played every day after school being paved over to make way for a shopping mall. Like Mullet Fingers, they removed or rearranged survey stakes in protest. "We didn't know what else to do," says Hiaasen. "We were little and the bulldozers were big" (*Kick* xv). *Hoot* gives him an opportunity to write a kind of alternative history in which his young characters ask themselves what they should or shouldn't do in a similar situation and then take appropriate action.

Roy's battle between his head and his heart is complicated by his family situation. His mother suffered a miscarriage when he was four. Now as an only child he considers it his special duty to avoid all activities that might give his parents any reason to worry about him. In addition, his father works in government law enforcement and he can't bear the thought of facing his parents through jail bars if he ever got caught doing something illegal.

Mullet Fingers, on the other hand, is already something of an outlaw who, having grown up in Florida, is tired of seeing what's been happening around him: "Ever since I was little," he tells Roy, "I've been watchin' this place disappear—the piney woods, the scrub, the creeks, the glades. Even the beaches, man—they put up all these giant hotels and only goober tourists are allowed. It really sucks" (172). His concern is infectious, as Roy, the newcomer to the state, soon comes to the same conclusion: "It wasn't just about the owls, it was about everything—all the birds and animals, all the wild places that were in danger of being wiped out" (205).

Hiaasen heightens the suspense by emphasizing the urgency of the situation. The actress who plays Mother Paula in TV commercials is scheduled to arrive for the groundbreaking ceremony in forty-eight hours. Once the bulldozers are unleashed, the battle will be lost and the owls will be killed. Roy, however, comes up with a new approach that might stop the project which up to now Mullet Fingers has only been able to delay. He visits City Hall to examine documents related to the building of the pancake house but discovers that the file containing the required construction permits is missing. He then searches the Internet and learns that burrowing owls are a protected species, and a special permit is required for any construction where they are found to be living. He borrows his mother's camera and gives it to Mullet Fingers hoping he might be able to take pictures that would prove that endangered owls are indeed nesting on the site.

This all leads up to the kind of feel-good scene at the groundbreaking ceremony that we don't ordinarily get in Hiaasen's adult novels. In a last-ditch attempt to disrupt the proceedings, Mullet Fingers squeezes his entire small body up to his neck in one of the holes the owls burrow in. If the bulldozers attempt to bury the owls, they'll have to bury him too. At this point, Roy and Bernice step up and join hands to protect Mullet. Then Bernice's entire soccer team joins them, followed by several more of their schoolmates who form a human barricade. When they begin singing "This Land Is Your Land," even Mother Paula joins in. This time the good guys win.

In Hiaasen's adult fiction, the focus is usually on the bad guys and readers get some satisfaction from the mainly comic ways they are punished for their evil deeds. In *Hoot*, the perspective shifts to the good guys, the kids who are fighting for their beliefs. Readers become emotionally attached to their efforts in a way they don't in the adult novels. Rather than simply enjoying a moment of satisfaction when the bad guys are defeated, readers of *Hoot* get to openly cheer the kids on to victory. In the end, the construction project isn't just delayed, it's abandoned after it is revealed that an Environmental Impact Statement was in fact completed that confirmed that protected owls were living on the property. But this being Florida, where it's crooked business as usual, all it took was the bribing of a local city councilman to have the document secretly removed from the file so construction could take place.

Hiaasen uses Roy to convey to the reader a sense of the natural beauty in Florida he has spent his entire career fighting to preserve. Roy is a reluctant newcomer to the state who had originally resisted the whole idea of moving away from Montana. But what he sees (and we see through his eyes) when Mullet Fingers brings him to a special place changes his mind: "Roy was dazzled by the wondrous quiet, the bushy old mangroves sealing off the place from the honking and hammering of civilization" (176). The sight of a lone osprey overhead, a school of tarpon swimming by, and a blue heron posing regally on one leg in a nearby tree reminds him of what he failed to notice while he was moping around being homesick for Montana. The realization that ospreys are as much at home in Florida as they were in Montana teaches him an important lesson: "Once you got away from all the jillions of people, Florida was just as wild as Montana" (205).

Hiaasen also uses Roy to address another issue that's especially important to many young readers—bullying. Because his family moves so often, Roy is often the new kid in school (Trace Middle School is the sixth school he's attended). This, combined with his small size, often makes him the target of bullies. Dana Matherson is the classic school bully. A lousy student (his father has to pay classmates to do his homework), his only hobbies are smoking and beating up smaller kids. Roy decides he has no choice but to stand up to Dana, who outweighs him by fifty pounds. In one physical confrontation, he even manages to break Dana's nose.

Hiaasen treats Dana the way he normally treats his bad guys: he ridicules him. How seriously can you take a bully whose threats after he's been hit in the mouth sound like this: "You and me got thome bithneth to thettle, Eberhardt.... You're going to be thorry you ever methed with me" (94). Or who finds himself stripped to his underwear and tied to the flagpole in front of school, as he is by Beatrice Leep. Whether smashing his hand into a bird feeder while trying punch Roy or getting locked out of his house dressed only in his baggy boxer shorts, he is brought down to size by constant humiliation.

Despite the seriousness of the issues it addresses, *Hoot* wouldn't be a true Hiaasen novel if it weren't also funny, though the humor is both tamer and calibrated to its young audience. For example, Roy's friend Garrett is understandably popular with his schoolmates because of his talent for making phony fart noises: his speciality is farting out the first line of the Pledge of Allegiance during homeroom. Much of the humor, however, comes at the expense of the adults in the novel. Poor patrolmen David Delinko is the butt of the joke after he falls asleep in his patrol car while he's on the job and the windows are painted black. He's also a bit of a stumblebum, but he's decent, dedicated, and in the end a supporter of the kids' efforts to save the owls.

Another authority figure isn't so lucky. Vice-principal Miss Hennepin is often on Roy's case. For example, she orders him to write a letter of apology to Dana for breaking his nose even though he acted in self-defense. However, the humorless woman fails to appreciate Roy's sarcastic retort—"Okay ... but who's going to help him read it"(20)?—the way Hiaasen's readers will. And once Roy points out the single black hair growing above Miss Hennepin's upper lip, the reader will likely agree with him that it's hard to take a person with a distraction like that very seriously. Her attempt at the end to try to take credit for encouraging the kids in their effort to save the owls prompts this well-deserved putdown: "Roy was always amused when grownups lied to make themselves look more important" (284).

In the end, not everything works out well. Mullet's reunion with his "proud" mother, who is faking it for the benefit of the TV cameras, leaves Roy and Beatrice with a feeling of "helpless disgust" (276). Shortly afterwards, when Mullet runs away again, his mother has him arrested after falsely claiming he stole a piece of her jewelry. He lasts only seventeen hours in juvenile detention before breaking out with the help of a fellow inmate, who just happens to be Dana Middleton. Dana is quickly recaptured and returned to the place where, given his criminal record, he belongs. Mullet, however, remains a runaway, though we have every reason to believe he will survive and be better off than he would be at home with his unloving, heartless mother.

After the novel's publication, longtime friend Jimmy Buffett called to tell Hiaasen how much his daughter loved the book and asked if he'd be interested in optioning it for a movie. He said his friend Wil Shriner, an actor and director of such TV shows as *Frasier* and *Everybody Loves Raymond*, might be interested in writing the screenplay. The three of them got together and agreed to proceed with the project: Shriner began writing the screenplay while Buffett pursued Hollywood financing. In 2006, the movie, directed by Shriner and with songs written by Buffett (who also played the role of science teacher Mr. Ryan), was released. The film features winning performances by its trio of young actors—Logan Lerman, Cody Linley, and Brie Larson, who would go on to win the Academy Award, the Golden Globe, and the Screen Actors Guild Award in 2015 for her performance in *Room*. It also includes a brief cameo by Hiaasen himself.

Hiaasen had a much happier experience with the film version of *Hoot* than he did with *Strip Tease*. This time around, he was far more personally involved, working with friends who shared his love of Florida and who were determined to ensure that the film remained as faithful to the novel as possible. Not all the battles Hiaasen and Shriner fought with the studio were successful, and the film's final scenes aren't as faithful to the book as the rest of the film is. But one battle they did win was especially important to Hiaasen. There was pressure from the studio to have Mullet Fingers reconcile with his mother at the end of the film and return to school. "I threw myself in front of that train with everything I could, and so did the director, to prevent that," he said (Marcus 112). "You're going to lose every kid who goes to the movie if you have him suddenly, blissfully assimilated," he argued. Mullet Fingers, he insisted, is a survivor and his story is inspiring. "It's not telling kids to leave home and live in the woods. It's the grown-ups who are a little thick about it" (113).

Despite a modest budget and some bruising battles with the studio, Hiaasen says he ended up feeling pretty good about the film: "No matter what happens at the box office, I know that everyone killed themselves to keep it as true to the book as they could. And that doesn't happen very often in Hollywood. The novelist is usually the last person they want to hear from, and I will always be grateful to Jimmy and Wil for involving me" (Beauregard).

Flush *(2005)*

Young Noah Underwood is spending an unusual Father's Day with his dad—in the local jail, where his father been confined since being arrested for deliberately sinking a boat. Worse, he won't let Noah's mother bail him out. Paine Underwood insists he's not a common criminal but a man of principle who, he admits, does sometimes gets carried away. (His reckless behavior earned him the childhood nickname, "Paine-in the Butt.") He has freely confessed to the crime of sinking the Coral Queen, a seventy-three-foot casino boat owned by Dusty Muleman. Late one night, he untied the ropes, drove the boat out of the basin where it was docked, and opened the seacocks, causing it to sink. To his way of thinking, however, he had no other choice: the Coral Queen has been flushing hundreds of gallons of human waste into the sea each night, poisoning the water at nearby Thunder Beach where kids swim and loggerhead turtles lay their eggs.

He intends to remain in jail until his trial, where he plans to expose Dusty Muleman's illegal dumping of waste. As he self-righteously explains to his son, "You know how many jails around this world are full of people who spoke up for what they believed in and lost their freedom? Lost everything they had? Look at Nelson Mandela.... He spent twenty-seven years in a South African prison. Twenty-seven years, Noah! A couple of weeks won't hurt me" (26).

In many ways, Blaine resembles *Sick Puppy*'s Twilly Spree, but with a family and without Spree's multimillion dollar inheritance. Like Spree, whenever he sees an injustice, he has a "bad habit of doing the very first thing that popped into his mind, no matter how foolish" (209). After witnessing a man beating his dogs with a bungee cord outside his parked RV, he rescues the dogs and flattens all eight tires on the vehicle. On another occasion, he chased down a fisherman who was stringing illegal gill nets in the protected Everglades National Park and trussed him up with his own net. That led to his boat captain's license being revoked, costing him a job he loved as a fishing guide and forcing him to become a cab driver.

But as the father of two young kids, his actions have consequences that seriously affect others. Bills begin piling up while he's unable to work because he's in jail and refuses to leave. Noah's mother complains that being married to her husband "is like having another child to watch after, one who's too big and unpredictable to put in time-out" (20). She has just about reached the end of her patience with his actions. He may fancy himself a political prisoner, but this time she can see him only as "a selfish jerk" (50) who needs to start behaving like a grown-up.

When Noah's younger sister Abbey overhears their mother talking with a lawyer about a divorce, she and Noah have something else to worry about in addition to their father's situation. To prove he isn't a looney troublemaker but just a guy "who cared about kids and the beaches and the things that lived in the sea" (57) and to change their mother's mind about a divorce, the two kids decide to do something. They begin looking for evidence that the Coral Queen, which has been refloated and is back in business, is flushing poop into the fresh water. (The kids' names are a tipoff to the roles they will play: Abbey was named after her father's favorite writer, Edward Abbey, famed environmentalist and author of the classic eco-thriller, *The Monkey Wrench Gang;* Noah will remind readers of the Biblical figure who saved his family and two of every animal from the destruction of the flood.) Noah begins sneaking out of the house late at night while his mother is sleeping to see if the Coral Queen is still dumping its waste. At first, he's disappointed to see that the boat appears to be properly pumping its sewage into storage tanks as required, but after a closer look, he discovers that the whole operation is a sham—the tanks are totally rusted out and won't hold anything.

During one of their nightly escapades, Norah and Abbey are accosted by a strange bald-headed man with a foreign accent. Abbey's a biter, which enables them to escape when she chomps down on his arm. Things take an even more ominous turn when Lice Peeking, a former crewman on the Coral Queen who agreed to give eye-witness testimony about the illegal dumping, disappears: the last person he was seen with was the bald-headed stranger who attacked Noah and Abbey, and the car he was driving is later found abandoned with the upholstery covered in blood. What have these kids gotten themselves into?

The second half of the novel becomes an adventure thriller as Noah and Abbey, with assistance from Lice's girlfriend Shelley, a bartender on the Coral Queen, launch Operation Royal Flush. Noah and Abbey pool their money, and use the $57.16 they scrape together to buy thirty-six one-ounce bottles of fuchsia food-coloring gel. They intend to dump the contents into the toilets on the Coral Queen, hoping it will produce a tell-tale streak in the water that will prove raw sewage is being flushed directly into the sea.

Complications, both comic and serious, follow. With Shelly's help, Noah sneaks aboard the Casino Queen and locks himself in a ladies' restroom to begin pouring the food coloring into the toilet. Unfortunately, it takes a long time for the gel to empty out of the bottle and he has seventeen of them. Suddenly, a cranky woman begins banging on the door, demanding entry while spewing "a string of cuss words that would have put my Grandma Janet into cardiac arrest" (182). After holding her off until he finishes his task, Noah jumps off the boat into the water where he has another scary encounter, this one with a huge slimy object he crashes into. Fortunately for him, it's only a harmless sleeping manatee.

5. Novels for Young Readers

Things become more dangerous after Abbey picks him up in a small dinghy. While he struggles to get the outboard motor started, Dusty Muleman and his bald-headed henchman appear on a nearby dock with a gun aimed at them. Only the miraculous (and highly improbable) appearance of a one-eyed pirate with a gold coin around his neck and an M-shaped scar on his cheek saves them when he disarms the gunman. The pirate turns out be the very same man who had previously appeared out of nowhere to stop a pair of bullies who were beating up Noah. Who is this mysterious guardian angel?

The *deus ex machina* role of last-minute savior in Hiaasen's adult fiction is ordinarily reserved for Skink, but apparently Hiaasen didn't feel the time was yet right to introduce his favorite character to children. Instead, he resurrects Noah's dead grandfather Bobby to play the role. Noah's family had been repeatedly told over the past ten years by the U.S. State Department that Grandpa Bobby had died and was buried somewhere in Colombia. They were wrong.

While enjoying a beer at a local bar in Colombia, he happened to see a story on satellite TV about his son Paine's arrest, so he immediately headed to Florida to see what he could do to help. But after rescuing his grandkids, there's little more for him to do, so he returns to Colombia to look for his stolen boat. However, he's not the only character in the novel who comes back to life, so to speak. Hiaasen puts to rest any fears his young readers might have had about the fate of the missing and feared-dead Lice Peeking. He shows up at the end and explains that he became scared after being threatened by Muleman's henchman and took off. The blood stains in the abandoned car? They were ketchup stains from the burgers he ate before he had to leave the car behind when it ran out of gas.

In the end, Noah and Abbey's victory for the good guys turns out to be only temporary. The Coast Guard shuts down the Coral Queen, but within weeks it's allowed to re-open after Muleman pays a $10,000 fine. It turns out he has an incriminating videotape he uses to blackmail the prosecutor's office into giving him only a token fine. But Hiaasen, that master of ironic punishment, comes up with a doozy for Muleman. The good kids may have lost the battle but thanks to another kid, they win the war. The Coral Queen burns down when Muleman's nitwit son accidentally ignites some firecrackers on board after carelessly tossing a lighted cigar away. Even worse for Muleman, arson investigators later find a fireproof lockbox amid the rubble containing $100,000 in cash. Dusty's partners, the Miccosukee Indians, sue Muleman for embezzlement.

Like so many villains in Hiaasen's adult fiction, Dusty Muleman is another example of the destructive power of greed. Already the richest guy around, he wants more. By law, gambling boats must remain three miles offshore, beyond Florida's boundary. He figures he can make more money from gambling if the customers don't get seasick, so he makes a deal with the Miccosukee Indians, who are allowed to have in-state casinos, to dock his boat in their marina. The reason he dumps the raw sewage into the sea is that it's simply cheaper than disposing of it properly. But what finally trips him up is another greedy mistake: skimming money from the gambling receipts to line his pockets even more.

Flush ends with Noah and his family fishing together in a small boat which takes them over the location of what's left of the Coral Queen now resting under twenty-two feet of water. As the sun begins to set over the Gulf of Mexico, they position themselves, hoping to witness the very elusive flash of green that is rarely visible at the moment the sun drops below the horizon. This time Mother Nature, perhaps in gratitude for their efforts on her behalf, rewards them with a momentary glimpse of the brief and brilliant phenomenon.

For only the second time (the first was in *Basket Case*), Hiaasen employs a first-person narrator in *Flush*. Having Noah tell the story has the benefit of directly placing the reader into the perspective of a young boy. This allows us to see others, especially adults, from a child's distinctive point of view, as for example in this description by Noah of his father's lawyer: "Mr. Shine looked about a thousand years old" (35). We also become emotionally closer to Noah than we did with the kids in *Hoot* as we are able to share from inside his head his worries about his jailed father as well as his fears about the possibility that his parents might split up.

Being restricted to Noah's perspective does, however, limit the humor in the novel. All of it must come from what Noah says or observes about the few other characters he actually interacts with. Still, several good examples of humor can be found in his descriptions: the noise Abbey makes while gargling and brushing her teeth "sounded like a duck swallowing a harmonica" (61); Shelly's face is smeared with so much zinc oxide that "it looked like she'd fallen nose-first into a frosted cake" (137); the word fuchsia sounds to him "like something you wouldn't want to step in" (159).

In many ways Noah is a chip off the old block. He has obviously taken to heart the lessons his father has taught him, among them that it's our duty to clean up after "brainless morons" and that "the smart humans owe it to every other living creature not to let the dumb humans wreck the whole planet" (139). He demonstrates this by wading into poop-filled water to retrieve an empty beer can and to scare a loggerhead turtle away from the filth. But he's also perceptive enough to recognize the limitations of his father's reckless approach to things: "Sometimes," he confesses, "it's like my father lives on his own weird little planet" (27); and after yet another of his father's high-minded speeches about truth and justice, he observes with a critical eye: "He paused, as if waiting for someone to applaud. We didn't" (97).

Flush sends a clear message that nature needs to be protected, and that children can play an important role in that effort. It also reminds us that ironically sometimes it takes a child's actions to expose the limitations of adult behavior. As David Aitchison said about the novel, "What begins as a story of childlike activism ends as a story of childhood activism" (182).

Scat *(2009)*

Mrs. Bunny Starch, the most-feared teacher at the Truman School, is trying her best to engage her biology students in a discussion of the day's reading assignment, but is having little success. She eventually zeroes in on a boy named Smoke, two years older than the rest of the class and a student at the private school only because of a generous donation by his grandmother. Unhappy at being assigned an essay to write as punishment for not being prepared, he becomes belligerent. He threatens Mrs. Starch, chews the end off the pencil she is waving at him, swallows it, and walks out of class.

The following day, she is taking the class on an all-day field trip to the Black Vine Swamp near the Big Cypress Preserve. Smoke, however, is absent. During the outing, a wildfire suddenly breaks out and Mrs. Starch hustles all the students to safety, then returns to the swamp to retrieve the asthma inhaler Libby Marshall had dropped along the way. Since she drove her own car to the site, the buses return to school without her. The next day, she doesn't show up at school and her distinctive blue Prius with a "Save the Manatee" license plate is found still in the parking lot.

Fears about her safety are temporarily put to rest when the asthma inhaler is dropped on the doorstep of Libby Marshall's home late one night and a phone message is received at school explaining that she is tending to a family emergency, even though she isn't known to have a family. But concerns about her safety arise again when a video one of her students, Nick

Waters, took on the field trip that he hoped captured the sighting of a rare Florida panther upon closer examination instead revealed a human form running through the woods. Could someone have intentionally started the wildfire? And could the culprit have been Smoke, who earned his nickname because of a history of deliberately setting fires? And who is that man in the dark knit hat seen driving Mrs. Starch's distinctive blue Prius?

Now that the reader has been hooked, Hiaasen begins to clear up the mysteries so he can get on to the main business of the novel. The reader learns that the wildfire was deliberately set by Jimmy Lee Bayliss, project manager for the Red Diamond Energy Corporation owned by Drake McBride. McBride is the latest in a long line of Hiaasen phonies. A lazy loser whose wealthy father has bought him a series of companies, all of which he has managed to ruin, he now pretends to be a Texas oilman.

He has obtained an oil-drilling lease in the Big Cypress Preserve, but finds no oil there. But then he learns two things: 1) there may be underground oil deposits in the section next to his, which is owned by the state of Florida; 2) The U.S. Government is looking to buy up all drilling rights for oil and natural gas in the Big Cypress Preserve to protect the vanishing wetlands from future damage. McBride's really not interested in oil anyway, just easy money. If he can provide evidence that there is oil underground, he figures the government will pay him a fortune *not* to pump it out. His plan is to illegally erect an oil-drilling platform on the state-owned section and secretly pipe the oil to his. Bayliss set the fire to scare the school kids off, fearful that they might stumble onto McBride's illegal operation. When an arson investigator begins snooping around, Bayliss obtains a backpack belonging to Smoke and plants it near the site of the fire, leading the police to conclude he was the arsonist.

The mysterious man in the knit hat that Nick had spotted driving Mrs. Starch's Prius turns out to be a character familiar to readers of *Sick Puppy*. It's Twilly Spree, the rich guy with a short temper who can't stand to see anyone trash the environment. He just happened to be camping out in Black Vine Swamp when Mrs. Starch brought the school kids on their field trip. Twilly hasn't changed much since his previous appearance. He's still a man with "good intentions but a rotten temper, which occasionally got him into hot water," although most of what he does is motivated by a love for Florida, "a place that was breaking his heart because it was disappearing before his very eyes" (164).

Twilly plays several important roles in the novel. It was he who discov-

5. Novels for Young Readers

ered that the Red Diamond company was preparing to begin illegal drilling for oil in the wetlands. Like Mullet Fingers in *Hoot*, he embarks upon a comic campaign of opposition: he captures one of Red Diamond's workers, strips off his clothes and glues him to a tree trunk; on another occasion, he spray paints the man orange from head to toe and ties him to the hood of his truck; finally, he removes the pink flags marking the future path of the illegal pipeline and rearranges them to spell a one-word message for McBride to see when he flies over the site in his helicopter: SCAT.

He also rescued Mrs. Starch after she became lost in the smoke from the fire when she returned to retrieve the student's asthma inhaler. And it is he who gives her a tiny panther kitten he found that had been separated from its mother during the fire. The reason for her absence from school is that she has been nursing the tiny panther with bottles of zoo milk Twilly has flown in. But if he can't locate the mother soon, the baby will likely die. Or the mother might be killed by McBride, who fears that if any evidence of panthers, an endangered species, is ever found in the area, the government will halt his oil drilling.

The dramatic highlight of the novel is the attempt to reunite the baby panther with its mother. On a fog-shrouded morning, Twilly sets out to find fresh panther scat. Smoke (who has now joined the group) will then track the panther, and Mrs. Starch, aided by two of her students, Nick Waters and Marta Gonzalez, will attempt to bring the kitten to its mother. The description of the group—"the five of them had learned to move together through scratchy brush and sodden marsh—in fluid unison, like a centipede or the muscles of a snake" (326)—reinforces an important point Hiaasen has been making in his previous kids' novels about the value of group action compared with solo efforts.

This collective effort proves crucial when the howl of the mother panther is followed by the sound of gunshots. Fortunately, the shots fired by Drake McBride miss the panther; unfortunately, one of the bullets strikes Mrs. Starch in the hip. Twilly and Smoke now have to get the badly injured woman to medical help before she bleeds to death, leaving Nick and Marta alone to deal with the kitten. After spotting the mother high above him in a dead pine tree, Nick starts scrambling up the tree. Halfway up, the branch he's on breaks, hurtling him toward the ground. Luckily, his sleeve catches on a branch, breaking his fall, but also breaking his right arm. Using only his left arm, he manages to climb back up the tree close enough to leave the kitten, still tightly clasped to his chest by her sharp claws, where its mother can see it. The last thing he witnesses before blacking out from the pain is the mother panther carrying her baby by the scruff of its neck to another tree.

Young Nick has had much more on his mind than simply solving a mystery or saving a panther kitten. His father's National Guard unit has been called up to fight in the Iraq war, and he constantly worries about his welfare. His father has been able to stay in touch with his family by e-mail, but when they stop coming Nick's fears grow. The news he finally gets is bad: the Humvee his father was riding in was struck by a rocket-propelled grenade launcher; he survived, but suffered severe injuries, including the loss of his right arm.

Nick is relieved his father didn't die, but worried about how he will adjust to the loss of his arm and how it will affect his job as the pitching coach for a minor league baseball team. He decides to bind his own right arm tightly behind his back with an Ace bandage, forcing him, like his father, to learn to do everything with his left arm. It's a struggle, but it's important that he show his support for what his father must go through. The training will also prove to be useful after he breaks his right arm in the fall from the tree; only a strong left arm, which he now has, enabled him to complete his mission.

In many ways, *Scat* is a novel about how misleading first impressions can be. To her students, Mrs. Starch is simply the "world's meanest biology teacher." She tolerates no nonsense, and her students live in constant fear of being called on, especially when they are unprepared. When Nick's best friend Marta Gonzalez once became so nervous she threw up in her classroom, Mrs. Starch assigned her a 500-word essay on the muscle groups used in the act of regurgitation. The kids are convinced she's a witch who lives alone in a house in the woods that is reputedly filled with stuffed dead animals and fifty-three poisonous snakes.

But then Nick and Marta get to see another side to her. (Her full name—Bunny Starch—symbolizes her two sides, the rigid and the lovable.) Yes, her house is filled with dead animals, but each mounted bird or reptile is a member of an endangered species that was accidentally killed or shot. She had them mounted because she feared she would never get a chance to see any of them alive in the wild. Watching her sing a tender lullaby to the baby panther while she nurses it with a bottle, plus learning that she has been privately tutoring Smoke, the unruly student who had threatened her in class, further challenges their negative impressions. If she at times acts like a mean witch, it's because she has to. As she explains to Nick and Marta:

5. Novels for Young Readers

> Look, my job is to fill young minds with knowledge, and certain fields of knowledge can be boring at times. *Really* boring. Which means I have to be tough in order to keep my students focused. I don't expect to win any popularity contests, but at least you'll be able to write five hundred intelligent words about the Calvin cycle when you finish my course [265].

That's probably why her students do exceptionally well on the biology questions on their SAT tests.

To highlight the qualities of a dedicated teacher like Mrs. Starch, Hiaasen includes a contrasting portrait of what a truly bad teacher looks like. At first, Dr. Wendell Waxmo, who takes over Mrs. Starch's biology class in her absence, seems to be a breath of fresh air. He cuts a colorful figure, dressed in a faded black tuxedo and sporting a bright yellow bow tie that bobs up and down whenever he talks. And he gets class going in an unconventional way by having the students *sing* the Pledge of Allegiance. Marta even passes a note to Nick that reads, "This is fantastic! He's crazy as a bedbug!" (99).

But once he begins teaching, it's clear he really is a lunatic. His method of instruction is quite simple (and simple-minded): he devotes each day of the week to a different page of the textbook (no matter what subject he has been assigned to teach), which the students are then ordered to focus on. It isn't long before Marta passes a second note to Nick, this one pleading, "I want Mrs. Starch to come back!" (161).

Worse than his clueless teaching methods is the way he treats his students, whom he routinely addresses as "You little termites." He enjoys bullying them, making them stand and sing ridiculous songs, or in the case of Smoke, publicly humiliating him for the quality of an essay. The students are finally spared any more of his lunatic antics thanks to Twilly Spree, who pays a visit to his home to demand that he immediately resign. "I'm much, much crazier than you are," he tells him. "Do *not* give me a reason to return here" (180).

Smoke (real name Duane Scrod, Jr., aka Duane the Dweeb) is a character who suffers not so much from negative first impressions as premature judgments. It's true that he has a troubled past. He was held back two years in elementary school and later expelled from his public middle school for a fight with his P. E. teacher during which he chewed off and swallowed the tip of his pinkie finger. He got into the Truman school only because of his wealthy grandmother's donations to the school. His nickname was earned because of a history of starting fires: he burned down a construction trailer at age ten and later torched a billboard on the interstate. All this, combined with the offensive behavior we witnessed in the opening scene, gives us little reason to doubt Mrs. Starch's assessment that he may be "just another dull lump with no talent and no future" (6).

Fortunately, like Mrs. Starch, there's more to the boy than his reputation suggests. The first surprise comes when Smoke shows up a school one day so neatly groomed and dressed that he "looked like the future president of the Student Council" (108). But it isn't just his appearance that has changed. His whole attitude is different. He tells Nick that after camping out in the woods by himself for a few nights, he came to the conclusion that he was headed in the wrong direction in his life. "It gets old," he confesses to Nick, "Not carin' about a damn thing in the world. So I decided to try it the other way" (111).

He still has a major problem to overcome: his history of setting fires plus evidence found at the scene of the wildfire—his backpack and handheld propane torch—lead the police to consider him the prime suspect. But he insists he's innocent, and what we learn about his past serves to cast further doubt as to his guilt. He did set fire to a billboard at age ten, but only because it featured an American Airlines advertisement for a bargain flight from Miami to Paris. His mother had just abandoned him and his father and had taken that very same flight to Paris, so he took his anger out on the billboard. And yes, around the same time he did set fire to a trailer at a construction site, but only after he witnessed a backhoe knocking down a tree that killed a raccoon and her three babies. Growing up as he did in a home without a mother and with a father who "didn't always have both oars in the water" (210) were difficulties it took him some time to overcome. But overcome them he did, and better late than never.

It's easy to understand why Smoke is a troubled boy once we meet his father, Duane Scrod, Sr., an unhappy man with troubles of his own. Setting fires must run in the family: Duane Sr., spent six months in jail after burning down the car dealership that refused to replace the transmission that blew in the SUV he had just purchased from them. During his stint in jail, he left his son home alone to fend for himself. However, as is the case with many of the other characters in the novel, there's more to his story than meets the eye.

Like his son, he too was thrown for an emotional loop when his wife abruptly left and moved to Paris to open a gourmet cheese shop. The antique piano shop he owned went bankrupt and he's now jobless. He spends his days listening to classical music and watching French cooking shows on TV, hoping to catch a glimpse of his wife whenever cheese is discussed. But like his son, he too begins to grow up and at the end of the novel he finds a job doing something he loves—teaching piano to young kids.

The portrait of Duane Scrod, Sr., is a good illustration of Hiaasen's skill in combining seriousness and humor. The emotional pain of a man who is spurned by his wife and then unable to cope with the demands of being a single father is meant to be taken seriously. But Hiaasen, who understands the value of comic relief, finds a way to lighten the situation simply by giving the man a pet macaw. Nadine isn't just an ordinary bird: this clever one can speak three languages, thus treating us to a regular chorus of trilingual squawks: "Bless you! "*À vos souhaits! Gesundheit!*" (23); "Why? *Pourquoi? Warum?*" (81); "Thanks a million! *Danke Schön! Merci Beaucoup!*" (255). She also performs cute little bird tricks, like pooping on her owner's shirt and ruffling the hair of visitors with her beak.

In addition to paying tribute to dedicated teachers like Mrs. Starch, Hiaasen also pays tribute to two other noteworthy figures. One is Skink, whose presence hovers over the novel in the person of his disciple Twilly Spree. Readers of *Sick Puppy* will also recognize that the unidentified friend who gave Twilly the vulture-beak necklace he wears around his neck and that he gives to Marta was Skink.

Hiaasen also salutes author Edward Abbey, this time much more directly than he did in *Flush*. There all we were told is that Abbey was named after one of her father's favorite writers, "some weird old bird who's buried out west in the middle of the desert" (*Flush* 5). In the very first conversation Twilly has with Nick in *Scat*, he mentions Abbey's eco-terrorist novel *The Monkey Wrench Gang*. The next day, Nick checks it out of the library, and later he and Twilly begin discussing it. When Twilly phones the U.S. Fish and Wildlife Service to report having seen a panther near the Red Diamond drilling site, he gives his name as George W. Hayduke, the name of the leader of Abbey's Monkey Wrench gang. Finally, before heading off to parts unknown, he mails Nick a copy of *Hayduke Lives!*, Abbey's sequel to *The Monkey Wrench Gang*, which he inscribes with this message: "*From your favorite monkey wrencher. We'll meet again*" (367).

Scat is the most tightly plotted of Hiaasen's kids' novels, and the most topical. It contains enough mystery and suspense to keep his young readers turning the pages, but at the same time it also addresses a pair of issues relevant in the lives of many of those young readers. The first is the damaging effects of a broken marriage, both on the abandoned spouse but even more dramatically on a ten-year-old boy. The second is the effect of our current wars in the Middle East on families, both in the constant fear they must live with about the safety of a loved one who is fighting as well as the struggle those who return with severe injuries face on a daily basis. *Scat* has plenty of laughs, but interspersed among them are some sobering realities.

Chomp *(2012)*

Chomp is the funniest of Hiaasen's kids' novels, thanks largely to the comic misadventures of Derek Badger, star of the popular TV reality show, *Expedition Survival!* He will remind readers of *Skin Tight* of Reynaldo Flemm, the sensationalist TV newsman who is a phony doofus like Badger. He was originally created for *Star Island*, but in the end that novel had enough comic phonies so he was excised from the book. In *Chomp*, he has the spotlight to himself and seldom fails to produce a laugh, all at his expense.

Lee Bluepenny (his real name) got his start in show business as a member of an Irish folk-dancing group. His big break came thanks to a broken toe: while in the hospital, he met a talent agent who was impressed by his good looks. Thanks also to an ability to swallow a live salamander without throwing up, he was cast as the lead in a wilderness survival show. With the new name of Derek Badger and a fake Australian accent modeled on famed crocodile hunter Steve Irwin, he soon became one of TV's most popular reality stars.

Each week, Derek would parachute into some dangerous wilderness area and armed only with a Swiss army knife and a straw would make his way to safety. He would eat whatever he could find—bugs, rodents, worms, tree bark fungus—to stay alive. None of this would be noteworthy if any of it was authentic and he was talented in any way. It isn't real and he's a total fake, which makes him a ripe target for ridicule.

Mickey Cray is a professional animal wrangler who has an exotic collection of creatures ranging from alligators and snakes to raccoons and a tortoise living in his backyard. However, a freak accident during a cold spell—the frozen body of an iguana fell on his head—gave him a concussion that has left him with pounding headaches and double vision. Because he's unable to work, his wife, a language teacher, has been forced to take a job teaching Chinese to American business executives in Shanghai for the next two months. She leaves her husband in the care of their son Wahoo (named not after the fish but after former Miami Dolphins linebacker and professional wrestler Wahoo McDaniel). The bills keep piling up, however, and the Crays are in imminent danger of losing their home. Help comes in the nick of time when Raven Stark, the production assistant on *Expedition Survival!,* calls looking to hire Mickey and his animals for the next episode of the show.

Derek Badger (whom Mickey soon begins referring to as Dork Badger and His Phoniness) proves to be a more difficult challenge than any of the animals he's used to wrangling. To begin with, he's a phony from his boots (which are covered with wet oatmeal to look like mud) to his tan (which is of the spray-on variety). The parachute jump that opens each show? Performed by a stunt double. What makes all this worse (but exceedingly funny) is his massive ego: he believes what's written in the script he's given to read and is convinced he really is a skilled survivalist. *Chomp* is filled with evidence to the contrary.

Derek is an easy target to ridicule. He sprains both ankles after leaping from a tree when a baby gecko scurries up his shorts. He nearly drowns when he ignores Mickey's advice about his pet alligator Alice and tries to ride her like a horse; failure to heed Mickey's warning about a sleepy snapping turtle results in the animal taking a bite out of his nose. Much of the humor arises from the contrast between the words he speaks on his show and the reality of what actually happens. For example, after a Florida mastiff bat is accidentally stunned and drops into his cheesecake platter, Derek prepares to eat the critter. "Now, please don't try this yourself," he warns his viewers, "wild bats can be vicious, and their teeth are needle sharp. Remember, I'm an experienced survivalist. I know how to handle these unpredictable rascals..." (186). And then the bat chomps down hard on his tongue. Scenes like these must of course be edited out of the broadcast, but they provide plenty of yucks when they are shown at the crew's annual end-of-the-season party.

The first part of the Everglades episode is filmed on a set Mickey had constructed on his property. Derek, however, now insists he wants to shoot the rest in the real Everglades. Only an offer of $8000 (the exact amount Mickey is behind on his mortgage) persuades him and his son to accompany Derek on this potentially dangerous adventure. (As Mickey sagely observes, "Slow and dumb doesn't mix well with wild and raw" (8)). While Mickey and Wahoo are loading their truck with supplies they just purchased at Walmart, Tuna Gordon, a classmate of Wahoo's, approaches and asks them for a lift. They become concerned when they notice her black eye, which she confesses her father Jared, with whom she lives in an old Winnebago parked at the far end of the Walmart lot, gave her after he got drunk again and beat her up. They decide to take her with them to the Everglades for her own safety.

The final third of the novel becomes a bit over the top as Derek and Jared, who has tracked his daughter down in the Everglades, both become a little cuckoo. Derek is a huge fan of vampire movies, especially those based on the Dark Night Trilogy (which one reviewer dismissed as "three of the most brainless books ever written in the English language" (173). After developing an infection from the bat bite, he begins to fear that he might be turning into a vampire himself. He takes off into the wilderness by himself like Dax Mangold, the hero of the Dark Night Trilogy, to "battle the terrible forces of the spirit underworld and to save his own soul" (175).

For the first time in his life, his fans would be surprised to learn, he spends a night alone in the wilderness. When a bolt of lightning strikes the metal helmet camera he's sitting on during a violent thunderstorm, leaving him with a bit of a shock and a small burn on his butt, he exclaims, "It's a mark!... The mark of the undead!" "Actually," the narrator corrects him, "it was the mark of the stupid, which is what you get for sitting under a tree during a thunderstorm" (215). He begins repeating the chant his hero Dax uses to fight off the vampires—"Eee-ka-laro! Eee-ka-laro! Gumbo mucho eee-ka-laro"—which happily also reminds him of éclairs, his favorite dessert.

Meanwhile, Jared is becoming increasingly drunk and dangerous. When he spots his daughter fleeing in an airboat, he fires his gun at her, hitting the boat's driver in the back. Then he forces Mickey at gunpoint to help him chase after his daughter. Eventually he loses all control—he clubs Mickey in the head with his pistol butt and then shoots him in the foot at point-blank range. Who can stop the monster Hiaasen now describes as "demented" and "drooling?" Only a vampire, or a man like Derek Badger who thinks he is one, who tackles Jared and bites him in the neck like a vampire.

While Derek Badger is the primary source of humor in *Chomp*, Tuna is responsible for the serious side of the novel. She introduces the issue of child abuse. Wahoo, who has only known loving parents, is freaked out that any adult could harm a child, but the fact remains that it is a widespread problem in our world. Unlike Derek, Tuna knows what surviving a situation of real danger is like. Tuna's father had promised her mother, whom not surprisingly he also beats, that he wouldn't lay a hand on Tuna while she's away in Chicago caring for her ailing mother. But he breaks that promise, and for the third time in her young life, Tuna has been forced to run away from home.

Beside that fact that Tuna and Wahoo both have names the same as a creature with scales, gills and fins, they share another connection involving the loss of a home: without the $8000 his father is promised for accompanying Derek to the Everglades, Wahoo would lose his; because Tuna's father drank away all the mortgage money on the home they once lived in, she has lost hers and is forced to live in a Walmart parking lot.

She is also indirectly responsible for the terrifying situation that develops when her drunken father comes to the Everglades to punish her for running away. Concerned about the welfare of her pet hamster, Tuna made the mistake of calling her father from a phone at a tourist shop in the Everglades to remind him to feed it. Using the caller ID on his phone, he is able to figure out her exact location.

Tuna is one of Derek Badger's biggest fans. She regularly watches his show on a TV set in the Walmart store near where she lives in the parking lot. Her inevitable disillusionment is especially painful as she gets to see with her own eyes what a fraud her TV hero really is: "She felt like a fool for ever thinking Derek's adventures—and his ruggedness—were real. He was no tough guy; he was just a Hollywood fake" (241). She's the kind of serious kid who on her own takes the trouble to memorize the Latin names of as many animals as she can. (One reason she does this is that it provides a temporary escape from the craziness of life with an abusive father.) Her reverence for scientific accuracy is a stark contrast to Derek Badger's total lack of respect for authenticity.

Happily, not all of Tuna's experiences are negative. She is the beneficiary of an eye-opening experience when she is given the opportunity to encounter real nature for the first time. Unlike Wahoo, who is fortunate enough to have grown up among a variety of wild animals, Tuna, like many children her age, suffers from what Richard Louv in his influential book *Last Child in the Woods* calls a "nature-deficit disorder." He contends that children today learn about nature only in school and have precious little contact with the real thing: "A kid today can likely tell you about the Amazon rain forest—but not about the last time he or she explored the woods in solitude, or lay in a field listening to the wind and watching the clouds move" (1). Tuna does have an interest in nature, but it is based mainly on what she learns from books. She can rattle off the Latin names of hundreds of animals without ever having had the opportunity to see most of them with her own eyes. That all changes when she goes to the Everglades for the first time with Wahoo and his father.

Not every child is given the opportunity to save the lives of burrowing owls or help a panther kitten be reunited with its mother. But everyone can still experience some of the wonderful things Tuna does, like listening to the croak of a great blue heron, or watching the casual ballet of zebra butterflies, or even picking a cocoa-striped snail from a bush. This isn't the fake world promoted by TV reality shows like *Expedition Survival!* Nor is it the antiseptic Disney version. Animals bite—Wahoo lost his thumb when a pet alligator accidentally bit it off while grabbing for the chicken he was holding for its dinner—and must kill others to survive, as Tuna learns when she sees a small bird in the mouth of a hungry python. But it's all real.

Chomp ends happily, especially for Tuna, who is finally freed from her father's violence—he'll likely spend the rest of his days in prison—and exhilarated by her encounter with Mother Nature. Tuna may be a victim, but like most of the female characters in Hiaasen's adult fiction, she is smart, quick-witted, resilient, and resourceful. She can also teach fake survivalists like Derek Badger a thing or two about what survival really means.

Skink—No Surrender (2014)

The novel's title signals what many of Hiaasen's readers have been hoping for—the unleashing of Skink on his young readers. His appearance comes, as it usually does, in a dramatic way.

Fourteen-year-old Richard Sloan is walking the beach one night as he often does, looking for mounds the loggerhead turtles have built for their eggs. Whenever he and his cousin Malley (who has inexplicably failed to show up and join him as she normally does) find one, they call the state wildlife office, which then sends an officer to mark off the location to protect the eggs. He approaches a marked-off area he hasn't noticed before and becomes curious when he hears a strange breathing sound and sees a soda straw sticking up out of the sand. He pulls the straw out and is shocked when a one-eyed giant of a man wearing a shower cap also comes bursting up out of the mound. He is at first understandably frightened by the old man, who tells him his name is Clint Tyree. But a quick bit of googling by Richard on his phone reveals that no one by that name is on the state registry of sex offenders. He is, however, surprised to read on Wikipedia that Clint Tyree is listed as being dead.

As young readers of the novel now learn, Clinton Tyree, better known as Skink, is the former governor of Florida who has been living for the past thirty years as a hermit in the woods. He tells Richard he's on the trail of a man named Dodge Olney who has already been arrested three times for stealing and then selling protected loggerhead eggs. Skink has buried himself in the sand in an area he has marked off as being the location of turtle eggs, and is patiently waiting for Olney to dig him up. As he explains to Richard, "The jailhouse experience has failed to rehabilitate him. I'll be taking a different approach" (6).

Richard tells Skink he's worried about his cousin Malley, who's also fourteen. She's a handful to raise and her parents have decided to ship her off to

5. Novels for Young Readers

an all-girls' boarding school in New Hampshire. When he later calls her parents to ask about her, they tell him that she suddenly remembered she needed to go to early orientation at the school and they had just dropped her off at the airport. But Richard finds out there is no early orientation at the school, and when the police review security camera footage at the airport, they observe Malley getting into a car with a strange man wearing a blond wig. Richard becomes even more alarmed when he subsequently finds out that she has apparently willingly gone off with a man she met on the Internet named Talbo Chock. When Richard learns that a U.S. Marine by that name was recently killed while serving in Afghanistan, he becomes even more concerned for Malley, who it now appears is in the dangerous clutches of a man who isn't who he pretends to be.

With the help of faithful friend Jim Tile, Skink obtains a car and invites Richard to join him in the search for Malley. Along the way, Richard gets a phone call from his cousin telling him she's OK. She also mentions seeing an ivory-billed woodpecker in a tree. Richard wonders why she mentioned that because he knows the bird is extinct and that there hasn't been a documented sighting in over eighty years. Skink, however, picks up on the fact that she's signaling her whereabouts: he too once saw the bird and knows its exact location—near the Choctawhatchee River close to Panama City. The two of them now head north on a road trip of several hundred miles to Florida's panhandle.

There isn't a whole lot to do during a long car ride except talk, which Skink and Richard spend a lot of time doing. The only action occurs when Skink takes a brief detour after spotting a motorist tossing an empty Budweiser can out the window. Skink follows the car to a restaurant parking lot and pours a six-pack of Bud into the gas tank before resuming the journey. Hiaasen later comes up with a way to give Richard something to do by having an eighteen-wheeler drive over Skink's right foot while he's attempting to rescue a baby skunk trying to cross the highway. Skink now has to teach Richard how to drive so they can continue. Richard is only five feet one and a half inches tall so he has to sit on some of the books Skink keeps in the car. In addition to following Skink's directions about how to drive, he has to heed his stern warning, "Don't fart on my Steinbeck," referring to the copy of *East of Eden* he's perched on.

After finally arriving at the river, Skink is able to buy a used canoe from an agreeable couple. Conversation continues between the ex-governor and the kid until Hiaasen devises a way to get Skink out of the picture, at least temporarily. A hungry alligator grabs a stringer of fish dangling over the side of their canoe and heads off down the river, dragging the canoe with it. Skink dives into the river to retrieve it, but fails to return, leaving Richard all by himself in the woods.

He eventually makes his way to the houseboat where Talbo is holding Malley prisoner, but once again little happens without Skink. At one point, Richard has the perfect opportunity to attack Talbo when he's bent over gutting some fish for dinner, but he talks himself out of doing anything. "I considered making a hero move for the nine-iron, but then what? The truth: When it came to fighting, I had no self-confidence and zero experience. Dad was opposed to violence of any sort, and it's one of the few things he was super strict about." And so, he confesses, "I didn't do a darn thing except stand there like a worthless wimp" (158). He's given a second chance when Talbo's hand is impaled by the spine of the catfish he's gutting, causing him excruciating pain. But once again he is unable to act: the sight of blood causes his knees to buckle and he nearly faints. Another opportunity lost.

When Talbo, whose real name we learn is Tommy Chalmers, pulls a gun on Richard, he acts instinctively, but he's no match for the bigger and stronger man, who begins pummeling him. The time is now ripe for the re-appearance of Skink, who is quite a sight, with wounds in his neck, a bite on his shoulder, and welts on his chest from his encounter with the alligator. His head is crowned with hydrilla weeds that made him look "like some sort of demented sea monarch" (176) and his beard is covered with leeches he picks off and pops into his mouth "like junior Twizzlers" (180).

Skink stops Tommy from beating Richard, but then Tommy pulls a gun and orders Malley to tie up both Skink and Richard. Skink is later able to use the knife Malley had secretly slipped to them to cut the rope, disarm Tommy, and then push Richard and Malley off the boat so they can swim to safety. As Richard looks back, he describes his hero with an image that (with some updating) might have come from Homer or Virgil:

> A fork of lightning split the clouds, a phenomenal silver-yellow pulse that froze Skink in place like the flash from an old-time camera. One arm was raised skyward, the hand open in a farewell wave. At the end of his other arm hung the thrashing, raging form of Tommy Chalmers.
> The governor's smile seemed to cast its own light.
> That insane movie-star smile. I swear I could still see it after the sky went black [198].

Skink now disappears again, so the two cousins make what will turn out to be an unnecessary trip to safety, one which is also delayed by a chapter-

5. Novels for Young Readers

long encounter with some feral pigs. Eventually they locate Skink's car and begin their long journey home. But then Richard suddenly decides he must go back and see if Skink needs help. The two retrace their steps until they finally find him. One again Richard's narrative slips into heroic mode:

> A lone man standing motionless on the water, his ragged reflection encircled in the liquid halo of an eerie bluish-purple sheen.
>
> Not *walking* on the water, Jesus-style, but just standing there, his bare feet (one of them mangled) clearly visible on the surface.
>
> Still impressive, right [239]!

It turns out that Skink is simply standing on the roof of the sunken houseboat. The three of them now set out after the missing Tommy. They eventually catch up with him, but the last time we see him he's in the jaws of an alligator that's happily swimming away with its dinner. That's also the final time we see Skink, whom Richard affectionately calls, "one of the coolest old farts ever" (275).

Because the narrative in *Skink—No Surrender* is restricted to Richard's first-person perspective and Skink is the only person he spends much time with, the result is largely a two-person book. And while the story is energized by Skink's presence, he ends up dominating the action. In Hiaasen's previous kids' books, the young characters played a much more active role in the story, whether it was saving burrowing owls, reuniting a panther kitten with its mother, or halting the flushing of sewage into the sea. Here Richard and Malley, who are a few years older than their counterparts in the previous novels, are largely passive characters. Malley is the teenage damsel in distress who must wait patiently to be rescued; Richard is unable to act when he's given not just one but two opportunities to act heroically. Only the fortuitous reappearance of Skink saves the two of them from the clutches of the bad guy.

The novel certainly has its delights, chief among them the relationship between the fourteen-year-old boy and the seventy-two-year-old ex-governor. Richard's father died when he was eleven. His mother recently married a man named Trent, a nice guy but anything but the father figure Richard needs. "Trent is my stepfather, and we're real cool," he says. "He treats me like a kid brother, and I treat him the same way. He's harmless and good-natured, and dumb as a box of rocks" (9). Skink becomes the guiding father the young boy needs. He teaches him how to drive, gives him a copy *Silent Spring*, Rachel Carson's classic 1962 book about the adverse effects of pesticides on the environment, and offers moral guidance about what he should do to make amends for a shoplifting incident he confesses to.

The instruction goes both ways. Skink plays his road-mix CD with songs by Creedence Clearwater Revival, Bob Dylan, and Led Zeppelin for Richard; Richard plays his iPod playlist for Skink, who likes the selections by the Black Keys and Jack Johnson, judges Adele not quite as good as Linda Ronstadt, and covers his ears and begins moaning "like a sick baboon" (103) when he hears a tune by Skrillex.

Richard also brings Skink up to date digitally. He explains to him what Wikipedia is and corrects him when he refers to Google as goggle. Sometimes, however, things get comically testy between student and teacher. When Richard mentions that Malley met Turbo in a chat room, Skink asks if that's something like a library. Richard explains that chat rooms are on the computer. "Come on, dude," he says, "they're virtual." "Stop calling me 'dude' or you'll virtually regret it," Skink fires back (67).

Hiaasen had heretofore employed single-word titles for his kids' books to distinguish them from his adult novels, which all have two-word titles. Using a three-word title may serve the purpose of signaling that *Skink—No Surrender* is unlike both his other kinds of fiction. His previous novels for kids were far more realistic than *Skink—No Surrender*, which is more like a fable or a fairy tale. Skink, for example, is all but superhuman here. Though Wikipedia claims he's dead, he's not. The first time we see him in the novel, however, it's as if he's rising up out of a sandy grave. He later emerges from what at the time appeared to be a watery grave. At one point he keels over after he suddenly begins chanting and dancing a jig, forcing Richard to begin performing CPR on his lifeless body. When Skink suddenly sits up, he complains that Richard has ruined a perfectly good trance. He also survives being hit by an eighteen-wheeler, a battle with an alligator, and twice being shot. The novel contains several other examples of contrived action and implausible behavior, which would be problematic in a realistic novel, but far less so in a fairy tale.

It differs from the earlier kids' books in other ways too. There's far less humor, with most of it coming from Skink. There's little satire in the novel, and the environmental theme that is usually in the forefront is largely pushed to the background here. There are several references to Rachel Carson and the sad reality of the extinction of so many species, but there's nothing for the kids to do about it. And while the problem of teenage girls being victimized by online predators is very a very real problem, it doesn't have quite the same widespread application to Hiaasen's audience of young readers that issues like bullying, child abuse, or worries about the safety of loved ones on active duty in far-off lands have.

5. Novels for Young Readers

Just before leaving the Choctawhatchee River, Richard is treated to the breathtaking sight of a beautiful fully grown ivory-billed woodpecker, the so-called "Lord God Bird" because that's what people said when they first saw one. That he is the third person in the novel to have actually seen with his own eyes one of the magnificent birds that is widely believed to be extinct is nothing short of miraculous. Could he have seen the last of its kind on the planet? Or the first of a new generation? Like a fairy tale, the novel gives the reader reason to hope it's the latter.

In addition to earning positive reviews and winning prestigious awards—*Hoot* was named a Newbery Honor book and *Flush* was included on the American Library Association's annual list of Best Books for Young Adults—Hiaasen's kids' novels have also been the subject of serious critical commentary. A pair of recent articles applaud his books for taking a new approach to the subject of environmentalism in children's literature.

In "Fighting Crime against Nature: Cross-Generation Environmental Activism in Carl Hiaasen's Young Adult Novels," Amy Cummins describes Hiaasen's kids' fiction as being "both subversive and mainstream" (8) in that he "convinces readers that radical action is acceptable to defend the environment when crimes occur against nature, and that children should lead this effort" (8). But unlike much of the literature in the genre that features young characters with "autonomy who challenge adults," Hiaasen's books make a strong case for a productive partnership between children and adults in achieving their environmental goals.

In "Little Saboteurs, Puerile Politics: The Child, the Childlike, and the Principled Life in Carl Hiaasen's Ecotage Novels for Young Adults," David Aitchison makes the case that *Hoot*, *Flush*, and *Scat* are "radical novels" that sanction "challenges to certain kinds of individualism, greed, and exploitation that thrive under our capitalist mode of production" (144). Like Cummins, he too welcomes Hiaasen's fresh approach to the genre: "In an era when the young adult book market is saturated with self-centered, escapist, and morbid fiction, Hiaasen makes a point of imagining young people with an expansive sense of who and where they are and what they might achieve" (156).

There's nothing dreary or didactic about Hiaasen's fiction for young readers. The novels are funny and entertaining with captivating stories, likable kids, and plenty of oddball adults. Most feature a pair of clever protagonists—a resourceful boy and a feisty female sidekick—who get things done. Hiaasen is also smart enough to pitch his message to his young readers in a way they can relate to. Rather than preach, "Save the Environment," he creates specific situations that are meaningful to them: e.g., who would want to kill cute little owls just to build another pancake house? Or, why is somebody dumping poop in the ocean where we swim?

Kurt Vonnegut, Jr., author of *Slaughterhouse-Five*, once said he wondered why people still bother to write books when those in power—presidents and senators and generals—don't read them. But then he realized that if you can catch people *before* they become presidents and generals and "poison their minds with humanity," you can "encourage them to make a better world" (Scholes 123). This is Hiaasen's strategy: remind young readers that nature is worth protecting and, more importantly, that they can do something about it. "Kids are born with a natural curiosity about nature and real compassion for wildlife.... I won't reach them all, but all it takes is one out of a hundred, one who becomes a purist and goes to the county commission meetings and hollers about some horrible development project" (Burke "Last").

What began as a one-book experiment has turned into something far more personally rewarding than Hiaasen had ever imagined. "Writing for kids was probably the smartest thing I ever did for my psyche," he says. "You get this tremendous response to the environmental message. Kids seem to be born with an innate passion for nature and wild things. It gives me hope, which is not something you get a lot of in the newspaper business. Kids have this unvarnished sense of right or wrong. They get the books; they get the humor" (Gilson).

6

Literary Influences

While Hiaasen has acknowledged the impact on him that comedians whose records he listened to with his dad when he was a kid (Mike Nichols and Elaine May, Bill Cosby, George Carlin) and books ranging from *Catcher in the Rye* to Woody Allen's *Without Feathers* had, the most important influences on his writing came from three novelists: John D. MacDonald, Joseph Heller, and Harry Crews.

John D. MacDonald was the most formative influence on *what* Hiaasen would write. Though not a native-born Floridian, MacDonald moved to Sarasota in 1952 and fell in love with the place. Over a career that spanned four decades until his death in 1986, he wrote some sixty-three novels, the most famous of which were the twenty-one novels about Travis McGee published between 1964 and 1985. McGee became a mouthpiece for MacDonald's opinions on a variety of subjects, but some of his most biting comments were aimed at the assault on Florida's natural beauty, which he saw being ravaged by overpopulation and unbridled development.

A self-described "salvage consultant" who helps people recover what has been stolen from them while also rescuing damsels in distress, McGee lived on a houseboat called "The Busted Flush" moored at Slip F-18, Bahia Mar in Fort Lauderdale, nor far from where Hiaasen lived. "Imagine the kick in discovering a clever action novel set in one's own hometown," he wrote in an introduction to a paperback re-issue of the series in 1994. "McGee and I ran on the same beaches, rambled the same roads, fished the same flats, ate at the same seafood joints, and avoided the same tourists" (viii).

But it wasn't Travis McGee he modeled himself on, it was his creator. "Most readers loved MacDonald's work because he told a rip-roaring yarn," he said. "I loved it because he was the first modern writer to nail Florida dead-center, to capture all its languid sleaze, racy sense of promise, and breath-grabbing beauty" (ix).

In *A Flash of Green* (1962), one of the first environmental novels published in America, MacDonald describes the battle between environmentalists who are trying to save a small bay on the West coast of Florida and local developers who want to fill it in so they can build a housing development there. One of his characters, who notes that the entire coastline is under siege by big-money developers, offers a parable that highlights the dire consequences of what is happening:

> Once upon a time there was a mountain peak with a wonderful view, so that people came from all over to stand on top of the mountain and look out. The village at the foot of the mountain charged a dollar a head to all tourists. But so few of them could stand on top of the mountain at the same time, they leveled the top of the mountain to provide more room and increase the take. This seemed to work, so they kept enlarging the area on top of the mountain. Finally they had a place up there that would accommodate ten thousand people, but by then the mountain was only forty feet high, and suddenly everybody stopped coming to see the view. This convinced them people were tired of views, so in the name of Progress and a Tourist Economy, they turned the flattened mountain into a carnival area, and every night you could see the lights and hear the music for miles around. They still attracted customers, but it was the kind of people who like carnivals instead of the kind of people who like beauty [189].

Elsewhere in the novel, MacDonald ridicules the effort to divert attention away from the disastrous consequences of such destructive actions:

> As the quiet and primitive mystery of the broad tidal bays disappeared, as the mangroves and the rookeries and the oak hammocks were uprooted with such industriousness the morning sound of construction equipment became more familiar than the sound of the mockingbird, the businessmen substituted the delights of pageants, parades and beauty contests [24].

Sprinkled throughout the McGee novels are bleak reminders of what progress has meant to Florida. The coastline has become so clogged with condominiums that McGee complains, "Had I not seen a boat for sale every few hundred yards, I would never have known I was within five hundred miles of salt water" (*Turquoise* 167). Thanks to the petrochemical stench produced by the "perpetual farting of the great god Progress" (*Empty* 32), the air has been poisoned. At one point McGee becomes so angry at the sight of chemical pollutants being belched into the air by a Borden phosphate and fertilizer plant that he stops to encourage his readers to write letters directly to members of the company's Board of Directors.

None of what happened to Florida had to happen. The fate of the state, McGee complains, is "in the hands of men whose sole thought was grab the money and run, cheap little politicians with blow-dried hair, ice-eyed old men from the North with devout claims about their duties to their share-

6. Literacy Influences

holders, big-rumped good old boys from the cattle counties with their fingers in the till right up to their cologned armpits" (xi).

Hiaasen never met MacDonald. He once sat near him and his wife at a Jimmy Buffett concert but couldn't summon up the courage to go over and introduce himself. Shortly before his death, MacDonald wrote a blurb for the cover of *Tourist Season*, Hiaasen's first novel, and also sent him a nice note about how much he enjoyed the book. He would also undoubtedly be heartened to know that Hiaasen has devoted his own writing to the very same thing Hiaasen praised him for doing: "MacDonald wanted his readers to do much more than see Florida. He seemed to want them to care about it as deeply as he did; celebrate it, marvel at it, laugh about it, grieve for it, and even fight for it" (x).

When Hiaasen first read Joseph Heller's comic masterpiece *Catch-22* as a teenager at his father's recommendation, he was blown away. He considers it "one of the most phenomenal novels in the English language" because of its ability to make the reader laugh while reading about one of the darkest subjects of all, war (Staskiewicz). What it taught him as a writer was that, "There are no limits. If you're good enough and if you believe enough, you can write about anything and make it funny and entertain" (Dunn). The comic novels he would write all reveal the strong influence of Heller's style of absurdist humor and stinging satire.

Catch-22 is both a hilarious comedy about war as well as a biting satire on all the nitwitted colonels and generals who see war mainly as a way to benefit themselves at the expense of the lives of so many of the young men under their command. John Yossarian is an Army Air Corps B-25 bombardier stationed on a small island off the coast of Italy during World War II. His main concern is simply trying to stay alive. The enemy, however, is not just the Germans who are attempting to shoot his plane down but also his superiors who keep raising the number of missions he must fly, steadily increasing the chances he will be shot down.

Heller's fictional world is a surreal one ruled by the absurdist logic of Catch-22, which states that anyone who is crazy must not be allowed to fly in combat. However, if you wish to be grounded so you don't have to fly any more dangerous missions, you must ask first. Here's the catch: If you do ask to be grounded, you can't be because anyone who wants to get out of combat duty isn't really crazy and therefore can't be grounded.

The novel is filled with comically absurd variations on the same maddening logic. For example, to forestall questions asked at meetings that the top brass don't want to answer, one colonel comes up with a rule stating that the only people who will be allowed to ask questions are those who never do. Soon, the only people who bother to attend are those who never ask questions, so the sessions are discontinued since it is impossible to educate people who never question anything.

Then there's this exchange between Major Major and a sergeant about when the men can see him in his office:

> "What shall I say to the people who do come to see you while you're here?"
> "Tell them I'm in and ask them to wait."
> "Yes, sir. For how long?"
> "Until I've left."
> "And then what shall I do with them?"
> "I don't care."
> "May I send them in to see you after you've left?"
> "Yes."
> "But you won't be here then, will you?"
> "No."
> "Yes, sir. Will that be all?"
> "Yes" [102].

Hiaasen's fictional world isn't as surreal as Heller's. His remains firmly rooted in the real world we all inhabit, and no matter how implausible some of what he describes might seem, he repeatedly reminds us that it is based on actual events. But he does follow Heller's example in other ways. One of Heller's favorite comic techniques is, like Hiaasen's, a statement that takes a corkscrew turn and ends with an unexpected punch line: "Nurse Cramer had a cute nose and a radiant, blooming complexion dotted with fetching sprays of adorable freckles that Yossarian detested" (173); "He got on well with his brothers and sisters, and he did not hate his mother and father, even though they had both been very good to him" (255).

Hiaasen also followed Heller's practice of creating comic biographies for many of his characters. Major Major is a prime example. At birth, his father gave him the middle name of Major, saddling him with the ridiculous name of Major Major Major. He also has to bear the burden of having an unfortunate resemblance to Henry Fonda, which forces him to go through life apologizing to everyone he meets for not really being Henry Fonda.

A man with few talents—"Even among men lacking all distinction he inevitably stood out as a man lacking more distinction than all the rest, and people who met him were always impressed by how unimpressive he was" (85)—four days after joining the Army, he's promoted to the rank of major by an IBM machine with a sense of humor. When he is later recommended for another promotion, the request is denied because the Army doesn't intend to lose the only Major Major Major Major it has.

Hiaasen was also likely influenced by Heller's acerbically satirical character portraits. Milo Minderbinder is a mess hall officer who goes into private business under the name of M & M Enterprises. As Hiaasen would often later do, Heller took something real—a statement by Charles E. Wilson, former head of General Motors, who reportedly said during his Senate confirmation hearings for the post of Secretary of Defense that, "What is good for General Motors is good for the country"—and exaggerated it for satirical purposes. Milo is in the business of war-profiteering and excuses everything he does as being good for all his shareholders, who exist in name only. His standard rationale is that, "What's good for M & M Enterprises is good for the country" (316).

For example, he first contracts with the American military to bomb the German-held bridge at Orvieto, then contracts with the German military to defend the bridge with antiaircraft fire. He charges both sides cost plus six percent, though he charges the Germans an additional thousand dollar bonus for every American plane he can shoot down on their behalf. As he explains it, "The Germans have the bridge, and we were going to bomb it, whether I stepped into the picture or not. I just saw a wonderful opportunity to make some profit out of the mission, and I took it. What's so terrible about that" (262)?

Car (1992) by Harry Crews is another novel that changed Hiaasen's life. He read it at age eighteen or nineteen when he was looking for new fiction set in his home state. Crews came up with a clever way to combine two American obsessions: love of cars and a desire to become famous. Thirty-year-old Herman Mack, "a dreamer of mad dreams" (17) whose family owns the largest car-wrecking business in Florida, one day declares, "I will eat a car. I will eat a car from bumper to bumper" (18).

A savvy entrepreneur arranges for the stunt to take place on a platform erected in front of his hotel, the largest in Jacksonville. Soon, TV cameras arrive to broadcast the event around the world. At six each evening, Herman eats a one-ounce piece of a brand-new Ford Mustang; at nine-thirty the following morning, he sits on a specially designed toilet and passes the piece of metal he ate the night before to the cheers of the gathered crowd.

"The whole concept was so warped," says Hiaasen, "I loved every word of it" ("On" 114). The novel showed how chaotic and bizarre Florida was becoming and fueled his own ambition to tell similar twisted stories. Like *Catch-22*, it confirmed his belief that, "basically anything's possible when you sit down to write. Anything."

7

Florida: Hiaasen's Muse

Carl Hiaasen maintains he needs to be angry to write, so it's a good thing he lives in Florida: "Living in Florida and having been born there, there's not a day that goes by that something doesn't piss me off" (Alter). His anger can be traced to when he was a young boy living an idyllic childhood on the edge of the Everglades, fishing from inner tubes, playing in the swamps, and catching snakes with his buddies. And then one day everything changed as the bulldozers began arriving to pave over his playground to make way for shopping malls. What happened to his neighborhood and to the rest of Florida as mindless development all but obliterated the natural beauty he grew up with has been the driving force behind all his writing.

No one can bring the old Florida back, but Hiaasen has devoted his entire writing career to reminding his fellow Floridians (and educating newcomers to the state) that what remains is worth fighting to preserve before it too disappears. The battle to save what's left has been a major theme in his reporting, his columns, and above all in some of the most raucously funny novels being written in America today.

Hiaasen admits that in his darker moments he sometimes fantasizes that the best thing to happen to Florida would be for "a force-five hurricane to blow through here and make us start all over again.... God didn't want condos on the beaches and some day he's going to tear the shit out of this place. That would be fine with me, separate out the people who really love this place" (Williams 14). In his writings, however, he takes a far more pragmatic approach by identifying the reasons behind the rape of Florida and exposing those who made (and are continuing to make) it happen.

Ironically, one cause of the problem is Florida's natural beauty itself. Who wouldn't want to live in a tropical paradise? People began arriving in record numbers, especially after the invention of air-conditioning made the summer months tolerable. But lack of intelligent planning and the desire of so many to cash in on the influx resulted in massive overpopulation and its dire consequences. "South Florida needs more people like the Sahara needs more sand," Hiaasen grumbles (*Dance* 217)—and yet they still come.

What facilitated the destruction was the vast army of lobbyists, lawyers, bankers, developers, building inspectors, inept planners, and corrupt politicians who have all embraced the belief that "the sound of bulldozers is the sound of money"(*Kick* 338), and damn the consequences. These are the folks who have turned a tropical paradise into what it is today: "Newark with palms trees" (*Tourist* 24). In Hiaasen's view, the main culprit is simply greed:

> In a place like Florida, there's no such word as 'enough'.... It's how many more people can we cram in and how much can we sell them and how much beach can we cut up into little tiny pieces and tell them this is their little piece of paradise. Florida is a place where growth itself is an industry. Basically, it's the operating mechanism of a cancer cell [Sutcliffe].

In *Sick Puppy*, Twilly Spree is devastated by the same kind of childhood experience that Hiaasen had. At age fourteen, he returned to Marco Island, a place where he fondly remembers collecting tropical seashells along the dune-fringed beaches when he lived there as a child. What he now sees horrifies him:

> The island had sprouted skyline: a concrete picket of towering hotels and high-rise condominiums. Waterfront, of course.... He hoped he was seeing a mirage, a trick of the fog and clouds, but when he glanced up, the hotels and condos were still there, looming larger than before. As the sun began to rise, the buildings cast tombstone shadows across the sand. Soon Twilly found himself standing in a vast block of shade—shade, on an open beach under a bright clear sky! He sunk to his knees and punched the hard-packed sand with both fists until his knuckles were skinned [*Sick* 24].

As he later explains to another character, "If you'd seen it when you were a kid and then now, you'd say it was a crime. You'd say somebody ought to have their nuts shot off for what they did. And you'd be right" (*Sick* 228). Hiaasen doesn't exactly shoot anyone's nuts off, but in his fiction he devises some outrageously fitting punishments for those who deserve it.

Hiaasen's novels include a few brief glimpses like this of what pre-development Florida once looked like:

> The vista from atop the poinciana was timeless and serene—a long string of egrets crossing the distant 'glades; a squadron of white pelicans circling a nearby bay; a pair of ospreys hovering kite-like above a tidal creek. It was a perfect picture and a perfect silence [*Nature* 225].

But his main strategy is to focus less on what has been lost and more on those actions that have resulted in, to quote the title of one of his collections of columns, a "paradise screwed." "They've taken everything that was perfect about Florida and destroyed it," he complains. "They've straightened the rivers, bulldozed the beaches, drained the Everglades. That to me is immoral.... I have no problem saying that most developers have the moral footing of drug dealers. It is the exact same thing" (Booth).

Among the worst offenders are all those elected officials who value the cash bribes they rake in more than natural beauty or who fail to even appreciate the beauty surrounding them. Congressman David Dilbeck in *Strip Tease* is guilty on both counts. As long as the bribes continue to come in he will gladly vote for whatever the Big Sugar growers in Florida want. He never for a moment agonizes over the far-reaching impact of cane growers flushing billions of gallons of waste into the Everglades because he "didn't understand what the fuss was all about. In truth, he didn't much care for the Everglades; it was torpid, swampy, crawling with bugs" (320).

Chaz Perrone in *Skinny Dip* is another example of the soulless cretins who aided and abetted in the destruction. He's a marine biologist who is hired by the owner of a huge farm operation to fake the readings of toxic levels in the water he's testing in the Everglades so his boss can continue to pollute it at will. How could he do this? Simple: "Nothing about nature awed, soothed or humbled him—not the solitude or the mythic vastness or the primordial ebb and flow. To Chaz, it was all hot, buggy, funky-smelling and treacherous" (*Skinny* 75).

It is largely the young characters in Hiaasen's novels for kids who still have a sense of openness that allows them to appreciate nature's beauty when they can still find it. In *Hoot*, young Roy Eberhardt, who had recently moved to Florida from Montana, is bowled over by an experience along a tidal creek: "Roy was dazzled by the wondrous quiet, the bushy old mangroves sealing off the place from the honking and hammering of civilization.... The creek was incredibly beautiful and wild; a hidden sanctuary, only twenty minutes away from his own backyard" (176). Not only does he agree to join his new friend Mullet Fingers in a campaign to save some burrowing owls from being buried under by bulldozers, he recognizes that the problem is bigger than that: it's all the birds and animals and wild places that are in danger of being wiped out if enough people don't do anything to stop it before it's too late.

Environmental devastation isn't the only crime that interests Hiaasen. Murder, kidnapping, robbery, corruption, fraud and assorted other criminal activities figure prominently in his novels. As the crime capital of America, Florida is fertile ground for a writer. "Miami is the best place in America to be a criminal," Hiaasen insists. "It is to hard-core felons what Disneyland is to Michael Jackson" (*Kick* 198). Sooner or later "every scheming shitwad in America turned up here ... such were the opportunities for predation" (*Skinny* 37). Hiaasen jokes that the police blotter in Florida "is a novel waiting to be written" (Beauregard). Thus is no surprise that an army of crime and mystery writers—John D. MacDonald, Charles Willeford, Elmore Leonard, Edna Buchanan, James W. Hall, Tim Dorsey, Tom Corcoran, Vicki Hendricks, Les Standiford, Randy Wayne White, Laurence Shames, John Lutz, to name but a dozen—have set their novels there.

Two recent essays on Hiaasen have suggested that South Florida has largely replaced Southern California as the symbol for much of what's wrong with contemporary America. According to Adam Gopnik, what he calls the "Florida-glare" crime novels of the past thirty years have supplanted the LA noir novels of the thirties and forties as a "mirror of American manners" (104) that captures the national condition. Crimes that in the noir tradition took place "melodramatically, at night," in Florida are now committed "matter-of-factly, in the middle of the day" (107). David M. Parker agrees, arguing that while Southern California as far back as Nathanael West's *Day of the Locust* (1939) has been presented as a "sprawling dystopia inhabited by narcissistic, self-indulgent people who deserve the consequences of fires and earthquakes," (307), today, thanks to writers like Hiaasen, Florida has become the new symbol of excess.

Why are so many Florida writers attracted to crime? In his preface to a collection of interviews with Florida crime writers, Steve Glassman jokingly suggests it might be because the outline of the state forms the shape of a gun. A better answer, he says, may be found in Florida's violent past: "From the very first Florida has been a land made noteworthy by crime. The Father of Spanish Florida murdered the putative Father of French Huguenot Florida" (3). Crime fiction, he goes on to say, "is the literary mode best able to investigate the social fabric of this state, which today still reflects its volatile past" (4).

Florida is also a rich source of weird behavior. Dave Barry once observed that, "If states were characters on *Seinfeld*, Florida would be Kramer: Every time it appears, the audience automatically laughs, knowing it's going to do some idiot thing" (4). To a writer like Hiaasen who is fascinated by examples of human folly and stupidity, South Florida is a "fountain of weird news" (Silet "Sun" 12) and a "24-hour freak show.... Inspiration rains down from the headlines every day" (Curley).

Hiaasen would like to take credit for having an extremely warped imagination, but he confesses that much of the craziness in his novels is simply ripped from the local newspapers. Readers outside the state assume he's making it all up; readers who live in Florida consider his books documentaries. Hiaasen says he simply takes what he reads about in the papers and then cranks up the absurdity just a bit. He also insists that he doesn't put anything in his novels, no matter how outrageous it seems, that couldn't actually happen. The problem is that it's hard to stay ahead of the curve of weirdness in Florida. He confesses he finds it frustrating when he's written something he thinks is about as sick as it gets and "the next day in the *Miami Herald* there's a headline that just makes me weep that I didn't think of it. It's worse than anything I could have thought of, you know, I mean, I just feel defeated" (Byrne).

With novels set in locations ranging from the panhandle to the Keys, Hiaasen has earned the title of Florida's "laureate of sun-kissed sleaze" (Sutcliffe). His love-hate relationship with the Sunshine State pretty much explains everything about him as a writer: "I can't imagine living anywhere as corrupt, overrun, mismanaged, and freak-infested as Florida," he says, but then adds, "I also can't imagine living anywhere as beautiful or so worth fighting for" (*Dance* 400).

8

Humor and Satire

Hiaasen's novels are often compared with those of Elmore Leonard, one of his literary heroes. Neither author writes traditional whodunits or conventional thrillers, although both freely borrow features for their own purposes. Neither uses an outline. Leonard once said that if he knew how his novel was going to end, there would be no point in bothering to write it. Both like to audition their characters to see how they talk and interact with one another, then allow them to shape the story. And finally, both prefer third-person narrative, which enables them to tell multiple stories they can use to fashion a fast-paced reading experience.

One significant difference between the two is that Leonard is primarily a storyteller who requires only a few characters and a situation before he begins writing. Before Hiaasen begins, he says he needs to be "ticked off about something. I have to have some sort of burr under my saddle before I can get rockin' and rollin' on these things. I have to be sustained by more than just an entertaining cast" ("How"). For him, storytelling and colorful characters are an effective way to make a point related to an issue he feels very strongly about. The "burr" under his saddle not only inspires the story, it also provokes the kind of stingingly absurd humor he's so good at.

Leonard is celebrated for humorous dialogue that arises naturally from his characters, many of whom are funny without necessarily being aware of it. Hiaasen, who has been described as "Elmore Leonard after several hits of nitrous oxide" (Bearden), has a much wider comic range. His humor comes from funny names, ridiculous characters, hilarious dialogue, outrageous plots, absurd situations, and the narrator's sarcastic commentary. But make no mistake about it. As funny as he is, Hiaasen is no mere jokester. For him, humor is serious business.

As far back as the satiric newsletter he wrote in high school, he recognized the value of using humor to make a serious point. Though he has often stated that his humor comes from anger, he avoids preaching or simply vent-ing. "Outrage in its natural state is not too salable," satirist Stan Freberg once wisely noted. "The hard part comes in covering the social message with the candy coating of humor. Otherwise, you end up as just another crackpot on a soap box" (Nachman 187). Hiaasen understands that if he can use humor to address a serious subject, readers who disagree with him might still be able to enjoy a few laughs.

Being funny, and especially being funny and serious at the same time, is hard work. Hiaasen never laughs or smiles while writing: "When I come home for lunch after writing all morning," he notes, "my wife says I look like I just came home from a funeral. This is not bragging. This is an illness. I've awakened in the middle of the night horrified over an adjective or adverb I used during the day" (Solomon). Writing humor is tricky business because it's so easy to fail. "If you're off by half a beat," Hiaasen says, "it can fall pretty flat" (Moore). And so he agonizes over every word, every bit of dialogue to get the tone just right. In response to a friend who once asked when he was ever going to write a serious novel, he replied, "You don't understand. This stuff is deadly serious to me" (Patterson).

A distinction needs to be made between humor and satire. Humor is designed to make you laugh; satire is designed to make you laugh *at* someone or something. Satire can be formally described as a "literary genre that uses irony, wit and sometimes sarcasm to expose humanity's vices and follies, giving impetus to change or reform through ridicule" (Murfin 426). Hiaasen employs all the aforementioned techniques plus burlesque, caricature, lampoon, parody, mimicry, and mockery to ridicule his targets. Politicians don't mind if you yell and scream at them. They get used to it. But they hate to be made fun of, so that's what Hiaasen aims to do: "I love to ruin their day," he says. "The more I can humiliate them in print, the happier I am" (Byrne).

Satires can range from a gentle needling to an all-out evisceration. Literary historians divide satire into two main types—Horatian and Juvenalian—named after two important early Roman satirists. Horace (65–8 BC) was a gentle satirist whose works took the form of helpful fatherly advice. Juvenal (c.55–c.127 AD) was known for his angry diatribes against his fellow citizens. Hiaasen's satires clearly fall into the Juvenalian category. Like Hiaasen, it was anger at what he saw around him that was the burr under Juvenal's saddle: "It is difficult NOT to write satire," he wrote. "What human being / Has such iron control of himself in this city of evil / As to hold his tongue" (Juvenal 18). Like Hiaasen, he too ridiculed examples of human greed, hypocrisy, and folly, and was also disgusted by the physical deterioration of

Rome itself, where grassy areas were being replaced by marble monuments, shoddy construction was rampant, and the streets were crowded with wheeled traffic.

Hiaasen differs from Juvenal in one key area. Juvenal's anger sometimes overwhelmed him, and he ended up writing a series of rants. Hiaasen never forgets that as angry as he is, expressing it through humor is a far more effective way of getting his message across to the reader. But whether he's making a serious point or simply having fun with his characters, his primary aim is to make his readers laugh.

In his book on satire, Dustin Griffin claims that satire is a form of witty sadism in the sense that, "both satirist and reader derive pleasure from participation in an act of rhetorical violence" (162). It is certainly true that Hiaasen derives great personal pleasure from humiliating his targets, but not only because of the suffering he causes them. He can also get satisfaction from the artful way he causes their discomfort. Similarly, Hiaasen's readers take pleasure at seeing his targets suffer well-deserved humiliation, while at the same time they can enjoy the entertaining way the attack is made.

Much of the humor in Hiaasen's novels is designed to be purely entertaining. It starts with something as simple as the Dickensian names he chooses for many of his characters: Dean Ryall Cheatworth, Race Maggad III, Minton Tweeze, Fremont Spores, Methane Drudge, Reynaldo Flemm, Palmer Stoat, Jon David Ambergrodt, Moldy Moldowsky. He tries to come up with names that have a certain look on the page and sound to the ear. "I want readers to read the name once and not forget it," he explains. "I don't want them to be at page 100 turning back to figure out who that character was" (Smith). But he wants to get a laugh too.

As for his plots, Donald E. Westlake, who knew a thing or two himself about how to tell a funny story, said that Hiaasen "would not waste your time with the kind of story that anybody could tell." His riotously funny plots, which defy easy summary, are marvels of comic inventiveness. He begins by assembling a rich assortment of loopy goofballs and creepy villains that he hopes will produce funny story lines he can then juggle into a fast-paced narrative. His outlandish characters and their zany behavior result in what Alan Gibbs calls "cartoon realism"(76), the model for which is far from Disney cuteness. Instead, as Adam Gopnik has suggested, his tales are closer in spirit to the work of famed animator Tex Avery, creator of Bugs Bunny and Daffy Duck: "fast and sinuous and able to get his grotesques down in Day-Glo colors and fastidiously minimal gestures" (105).

8. Humor and Satire

Inspired by the example of Joseph Heller's *Catch-22*, one of his most influential literary models, Hiaasen fills his novels with hilarious examples of absurd human behavior. Some—like the woman who crashes her car while shaving her pubic area, or the guy who steals wheelchairs for a living—are based on actual incidents he reads about in the newspapers. Most, however, are products of his own twisted imagination: e.g., the drunken man who is kicked out of the KKK for accidentally setting the Klan leader on fire instead of the cross he was trying to light; the extremely hairy man who is shot by a poacher who mistakes him for a bear, leaving him with a bullet painfully lodged in his butt crack causing him to become addicted to fentanyl patches which he steals from the backs of sedated cancer patients.

He even finds a way to wring some absurd ironic humor out of tragic events: a man is killed by a sky diver who falls on him while he's practicing fly casting in his backyard; a Formula 1 race car driver is run over and killed one sunny afternoon while jaywalking on Bleecker Street in Greenwich Village; a racist keels over dead from a heart attack while trying to scrape an "Obama for President" bumper sticker off a neighbor's car.

Hiaasen is also a gifted caricaturist. In his columns, the targets of his satire are real individuals whom he identifies by name, which limits him to their actual behavior. In his fiction, he is free to create characters whose behavior can be as outlandish as he wishes. As a columnist, even if he knew about the private sexual habits of an individual, he wouldn't be able to mention them in print. But in a novel if he wants to ridicule a U.S. Congressman who makes love to a woman's laundry lint or a land developer who is paying a pair of prostitutes to undergo a series of plastic surgeries to satisfy his fantasy of having identical twin real-life Barbie dolls, he's free to do so.

He usually begins with behavior he wants to expose—polluting, bulldozing nature, trashing the environment, taking bribes, fraud of all kinds—and then creates a character to represent that evil. He devises a hilarious back story for that character and then keeps adding additional comic details. Though the exaggerations sometimes push the bounds of believability, the crimes these characters represent are anything but unusual or unrealistic.

His colorful characters are reminiscent of those of another Southern writer, Flannery O'Connor, whose creations are often described as "grotesques." O'Connor, a Roman Catholic writer who knew her audience did not necessarily share her religious beliefs, developed a method of exaggerated characterization that was aimed at grabbing the reader's attention: "To the hard of hearing you shout," she said, "and to the almost blind you draw large and startling figures" (113). If in his humor Hiaasen can be described as being like Elmore Leonard on nitrous oxide, in the creation of his outlandish characters he can also be described, as Julie Sloan Brannon has done, as being "like O'Connor on speed" (48). Hiaasen simply takes things a step further than O'Connor, pumping up similarly outsized characters with exaggerated features that certainly command the reader's attention.

Some of Hiaasen's characters are physically grotesque: Chemo in *Skin Tight* is six-foot-nine, has a severely disfigured face and a Weed Whacker attached to his arm; Snapper in *Stormy Weather* has a badly misaligned jaw that is further misshapen when The Club, a car-theft protection device, is clamped to it; Tool in *Skinny Dip* is so matted with thick body hair that he is mistaken for a bear and is shot by a hunter.

However, the real grotesques in Hiaasen's fiction are those of the moral kind—land developers, polluters, politicians on the take who have no sense of the value of anything other than money. Hiaasen has little interest in cold-blooded killers or armed robbers. He is instead drawn to supposedly upstanding citizens who should know better—wealthy businessmen, elected public officials, doctors, etc. What is so grotesque about them is moral rather than physical: it is the corruption in their souls. How can you blithely bulldoze over a beautiful piece of nature just so you can build another pancake restaurant or shopping mall? What would possess a wealthy farm owner to continue flushing pesticides into the Everglades or a casino-boat owner to dump raw sewage directly into the ocean near a public beach? Simple greed. These are the true criminals in his books and for villains like them, no punishment is too outrageous.

What holds everything together in Hiaasen's novels is the distinctive voice of the narrator, which is anything but a simple objective reporter of character and action. It has a distinct personality, one characterized by a relentlessly sardonic attitude towards the characters it describes. While some notable comedians like Jonathan Winters and Robin Williams have a rare talent for on-the-spot improvisation, others like Richard Pryor, George Carlin, and Chris Rock rely more on two things: 1) cleverly crafted lines they have tested and refined over and over again; and 2) a stage persona with a distinctive comic voice to deliver them. The same is true of Hiaasen. He does all the behind-the-scenes hard work of carefully shaping his sentences and perfecting the language, timing, tone, and pace of everything. Then he hands it over to his narrator whose delivery makes it all sound so effortless. Characters and actions are recounted in a deadpan voice that never seems the least bit surprised by the craziness it recounts.

8. Humor and Satire

It's a perfect vehicle for delivering goofy similes—"chatty as a cockatoo on PCP" (*Skinny* 5); "flapping like a spastic fruit fly" (*Razor* 89); "blinking like a toad in a puddle of piss" (*Bad* 147); "sweating like a constipated sumo wrestler" (*Star* 54); howling "like a bobcat in a stump grinder" (*Razor* 308)—and statements that veer off into an unexpected stinging putdown—"Of the millions of people who weren't sure which direction the Gulf Stream ran, he was probably the only one to have an advanced degree in a marine science" (*Skinny* 57); "Bodean Gazzer hadn't had sex in eleven months, his excuse for celibacy being that it was against the Bible to consort with nonwhite women, and all the white women he met demanded too much money" (*Lucky* 267).

What makes Hiaasen such an effective satirist? 1) It comes to him naturally in terms of his outlook on things, which he describes as "pointed and confrontational" (Silet "Sun" 11); 2) He's been honing his skill for almost fifty years, beginning with the alternative newsletter he created in high school; 3) His primary targets—greedy developers with an utter disregard for nature, polluters, corrupt politicians, incompetent doctors, frauds and phonies of every stripe—are ones that most readers would readily agree ought to be humiliated; 4) He is flexible, able to adapt his satire to his different audiences, i.e., readers of his newspaper columns, his adult fiction, his kids' novels; and 5) He is genuinely funny. Not every satirist can hit the mark while being as consistently entertaining as he is.

Hiaasen is widely celebrated as a serious environmental advocate, an old-fashioned moralist, and a scold of bad behavior. But above all else, he's an entertainer. The ratio between humor and satire varies from book to book, but what never changes is his ability to give his readers plenty to laugh about.

9

An Interview with Carl Hiaasen

DG: You have said that you learned to read at age four. How did you manage to do that at such an early age?

CH: When I was growing up we had two newspapers delivered to the house, the *Miami Herald* in the morning and the *Fort Lauderdale News* in the afternoon. The Yankees had their spring training in Fort Lauderdale, so I became a baseball fan when I was pretty young and would rush out to get the sport scores every day. We always had newspapers in the house so I learned to read by reading aloud to my mom and dad. I kind of figured it out that way. By the time I got to first grade I already knew how to read, so they advanced me a grade in school.

DG: You asked your dad for a typewriter when you were six. What inspired you to begin writing?

CH: Most writers I know will tell you the same thing—it was the joy of reading and the whole aspect of storytelling. I remember writing stories at an early age, little funny things. Once my dad got me the typewriter, it was sports stories, just whatever was going on in the neighborhood in the kickball league or softball. I would come home and type up whatever happened at the game and give it to my friends. I remember the fun of putting one sentence after another and creating something, as well as the instant feedback of having someone want to read it.

We always had books in the house and my parents encouraged me to read, but there was no prescribed reading. I enjoyed reading fiction very early on. At third grade in our meager school library they had these instant sports biographies of Willy Mays and Hank Aaron and Mickey Mantle which I burned through. I'm sure they weren't particularly well written but nonetheless it was fun going in there and reading. The natural next step is inspiring you to do the same thing. You read something, you close the book and look at the author's name, and you start wondering: How did he get a gig like this?

9. An Interview with Carl Hiaasen

How cool would it be to be able to write something like this? And then you start thinking about doing it yourself.

DG: What do you remember about writing your own stories?

CH: In middle school we had a very long bus ride, so I would write stories in longhand in a spiral notebook that I thought were funny and showed them to my friends on the bus. In high school I started a little underground newsletter, *More Trash*, that was typed on an old typewriter and run off on a mimeograph machine in the school office. I'd just hand out copies in the halls. It was supposed to be sort of informational to augment the lame high school newspaper we had, but I turned it into a commentary. It was really just a smart-ass rag, but I remember the kids would stop me in the hall and tell me how funny it was and how much they liked it. I remember that the administration of the high school wasn't very happy, and I liked the way that felt too.

DG: Where did you get your sense of humor from?

CH: My dad was a pretty serious dude. He did have a great sense of humor, but he wasn't what you would call a mirthful Norwegian. There aren't a lot of those. But I do remember when I was young he would bring home comedy albums and play them. We listened to Bob Newhart, Alan Sherman, Shelly Berman, and Jonathan Winters, who was a genius. My dad brought home the first Bill Cosby album that came out. We lived in Plantation, which you would never call a diverse community, and we were way out west by the Everglades. It wasn't like we were in the middle of the cultural stream or a diverse area. We would listen to them and he loved them.

I also remember watching Ed Sullivan and Dean Martin's Variety Show and they'd always have a comic on. One of those shows was where we first saw George Carlin, and I remember my dad bringing home a couple of his albums, which at the time could be fairly shocking. He was a pretty straitlaced guy and so was my mother, who was raised in a strict Catholic house and was trying without success to raise us the same way. Those were great times. It wasn't a somber household, but at the same time my dad wasn't the kind of guy to crack a lot of jokes. But he loved humor.

I never consciously said I want to grow up and be a stand-up comic. But what I'd get from listening to these comedians is a sense of timing. How a joke works. I remember when I was in my freshman year in college at Emory, I thought my dream job would be to write jokes for the *Tonight Show*. I would send stuff to Johnny Carson's office hoping someone would notice and want me to come out and be a writer. They never did, but then I was only seventeen years old.

While at Emory I was also writing a humor column. Even then I was interested in the structure not of how a joke sounded to the ear when it was spoken but the way it landed on the page, the way it had to be written to get a laugh. Somehow instinctively you know when a line is going to get a laugh. It has the right rhythm, the right word. You start to learn what's funny and what isn't. Once I began doing a newspaper column my idols were Art Buchwald and Russell Baker. I remember I once collected a bunch of my sophomoric college columns and sent them to Buchwald never expecting to hear back. But I did get a beautiful two-sentence letter from him saying, "Dear Carl, Your columns are very funny. If you keep writing them I'll have to kill you."

DG: You've said that you never laugh while writing something funny and that after a day of writing, you look like you've just come from a funeral. Why is writing comedy so difficult?

CH: I've talked to Dave Barry about it a little bit, and he's one of the funniest guys around. He says the same thing, it's really serious stuff. Both of us have talked about how you know when a line you've written is funny. Some part of your brain is laughing and saying, "That works, don't change a comma, don't change a syllable." But at the time you're writing it, you're dead serious because it's so easy to flop, to have a line fall dead on the page. If you're off by just a little bit, whether it's a piece of dialogue or just a throwaway part of a sentence, then it's all the way wrong. It's flat and doesn't work so you agonize and work it over and over.

If you're a conscientious writer and you're looking at something you wrote for the fifteenth or twentieth time, and frequently that's how many times I'll go through a chapter until I get it where I want, there's nothing fresh in it so you're not laughing. You still have to have enough trust in yourself to know that it works or doesn't work. You may not be laughing, but you damn well better know if you're funny or not.

DG: You were an English major at Emory and while there helped write two novels for a doctor friend named Neil Shulman. Were you yourself thinking about becoming a novelist at that time?

CH: I knew I wanted to write. I was just seventeen or eighteen when I met Neil for the first time. He just had a big stack of papers and said, "I want to make this into a book." There were a lot of funny stories in there, but it was going to be a structural challenge and would also involve polishing dialogue, bringing characters together, and working on storylines. I had never tackled anything as big as that before. Also, it was a piece of his life, not mine, so I had a big responsibility, but I think at the back of my mind I probably thought it would be fun to do this someday on my own.

I didn't know if the book, *Finally.... I'm a Doctor*, was ever going to be published. When he called me a couple of years later and said Scribner's was going publish it, I was blown away. I was thrilled for him because he had worked so hard at getting it published, but I also thought to myself, "Maybe I can figure out how to do this." We later did another one, and that one was made into a movie. By that time I was a full-time reporter, so I couldn't really give any thought to going out and starting to write novels. That didn't come until later when I met Bill Montalbano.

DG: Most crime writers tend to write a series of books with the same main character. With the exception of your last two novels, you create new characters for each of your books. Why did you decide not to use a series character?

CH: After *Skin Tight* came out, my editor liked the character of Mick Stranahan and said why don't we just do a series with him. I didn't want to do that. I liked some characters well enough and thought I could bring them back and have them appear in different novels, but that's a little different. I always wanted to start from scratch with a clean protagonist. I wanted to stay fresh and felt using the same character would get stagnant after a while and I would get weary of it.

I know the most commercially successful novelists have characters they can bring out every year. It's a great source of security knowing that the audience is waiting for that character. They're reliable and the readers love them. But I'd get bored. The danger when you bring the main character back several times in a row is that you start assuming your reader knows the character backwards and forwards, so you tend to get a little lazy. Secondly, you start putting them into a mystery or crime formula, which I've never used. I don't consider myself either a mystery novelist or a crime novelist, although there are elements of both in my novels.

DG: Instead of using an outline, you create a fresh group of characters each time and let them determine the story. What are the hazards of such an approach?

CH: The hazards of doing that are evident in the first draft of every chapter I write. There is a security in knowing where something is going. I usually have a premise in my mind. I see a diving board and though I'm not sure what's at the bottom, I know that's the board I'm jumping off of. The hazards are that you lose control of the characters and/or the plot. The fun of it for me is being surprised by the characters, though they can also lead you astray and you have so many strings to tie together at the end that it becomes more challenging.

When Bill Montalbano and I were writing, we had an outline because we were writing separately and we had to stay in synch. He was working on this character, I was writing on another character, or he was on chapter seven and I was on chapter eight. So by necessity we had to be organized. Many times he was in another part of the world and there was no Internet. We were flying blind until we'd get back together again to edit each other and the whole piece. I envy in some way the discipline of having an outline when you know what is in every chapter and you know how the book is going to end. It's a road map and you can write a lot faster like that. On the other hand, it's so much fun to not know. About a third of the way through, when I have the cast pretty well assembled, I probably have a good sense of who is going to be standing in the last act. How everything shakes down, I don't know. I depend a lot on the characters to lead me to the possibilities. At the same time, I'm always poaching from newspaper stories and getting weird ideas from real news events that I'm trying to weave in. I'll see a story about a weird character and think this guy opens up a whole new subplot possibility.

It's a high-wire act and is very stressful, especially when you're two-thirds of the way through and you still don't know how the novel is going to end. The last third of the book is brutal because I'm trying to pull it all together. Sometimes the end comes in a flash and it works out great. I've thought about spending more time trying to organize a plot in my mind before I get going, but it just doesn't suit my style. I don't think that while you're writing humor and satire, outlining is necessarily a good thing. I've always felt that outlines were like writing in handcuffs and I didn't enjoy that.

DG: Stand-up comics get an immediate response to their humor when the audience laughs. How do writers get that kind of response that tells them their humor is working?

CH: I've had the pleasure of being in an airport and seeing somebody reading one of my books. At first, I was horrified and wanted to run the other way. But I've actually seen a person laugh while reading it. There's no better feeling—I don't know who that person is or where they're going, but for at least one little part of their day they were getting some pleasure out of something I wrote. One value of book tours is that you get to meet your readers and that part is fun, hearing what they like about your book or what it meant to them. This is especially true of kids, who are incredibly loyal and frank and insightful. That's what keeps you going, that feedback. Generally, you're just a bundle of insecurity.

DG: Your books all have a complicated narrative with frequent shifts from one story to another. How do you juggle so many story lines? Do you write one subplot and then break it up, or do you keep switching story lines as you write?

CH: The best analogy is writing in scenes. Sometimes I'll experiment with a story line that doesn't go anywhere and I'll have to start over with another. But the best way to describe it is you reach a high point or a point of high momentum with one character in one scene and then you cut, like a smash cut, to another scene. That's how the story line propels itself. But I don't write the novel in advance. A lot depends on the characters and what they're up to and what I think they're capable of doing or pulling off. Sometimes I feel like they are sort of streaming out of control on me and they all have to lead back to the same place. That's the thing I always have to keep in mind as I send these strangers off: in the end they all have to come together somehow and I don't know how that is. I want to keep them manageable, but it's tricky and some days I do it better than others and in some books I do it better than others. I'm always amused when critics infer that I know what I'm doing with these things. Frequently, I start out and I don't know, I'm counting on something to click and it's all going to make some sense.

DG: Have you ever had to abandon a novel because it wasn't working?

CH: No. In the newspaper business you don't have that luxury. Your editor doesn't want to hear that the story you're writing isn't working and he needs it by tomorrow morning. So you just don't quit on things. The other part of newspaper training is that you never throw anything away—you're gathering stuff you may not use in the story for tomorrow's paper, but you may use it on the weekend. So I think my instinct is not to throw anything away.

Also, I sort of have this deadline sense. I don't want to waste a couple of months of my life writing five chapters I'm going to throw away. There was a time when you were young and there wasn't an editor waiting for your manuscript that you might have the luxury of being able to say, "This sucks, I'm going to throw it away." Now, when there's a lot at stake and there are people waiting—the graphics department is waiting to do the jacket, and they want to put it in the catalog—you up your game to the point where you're going to make it work. I've been lucky enough to have some of the best editors ever, so it's not like they are cracking the whip, but you just feel, "OK, I'm going to do what I have to do to make it work."

DG: Has the process of writing a novel changed for you over time?

CH: When I was working with Bill Montalbano, we were working on typewriters. We were literally cutting and pasting and gluing papers together and using magic markers. It was a much more cumbersome process to revise and edit, improve and polish. Now with a computer and a word-processing program there's really no excuse to have even a misplaced adjective. Also, fact-checking is now so luxurious with Google. The other day I needed to know the size of the Crow Indian reservation in Montana. In the old days that was a trip to the library. Now it's two seconds on the Internet. There's no excuse now to screw up. If you screw up, it's because you're lazy.

DG: Which of your novels gave you the most trouble to write? Which the least?

CH: *Tourist Season* was probably the easiest because I had nothing to lose and it was a story I wanted to tell. It was fun and I didn't even know if it was going to be published. I felt more freedom and less risk with that novel. If I look back on what was going on in my life at the time, I could tell you that some were incredibly difficult to write. Writing is what gets you through some tough times and I think after my divorce it was a very difficult time. The only thing that was anchoring me to what would pass for sanity was the novel I was working on at the time, *Lucky You*. That's not a reflection on my ex-wife at all. We get along fine. It's just an obstacle to any kind of writing if you have a lot of stuff going on in your personal life. I think it's a particular obstacle if you're trying be funny and the stuff in your life isn't particularly funny. It's challenging. I was reluctant to look back on that particular book very much because I was afraid it wasn't what it should have been. But the book turned out fine. However, you do associate a particular work with what you remember you were going through at the time.

DG: What role do editors play in your writing process?

CH: I was with a wonderful editor named Neil Nyren for my first three novels. He was terrific. I didn't have any inclination to leave Putnam's. In fact, they wanted me to stay. They do a great job with commercial fiction, and I think they would have loved for me to write a Mick Stranahan series. I'm just not wired to do that—or maybe not disciplined enough. I can't stay enamored of one character that long. My agent, Esther Newberg, said that Sonny Mehta, who was with Knopf, the most prestigious publishing house, wanted to meet me. She said he loved *Double Whammy*. So I met with him and told him that the problem with my books is they don't fit into any category. He said, "I wouldn't want to publish them if they did." So I said I'd like to try a book with him. And that's how we got started.

Twice he's said, "I like the character, but it just doesn't fit in the novel." It was a pain in the ass going back and erasing the footprints of a character in the novel. But both times he was right. His sensibilities are so good that I trust him and I'll go back and work, work, work until he thinks it's good enough. In terms of shaping the novel, I'll usually send the first five chapters and he'll send me some responses. When I ask if I should go back and rewrite, his response is always the same: "Just keep writing." The newspaper person in me wants to say, I can go back and fix this right now. He says no, don't lose the momentum, just keep writing. I'm very blessed to have been involved with the people I have been with from the beginning. I am so lucky. I haven't had any bad experiences to talk about, as some writers do.

Bibliography

Works by Carl Hiaasen

Novels for Adults [original publication dates are in brackets]

Bad Monkey. New York: Knopf, 2013 [2013].
Basket Case. New York: Knopf, 2002 [2002].
Double Whammy. New York: Grand Central Publishing, 2005 [1987].
Lucky You. New York: Knopf, 1997 [1997].
Naked Came the Manatee [with Elmore Leonard, Dave Barry, et al.]. New York: Putnam, 1996. [1996].
Native Tongue. New York: Knopf, 1991 [1991].
Nature Girl. New York: Knopf, 2006 [2006].
Razor Girl. New York: Knopf, 2016 [2016].
Sick Puppy. New York: Knopf, 2000 [2000].
Skin Tight. New York: Berkley Books, 2010 [1989].
Skinny Dip. New York: Knopf, 2004 [2004].
Star Island. New York: Knopf, 2010 [2010].
Stormy Weather. New York: Knopf, 1995 [1995].
Strip Tease. New York: Knopf, 1993 [1993].
Tourist Season. New York: Warner Books, 1987 [1986].

Novels for Young Readers

Chomp. New York: Ember, 2013 [2012].
Flush. New York: Knopf, 2007 [2005].
Hoot. New York: Knopf, 2002 [2002].
Scat. New York: Knopf, 2009 [2009].
Skink—No Surrender. New York: Ember, 2015 [2014].

Novels Written with William D. Montalbano

A Death in China. New York: Atheneum, 1984 [1984].

Powder Burn. New York: Vintage/Black Lizard, 1998 [1981].
Trap Line. New York: Vintage Crime, 1998 [1982].

Short Stories

"The Edible Exile." Byliner, 2013. Kindle Edition.
"Tart of Darkness." *Sports Illustrated.* 18 Feb. 2003.

Nonfiction Books

Assume the Worst: The Graduation Speech You'll Never Hear. Illustrated by Roz Chast. New York: Knopf, 2018.
The Downhill Lie: A Hacker's Return to a Ruinous Sport. New York: Knopf, 2008.
Team Rodent: How Disney Devours the World. New York: Ballantine, 1998.

Journalism

"The Bird Snatchers." *Miami Herald Tropic.* 10 Oct. 1982: 9–12.
Dance of the Reptiles: Selected Columns. ed. Diane Stevenson. New York: Vintage, 2014.
"Dangerous Doctors: A Medical Dilemma." *Miami Herald.* 25 Feb.-3 Mar. 1979.
"Key West: Smuggler's Island." *Miami Herald.* 16–21 Mar. 1980.
Kick Ass: Selected Columns of Carl Hiaasen. ed. Diane Stevenson. Gainesville: University Press of Florida, 1999.
"Killer: The Life and Death of a Cocaine Cowboy." *Miami Herald Tropic.* 3 Jan. 1982: 9–19.
"A Nation for Sale: Corruption in the Bahamas." *Miami Herald.* 23–28 Sept. 1984.

Bibliography

"North Key Largo: The Last Stand." *Miami Herald*. 25-27 July 1982.

Paradise Screwed: Selected Columns of Carl Hiaasen. ed. Diane Stevenson. New York: Putnam, 2001.

Miscellaneous Nonfiction

"Books that influenced me, changed me, surprised me." *Live Talks Los Angeles*. 13 Aug. 2010. Web. 10 Jan. 2017.

Foreword. *I'll Sleep When I'm Dead: The Dirty Life and Times of Warren Zevon*. By Crystal Zevon. New York: Ecco, 2007.

"How I Write." *The Writer* 116:6 (June 2003): 66.

"Inside the Box: Carl Hiaasen." *MidCurrent*. 11 Sept. 2011. Web. 14 Aug. 2017.

Introduction. *The Best American Mystery Stories 2007*. ed. Carl Hiaasen. New York: Houghton Mifflin, 2007: xiii-xvi.

Introduction. *The Quick Red Fox*. By John D. MacDonald. New York: Fawcett, 1995.

"John D. and Me: Carl Hiaasen." *Ticket Sarasota*. 15 July 2016. Web. 13 Sep. 2017.

"The Last Days of Florida Bay." *Sports Illustrated*. 18 Sept. 1995: 76-87.

"Last of the Falling Tide." In *Heart of the Land: Essays on Last Great Places*. ed. Joseph Barbato and Lisa Weinerman. New York: Pantheon, 1994: 71-77.

"The O.J. Effect." In *Deadline Artists: Scandals, Tragedies, and Triumphs*. ed. John Avlon, Jesse Angelo, and Errol Louis. New York: Overlook Press, 2012: 123-24.

"On *Car* by Harry Crews." In *The Books That Changed My Life: Reflections by 100 Authors, Actors, Musicians, and Other Remarkable People*. ed. Bethanne Patrick. New York: Regan Arts, 2016: 114-226.

"Real Life, That Bizarre and Brazen Plagiarist." *New York Times*. 24 Apr. 2000. Web. 12 Jan. 2017.

Selected Videos

"BookExpo America 2014: Carl Hiaasen." *YouTube*. 30 May 2014. Web. 15 May 2017.

"Carl Hiaasen: Art & Ideas at the Jewish Community Center of SanFrancisco." *YouTube*. 13 Sep. 2016. Web. 26 Aug, 2017.

"Carl Hiaasen: 2016 National Book Festival." Library of Congress. *YouTube*. 1 Dec. 2016. Web. 26 May 2017.

"Carl Hiaasen—*Star Island*." WGBHForum. *YouTube*. 2 Aug. 2010. Web. 25 April 2017.

"Carl Hiaasen in Conversation with Carolyn Kellogg." *Live Talks Los Angeles*. Vimeo. 13 Sept. 2010. Web. 12 April 2017.

"Carl Hiaasen takes us on a journey through his creative process." Florida International University. *YouTube*. 10 Apr, 2013. Web. 24 Mar. 2017.

"Carl Hiaasen Talking About Writing: Interview with Stacey Cochran." *The Artist's Craft*. *YouTube*. 31 Jan. 2013. Web. 15 Jan. 2017.

"A Conversation with Linwood Barclay." Appel Salon-Toronto Public Library. *YouTube* 20 Sept. 2016. Web. 25 April 2017.

"An Evening with Carl Hiaasen." *Southern Voices*. *YouTube*. 7 Mar. 2008. Web. 26 Apr. 2017.

"Florida: 'A Paradise of Scandals.'" *60 Minutes*. *YouTube*. 17 April 2005. Web. 12 Jan. 2017.

"Florida Sunshine Coalition Summit with Guest Speaker Carl Hiaasen." *YouTube*. 20 Nov. 2015. Web. 23 Mar. 2017.

"Margaret Atwood & Carl Hiaasen: Live from the New York Public Library." *YouTube*. 17 Sept. 2013. Web. 22 Oct. 2017.

"Talking Volumes 2016: Carl Hiaasen." MPR.org. *YouTube*. 21 Sept. 2016. Web. 25 April 2017.

"WSJ Book Club: Carl Hiaasen on 'Money.'". *YouTube*. 21 Jan. 2015. Web. 25 May 2017.

"Panel Discussion on Life and Politics in Florida: Carl Hiaasen and Dave Barry" Rancho Mirage Writers Festival. C-SPAN. 28 Jan. 2017. Web. 21 Feb. 2017.

Website

carlhiaasen.com

Secondary Sources

Acree, Cat. "Florida: Stranger than fiction." *BookPage*. 26 Mar. 2012. Web. 8 Dec. 2017.

Adams, Tim. "Scourge of the Scumbags." *Observer* (London). 1 July 2000. Web. 16 Aug. 2017.

Aitchison, David. "Little Saboteurs, Puerile

Bibliography

Politics: The Child, the Childlike, and the Principled Life in Carl Hiaasen's Ecotage Novels for Young Adults." *Children's Literature Association Quarterly* 40:2 (Summer 2015): 141–160.

Allen, Jamie. "Hiaasen Nightmare: Disney Devours the World." *CNN Interactive*. 29 May 1998. Web. 27 Oct. 2017.

Alter, Alexandra. "Satirizing the Sunshine State." *Wall Street Journal*. 21 July 2010. Web. 27 June 2017.

Ashbrook, Tom. "The World According to Carl Hiaasen." *WBUR On Point*. 7 Feb. 2014. Web. 24 Feb. 2017.

"Author Talk." *Bookreporter*. 30 July 2010. Web. 15 Aug. 2017.

Baker, Greg. "Doc Hiaasen and the Real Hollywood Story." *Miami New Times*. 21 Aug. 1991. Web. 27 Feb. 2017.

Bancroft, Colette. "Wacky Florida is Unending Inspiration for Bestselling Writer Carl Hiaasen." *Tampa Bay Times*. 19 March 2011. Web. 3 Apr. 2017.

Barry, Dave. *Best. State. Ever: A Florida Man Defends His Homeland*. New York: G. P. Putnam's Sons, 2016.

Bass, Erin Z. "Carl Hiaasen on His Motley Crew of Misfits." *Deep South Magazine*. 24 Oct. 2014. Web. 2 Feb. 2017.

Bearden, Michelle J. "PW Interviews: Carl Hiaasen." *Contemporary Literary Criticism Select*. 16 Aug. 1993. Web. 8 July 2017.

Beauregard, Sue-Ellen. "The Booklist Interview: Carl Hiaasen." *Booklist*. 1 May 2006: 53.

"Biography: Carl Hiaasen." *Scholastic*. 2013. Web. 6 Jan. 2017.

Blankenship, Gary. "Only in Florida Can Fact Outdo Fiction." *The Free Library*. 15 July 2003. Web. 13 May 2017.

Boedeker, Hal. "Carl Hiaasen Shares Favorite Florida Story." *Orlando Sentinel*. 31 Oct. 2016. Web. 28 Nov. 2017.

Bonner, Michael. "An Interview with Carl Hiaasen: "I Want to be Able to Turn Over Rocks and Shine a Spotlight on These Cockroaches." *Uncut*. 27 Aug. 2013. Web. 12 Feb. 2017.

Booth, William. "He Came From The Swamp." *Washington Post*. 4 Mar. 1992. Web. 2 Feb. 2017.

Bowman, David. "Carl Hiaasen." *Salon*. 31 Jan. 2000. Web. 2 Feb. 2017.

Bowman, Robert. "The Legacy of Florida Tourism: Labor and Leisure in Carl Hiaasen's *Native Tongue*." *Florida English Studies* 51:1 (Winter 2016): 9–12.

Brannon, Julie Sloan. "The Rules Are Different Here: South Florida Noir and the Grotesque." In *Crime Fiction and Film in the Sunshine State: Florida Noir*. ed. Steve Glassman and Maurice O'Sullivan. Bowling Green: Bowling Green Popular Press, 1997: 47–63.

Brunet, Rob. "Rob Brunet Interviews Carl Hiaasen." *The Thrill Begins*. Undated. Web. 8 Aug. 2017.

Burke, Monte. "Carl Hiaasen on Writing, Ben Carson, Fishing and the Enduring Appeal of Skink." *Forbes*. 9 Nov. 2015. Web. 5 May 2017.

_____. "Carl Hiaasen: The Last Great Howler." *Garden&Gun*. April/May 2013. Web. 28 Mar. 2017.

Byrne, Jennifer. "Interview with Carl Hiaasen." *Foreign Correspondent*. 16 May 2001. Web. 7 Mar. 2017.

Byrne, Larry. "Fighting the Good Fight on All Fronts: Carl Hiaasen and the Rhetoric of Ecocriticism." In *Florida Studies: Proceedings of the 2008 Annual Meeting of the Florida College English Association*. ed. Claudia Slate and April Van Camp. Newcastle upon Tyne: Cambridge Scholars Publishing, 2009: 181–189.

Callendar, Newgate. "Crime." *New York Times Book Review*. 10 Jan. 1982. Web. 4 Feb. 2017.

"Carl Hiaasen." *Current Biography Yearbook 1997*. ed. Elizabeth A. Schick. New York: H. W. Wilson, 1997: 221–224.

"Carl Hiaasen: By the Book." *New York Times Book Review*. 31 May 2012. Web. 25 Feb. 2017.

Charles, Ron. "We Interview; Carl Hiaasen." *Washington Post*. 21 May 2006. Web. 7 Apr. 2017.

Cheakalos, Christina. "Hurricane Hiaasen." *People*. 15 May 2000. Web. 10 Jan. 2017.

Colavito, J. Rocky. "Carl Hiaasen." *Dictionary of Literary Biography. Vol. 292: Twenty-First-Century American Novelists*. Edited

Bibliography

by Lisa Abney and Suzanne Disheroon-Green. Detroit: Gale, 2004: 155–163.

"A Conversation with Pete Hamill and Carl Hiaasen." *Mulholland Books.* 5 May 2011. Web. 20 Apr. 2017.

Cooke, Alistair. *Alistair Cooke's America.* New York: Alfred A. Knopf, 1973.

Crews, Harry. *Car.* New York: Pocket Books, 1973.

Crooks, Pete. "Extended Interview with Carl Hiaasen." *Pete's Popcorn Picks.* July 2010. Web. 7 Feb. 2017.

Cummins, Amy. "Fighting Crime against Nature: Cross-Generation Environmental Activism in Carl Hiaasen's Young Adult Novels." *Storytelling: A Critical Journal of Popular Narrative* 10 (2010): 7–18.

Curley, Nick. "Interview with Carl Hiaasen." *Barnes & Noble Review.* 24 Sept. 2014. Web. 23 Oct. 2017.

Davies, Dave. "Florida-Grown Fiction: Hiaasen Satirizes The Sunshine State." *Fresh Air.* 13 June 2013. Web. 15 Jan. 1017.

Dunn, Adam. "PW Talks with Carl Hiaasen." *Publishers Weekly.* 12 Nov. 2001. Web. 8 Mar. 2017.

Dunn, Stephanie. "Carl Hiaasen on His Latest Skink Novel and Why He Won't Do Vampires." *Ocean Drive.* 1 Sept. 2014. Web. 10 Sept. 2017.

Ferguson, Euan. "He's all the rage." *Guardian* (London). 17 Mar. 2001. Web. 8 Mar. 2017.

_____. "My humour has always come from anger." *Guardian* (London). 5 Mar. 2011. Web. 22 Aug. 2017.

Foglesong, Richard E. *Married to the Mouse: Walt Disney World and Orlando.* New Haven: Yale University Press, 2001.

Frail, T. A. "Carl Hiaasen on Human Weirdness." *Smithsonian Magazine.* Aug. 2010. Web. 14 July 2017.

Franklin, Daniel P. *Politics and Film: The Political Culture of Film in the United States.* Lanham: Rowman & Littlefield, 2006. p 203

Freeman, Hadley. "Sunshine Satirist." *Guardian* (London). 23 Oct. 2004. Web. 7 Mar. 2017.

Gibbs, Alan. "'Listen to Him, Mr. Take-Charge'; Gender Politics and Morality in Carl Hiaasen's Crime Novels." In *Writing America into the Twenty-First Century: Essays on the American Novel.* ed. Elizabeth Boyle and Anne-Marie Evans. Newcastle upon Tyne: Cambridge Scholars, 2010: 76–91.

Gilson, Nancy. "Carl Hiaasen: Fla. Novelist Crazy about Home State." *Columbus Dispatch.* 25 Oct. 2015. Web. 5 May 2017.

Glassman, Steve, and Maurice O'Sullivan, eds. *Crime Fiction and Film in the Sunshine State: Florida Noir.* Bowling Green: Bowling Green Popular Press, 1997.

_____. *Florida Crime Writers: 24 Interviews.* Jefferson, NC: McFarland, 2008.

Gopnik, Adam. "In the Back Cabana." *New Yorker.* 10 & 17 June 2013: 104–107.

Green, Graeme. "Carl Hiaasen: 'I love to go way out on the edge.'" *Wanderlust Magazine.* nd. Web. 2 Mar. 2017.

Griffin, Dustin. *Satire: A Critical Reintroduction.* Lexington: University Press of Kentucky, 1994.

Gulli, Andrew F. "Interview with Carl Hiaasen." *Strand Magazine.* 6 July 2013. Web. 2 Mar. 2017.

Haferkamp, Leyla. "'Somebody's got to get angry.' Ecoterrorism in the Work of Carl Hiaasen." *REAL: The Yearbook of Research in English and American Literature* Vol 26 (2010): 41–52.

Hamill, Denis. "Star-Crossed, Sun-Kissed Bottom Dwellers Carl Hiaasen Dissects Floridian Low Life in Laughing High Style." *New York Daily News.* 7 Dec. 1997. Web. 8 June 2017.

Harris, Jason Marc. "Absurdist Narratives in the Sunshine State: Comic, Criminal, Folkloric, and Fantastic Escapades in the Swamps and Suburbs of Florida." *New Directions in Folklore* 10:1 (2002): 32–84.

Harris, Mark. "Skinny Dip." *Entertainment Weekly.* 16 July 2004. Web. 1 Aug. 2017.

Heller, Joseph. *Catch-22.* New York: Dell, 1985.

Hillerman, Tony. "Terrorists and Beauty Queens." *New York Times Book Review.* 16 Mar. 1996. Web. 5 May 2017

_____. Quoted on Dust Jacket of *Native Tongue.* New York: Knopf, 1991.

Holahan, David. "Not a Lot of Redeeming Value." *Baltimore Sun.* 9 Aug. 1993. Web. 27 Apr. 2017.

Hoover, Emily. "Carl Hiaasen offers tools for upcoming writers." *Flagler College Gargoyle*. 2014. Web. 7 Mar. 2017.

Howard, Hugh. "The Trashing of the Planet, Writ Large: Carl Hiaasen." In *Writers of the American South: Their Literary Landscapes*. New York: Rizzoli, 2005: 135–145.

Huang, Jim. "Carl Hiaasen." In *St. James Guide to Crime and Mystery Writers*. ed. Jay P. Pederson. Detroit: St. James Press, 1996: 510–11.

Hubin, Allan J. "AJH Reviews." *Armchair Detective* 22:1 (Winter 1989): 24.

Hynes, James. "Carl Hiaasen: Sick Puppy." *Boston Review*. 1 Feb. 2000. Web. 19 June 2013.

Jones, Malcolm. "Hiaasen: Florida's Funniest Man." *Newsweek*. 11 Mar. 2006. Web. 29 Oct. 2017.

Jones, Malcolm, Jr. "More Trouble in Paradise." *Newsweek*. 6 Sept. 1993: 53.

Jordan, Peter. "Carl Hiaasen's Environmental Thrillers: Crime Fiction in Search of Green Peace." *Studies in Popular Culture* 13:1 (1990): 61–71.

Juvenal. *The Satires of Juvenal*. Translated by Rolfe Humphries. Bloomington: Indiana University Press, 1958.

Kenen, Joanne. "Carl of the Wild." *American Journalism Review*. Oct. 1993. Web. 10 Jan. 2017.

Kerridge, Richard. "Narratives of Resignation: Environmentalism in Recent Fiction." In *The Environmental Tradition in English Literature*. ed. John Parham. Aldershot: Ashgate, 2002: 87–99.

Kogan, Rick. "On The Water With Author Carl Hiaasen." *Chicago Tribune*. 24 Sept. 1995. Web. 23 Jan. 2017.

Kroft, Steve. "Florida: 'A Paradise of Scandals.'" *60 Minutes*. 17 Apr. 2005. Web. 2 Feb. 2017.

Lee, Luaine. "Spotlight on Carl Hiaasen." *Baltimore Sun*. 5 May 2006. Web. 10 June 2017.

Leopold, Todd. "Carl Hiaasen Reports from 'Paradise.'" CNNwww/Entertainment. 9 Nov. 2001. Web. 1 Mar. 2017.

Levy, Art. "Icon: Carl Hiaasen." *Florida Trend*. August 2015. Web. 10 June 2017.

Liang, Adrian. "True-life Source Material Is Fabulously Bizarre." *Omnivoracious: The Amazon Book Review*. 8 Sept. 2016. Web. 22 Oct. 2017.

Linskey, Annie. "Hiaasen's 'Skinny Dip': Nibbling the Everglades." *Baltimore Sun*. 4 July 2004. Web. 25 Aug. 2017.

Louv, Richard. *Last Child in the Woods: Saving Our Children from Nature-Deficit Disorder*. Chapel Hill: Algonquin Books, 2005.

MacDonald, Jay. "Carl Hiaasen: Florida's still crazy after all these years." *BookPage*. 6 Sept. 2016. Web. 3 Mar. 2017.

_____. "Carl Hiaasen takes a bite out of crime against the environment." *BookPage*. Jan. 2000. Web. 3 Mar. 2017.

MacDonald, John D. *The Dreadful Lemon Sky*. New York: Fawcett, 1975.

_____. *The Empty Copper Sea*. New York: Fawcett, 1978.

_____. *A Flash of Green*. New York: Fawcett, 1962.

_____. *The Turquoise Lament*. New York: Lippincott, 1973.

Marcus, Leonard S., ed. *Funny Business: Conversations with Writers of Comedy*. Somerville, MA: Candlewick Press, 2009: 105–117.

Maslin, Janet. "Everglades Sightings: Greedheads and Goons." *New York Times*. 16 Nov. 2006. Web. 11 Oct. 2017.

_____. "Her Marriage Had Taken a Dive, but She Sure Could Swim." *New York Times*. 2 July 2004. Web. 12 Sept. 2017.

McGrath, Charles. "It's Florida. It's Hiaasen. It's Golf?" *New York Times*. 6 May 2008. Web. 19 Aug. 2017.

McLellan, Joseph. Review of *Death in China*. *Washington Post Book World*. 6 May 1984. Web. 9 Feb. 2017.

McMahon, Bucky. "The Anger Artist." *GQ*. June 1996: 92–98.

Middlemas, Mary. "An Interview with Carl Hiaasen." *Chattahoochee Review* 16:3 (1996): 88–104.

Miller, Martin. "Oh, He's a Basket Case, All Right." *Los Angeles Times*. 25 Jan. 2002. Web. 1 Feb 2017.

Mitgang, Herbert. "A Death in China." *New York Times Book Review*. 24 June 1984. Web. 14 Feb. 2017.

Moore, Clayton. "Celebs take a tumble in Hi-

Bibliography

aasen's 'Star Island.'" *Denver Post.* 12 Aug. 2010. Web. 19 Aug 2017.

Morris, Bob. "Hiaasen Doubles Fun in Whammy." *Orlando Sentinel.* 17 Jan. 1988. Web. 24 Mar. 2017.

Murfin, Ross, and Supryia M. Ray. *The Bedford Glossary of Critical and Literary Terms.* 2nd ed. New York: Bedford/St. Martin's, 2003.

Nachman, Gerald. *Seriously Funny: The Rebel Comedians of the 1950s and 1960s.* New York: Pantheon, 2003.

Navarro, Mireya. "Carl Hiaasen; Can Success and Satire Mix?" *New York Times.* 4 July 1996. Web. 1 Feb. 2017.

O'Connor, Flannery. *Conversations with Flannery O'Connor.* ed. Rosemary M. Magee. Jackson: University Press of Mississippi, 1987.

Ott, Bill, and Brad Hooper. "A Hard-Boiled Gazetteer to Florida." *Booklist.* 1 May 2001. Web. 30 Jan. 2018.

Panos, Alexandra. "Beyond Sanctioned Activism in Carl Hiaasen's *Flush*: Sacrifice Zones in Realistic Fiction." *Journal of Children's Literature* 43:1 (Spring 2017): 6–15.

Parker, David M. "Is South Florida the New Southern California? Carl Hiaasen's Dystopian Paradise." *The Florida Historical Quarterly* 90:3 (Winter 2012): 306–323.

Patterson, Troy. "Mystery writer on sand, sun, and 'Skinny Dip.'" *Entertainment Weekly.* 30 July 2004. Web. 12 July 2017.

Patton, Jessica Rae. "Carl Hiaasen: Delightfully Juvenile." *Teaching Pre K-8 Magazine* 36:1 (Aug/Sep 2005): 62–64. Web. 12 Nov. 2017.

Phillips, Dana. "Is Nature Necessary?" *Raritan* 13:3 (Winter 1994): 78–100.

Pleasants, Julian M. "Interview with Carl Hiaasen." In *Orange Journalism: Voices from Florida Newspapers.* Gainesville: University Press of Florida, 2003: 245–276.

Reardon, Patrick T. "Hiaasen's Humor on Target: Author's 'Basket Case' Tackles Journalism's 'Suits.'" *Chicago Tribune.* 23 Jan. 2002. Web. 10 July 2017.

Rich, Frank. "The Rodent Rules." *New York Times.* 6 May 1998. Web. 19 Aug. 2017.

Richards, Linda. "January Interview with Carl Hiaasen." *January Magazine* (Jan. 2002). Web. 10 Jan. 2017.

Rife, Susan L. "BOOKS: Carl Hiaasen's 'Nature Girl.'" *Ticket Sarasota.* 28 Dec. 2006. Web. 24 Aug 2017.

_____. "Columnist Carl Hiaasen Aims to Connect with Readers' Frustrations." *Ticket Sarasota.* 13 Mar. 2014. Web. 20 Sept. 2017.

_____. "You Really Can't Exaggerate Florida Too Much." *Ticket Sarasota.* 14 Mar. 2014. Web. 20 Sept. 2017.

Rosenbaum, Ron. "Hurricane Hiaasen." *Vanity Fair.* Sept. 1993: 124–136.

Roth, Philip. *Reading Myself and Others.* New York: Farrar, Straus and Giroux, 1975.

Royce, Graydon. "The Voice of Florida is a Norwegian? Carl Hiaasen Talks about His Latest, 'Razor Girl.'" *Minneapolis Star Tribune.* 10 Sept. 2016. Web. 11 Oct. 2017.

Salustri, Cathy. "The Man who Invented Skink." *Creative Loafing Tampa.* 1 Mar. 2017. Web. 22 Aug. 2017.

Santella, Chris. "Carl Hiaasen: Making Sense of the Madness." In *Why I Fly Fish: Passionate Anglers on the Pastime's Appeal and How It Has Shaped Their Lives.* New York: Stewart, Tabori & Chang, 2013: 45–50.

Schindehette, Susan. "Tree Hugger from Hell." *People Magazine.* 21 Oct. 1991. Web. 13 Feb. 2017.

Scholes, Robert. "A Talk with Kurt Vonnegut, Jr." In *The Vonnegut Statement.* ed. Jerome Klinkowitz and John Somer. New York: Delacorte, 1973.

See, Caroline. "March Madness." *Washington Post.* 10 Nov. 2006. Web. 24 Aug. 2017.

Seymour, Gene. "Crazy From the Heat: In Mystery Novelist Carl Hiaasen's Florida, Crocodiles Eat Tourists, Eco-Terrorists Kidnap the Orange Bowl Queen, and Mickey Mouse is Filthy Vermin." *Los Angeles Times.* 17 Nov. 1991. Web. 10 Feb. 2017.

Shackle, Samira. "The Books Interview: Carl Hiaasen." *New Statesman.* 17 Mar. 2017. Web. 13 Feb. 2017.

Shacochis, Bob. "Code Orange." *Outside Magazine.* 1 Aug. 2004. Web. 12 Jun 2017.

Shea, Roz. "Trap Line is the Second of the Hiaasen Treasures." *Bookreporter.* 23 Jan. 2011. Web. 14 Feb. 2017.

Bibliography

Sherrill, Robert. "Dade Ain't Disney." *Nation*. 6 Mar. 2000: 23–30.

Silet, Charles L. P. "Carl Hiaasen." In *Speaking of Murder: Interviews with Masters of Mystery and Suspense* Vol. II. ed. Ed Gorman and Martin H. Greenberg. New York: Berkley, 1999: 66–77.

_____. "Sun, Sand and Tirades: An Interview with Carl Hiaasen." *Armchair Detective* 29 (Winter 1996): 9–18.

Smith, Kat. "No Surrender: Q&A with Carl Hiaasen." *Naples Illustrated*. 1 Dec. 2015. Web. 24 June 2017.

Solomon, Deborah. "Miami Voice." *New York Times*. 25 July 2004. Web. 1 Mar. 2017.

Stanton, David Duwe. *The Miami Herald and the Miller Effect: Literary Journalism in the 1980s*. M. A. Thesis. University of Florida. 2005.

Staskiewicz, Keith. "Carl Hiaasen on Movie Adaptations, Dostoevsky, and Buying his Own Work." *Entertainment Weekly*. 12 Aug. 2010. Web. 25 July 2017.

Stevenson, Diane. Introduction. *Kick Ass. Selected Columns of Carl Hiaasen*. ed. Diane Stevenson. Gainesville: University Press of Florida, 1999: xiv–xxiv.

Sutcliffe, Thomas. "Carl Hiaasen: Who says that Crime Doesn't Pay?" *Independent* (London). 6 Mar. 2002. Web. 22 April 2017.

Szubinska, Barbara. "Hiaasen's *Sick Puppy* and Dystopia: An Ecofeminist Perspective. *Storytelling: A Critical Journal* 8:1 (Summer 2008): 37–45.

Tamber, George J. "Author Carl Hiaasen Discusses Golf, Nerves and the Shanks." *Kwese ESPN*. 15 May 2008. Web. 15 Nov. 2017.

Taylor, Elizabeth. "Writing for Young People Isn't Much of a Stretch for Author Carl Hiaasen." *Chicago Tribune*. 11 Dec. 2005. Web. 28 Sept. 2017.

Trimborn, Harry. "Something Fishy Baits a Raucous Florida Thriller." *Los Angeles Times*. 2 Mar. 1988. Web. 25 Mar. 2017.

Van Kampen-Breit, Doris. "Hooting and Shooting at the Carpetbaggers: Carl Hiaasen's Revolt against Greed in Florida-Land." In *Florida Studies: Selected Papers from the 2012 and 2013 Annual Meetings of the Florida College English Association*. ed. Paul D. Reich and Andrew Leib. Newcastle upon Tyne: Cambridge Scholars, 2014: 103–111.

Walker, Walter. "Double Whammy." *New York Times Book Review*. 6 Mar. 1988. Web. 25 Mar. 2017.

Wappler, Margaret. "Ready to Give a Hoot." *Los Angeles Times*. 30 Apr. 2006. Web. 10 Oct. 2017.

Weeks, Linton. "Land Shark." *Smithsonian*. June 2003: 88–91.

Weich, Dave. "A Kinder, Gentler Carl Hiaasen: Still Pissing People Off." *PowellsBooks*. 15 Nov. 2005. Web. 3 July 2017.

Westlake, Donald E. "Mess Over Miami." *New York Times*. 29 Aug. 1993: 6.

Williams, John. *Back to the Badlands: Crime Writing in the USA*. London: Serpent's Tail, 2007.

Wolfe, Alexandra. "Carl Hiaasen: The Best-Selling Author on How Truth Is Really Stranger Than Fiction—Especially in Florida." *Wall Street Journal*. 8 June 2013. Web. 15 May 2017.

Wolfe, Linda. "Crime/Mystery: In the Amazing Kingdom of Thrills." *New York Times*. 20 Oct. 1991. Web. 22 Apr. 2017.

Woods, Sean. "Carl Hiaasen's Life Advice." *Men's Journal*. nd. Web. 16 June 2017.

"Writer Pulls No Punches Fighting for State He Loves." *Los Angeles Times*. 7 Oct. 2000. Web. 9 Mar. 2017.

Zane, J. Peder. *The Top Ten. Writers Pick Their Favorite Books*. New York: Norton, 2007.

Index

Abbey, Edward 44, 142, 151
Aitchison, David 145, 161
Alexie, Sherman 133
Alistair Cooke's America 118
Allen, Woody 163
Allende, Isabel 133
Apatow, Judd 118
The Armchair Detective 52
Ashe, Penelope 77
Atwood, Margaret 133
Avery, Tex 176
awards 8, 9, 13, 14, 23, 64

Bad Monkey 119–124, 126, 127
Baker, Russell 182
"The Ballad of Skip Wiley" (song) 46
Barry, Dave 9, 10, 18, 77, 172, 182
Basilica 39
Basket Case 10, 91–98, 120, 144
"Basket Case" (song) 10, 92
Bergman, Andrew 70
Berman, Shelly 181
Big Cypress Preserve 145, 146
Big Pine Key 123
Big Sugar 68, 69, 171
"The Bird Snatchers" 17
Bloor, Edward 133
Bond, James 5
Bosch, Hieronymous 11
Bowman, Robert 60
Branham, Bob 4
Brannon, Julie Sloan 178
Buchanan, Edna 13, 77, 172
Buchwald, Art 182
Buffett, Jimmy 10, 46, 139, 140, 165
Bugs Bunny 176
Bunker, Archie 78
Burke, J. Herbert 68

Calandra, Denis 83
Car 167–168
Carlin, George 4, 163, 178, 181
Carrey, Jim 133
Carson, Johnny 181
Carson, Rachel 159, 160

Carter, Jimmy 25
Cassadaga 81
Castro, Fidel 77, 128
Catch-22 4, 5, 105, 165–167, 168, 177
Catcher in the Rye 163
celebrity culture 112, 113, 114, 115, 117, 118
Chabon, Michael 133
Charlie Wilson's War (film) 105
Chemo 53, 54, 55, 57, 116, 117, 118, 178
childhood 3, 4, 121–22, 136, 169, 180, 181
Chitty-Chitty-Bang-Bang 133
Choctawhatchee River 157
Chomp 130, 152–155
Clapton, Eric 32
Clarkson, Kelly 133
Clizer, Fenia 10
Clizer, Ryan 10
Cocoa Today 7, 13
Coen Brothers 118
collaborations 1, 6, 8, 10, 14, 15, 16, 34–39, 77, 91, 92, 94, 182, 183, 184, 186
college 5–7, 182
columnist 6, 17–25, 71, 72, 177, 182
The Comedians 90
Como, Perry 32
Connelly, Michael 13
Conrad, Joseph 41
Cooke, Alistair 118
Corcoran, Tom 172
Cosby, Bill 4, 133, 163, 181
Crews, Harry 167–168
Cummins, Amy 161
Curtis, Jamie Lee 133

Damon Runyon Award 23
Dance of the Reptiles 23
"Dangerous Doctors: A Medical Dilemma" 14, 54
Day of the Locust 172
A Death in China 36–37, 39
de Leon, Ponce 61
Deliverance 46, 109
Depp, Johnny 119
deus ex machina 104, 143
Dickens, Charles 13

Index

Dismal Key 107, 108, 109, 110, 111
Disney Company 24–29, 62, 176
Disney World 25, 28, 29, 59, 60, 81
Disneyland 172
Doc Hollywood 6
La Dolce Vita 115
Donald Duck 176
Dorsey, Tim 172
Double Whammy 4, 8, 46–52, 54, 56, 186
The Downhill Lie: A Hacker's Return to a Ruinous Sport 29–32
Dreyer, John 29
Duck Dynasty 130, 132
Duffy, Brian 15, 17
Duke, David 83

Edinburgh Festival Fringe 83
Els, Ernie 32
Emory University 5, 6
The Emory Wheel 6
environment 1, 15, 19, 20, 23, 58, 68, 84, 96, 133, 161, 162, 163, 164, 171, 179
Ernie Pyle Lifetime Achievement Award 23
Everglades 3, 4, 49, 61, 100, 103, 153, 154, 155, 171
Everglades City 105

family 3, 6, 10, 32, 33, 122
Fanjul brothers 69
Fellini, Federico 115
Field and Stream 5
"Fighting Crime Against Nature: Cross-Generational Environmental Activism in Carl Hiaasen's Young Adult Novels" 161
Finally...I'm a Doctor 6, 183
fishing 9, 30, 50
A Flash of Green 163
Fleming, Ian 5, 133
Florida 19, 20, 26, 45, 58, 59, 71, 111, 138, 146, 163, 164, 165, 168, 169–173
Florida Keys 32, 33, 119, 173
Florida Lifetime Achievement Award in Writing 23
Flush 140–145, 151, 161
Fly Rod & Reel Magazine 9
Fogelsong, Richard E. 28
Fort Lauderdale 3, 48, 64, 163, 180
Fort Lauderdale News 180
Fox, Michael J. 6
Franklin, Daniel P. 70
Freberg, Stan 175
Funny Thing About Murder: Modes of Humor in Crime Fiction and Films 1

Gainesville Sun 7
García Márquez, Gabriel 13
Gibbon, Edward 118
Gibbs, Alan 110, 176

Gilligan's Island 109, 111
Glassman, Steve 172
Golden Raspberry Award 7
golf 29–33
González, Elián 19
Gopnik, Adam 172, 176
Gould, Stephen Jay 25
Graham, Gov. Bob 14, 15
Greene, Graham 90
Griffin, Dustin 176
Grisham, John 133

Hall, James W. 172
Hamill, Pete 10, 22, 25
Hanks, Tom 105
Hardy Boys 5
Harrelson, Woody 115
Harvey Penick's Little Red Book 31
Hayduke Lives! 151
Heart of Darkness 41
Heller, Joseph 4, 5, 105, 163, 165–167, 177
Hemingway, Ernest 13, 89
Hendricks, Vicki 172
Hersh, Sy 97
Heywood Broun Award 14
Hiaasen, Barbara 3
Hiaasen, Carl: awards 8, 9, 13, 14, 23, 64; childhood 3, 4, 121–22, 136, 169, 180, 181; collaborations 1, 6, 8, 10, 14, 15, 16, 34–39, 77, 91, 92, 94, 182, 183, 184, 186; college 5–7, 182; columnist 17–25, 71, 72, 177, 182; family 3, 6, 10, 32, 33, 122; high school 5, 181; investigative reporting 14–18, 54, 61; journalism 13–24, 54, 96, 97, 112; marriage 6, 10; on writing 174–176, 181–187
Hiaasen, Carl Andreas 3
Hiaasen, Judith 3
Hiaasen, K. Odel 3
Hiaasen, Patricia (Moran) 3
Hiaasen, Quinn 10, 32
Hiaasen, Rob 3, 122
Hiaasen, Scott 6, 10, 33
high school 5, 181
Hillerman, Tony 8, 45
History of the Decline and Fall of the Roman Empire 118
Holes 133
Hoot 8, 9, 97, 133–140, 144, 147, 161, 171
Hoot (film) 11, 139, 140
Horace 175
How I Play Golf 31
Hubin, Allan J. 52
Hurricane Andrew 71, 72

Independent Florida Alligator 6, 7
Ingalls, Clyde 4, 51
investigative reporting 8, 14–18, 54, 61
Islamadora Fall Fly Fishing Tournament 9

Index

Jackson, Michael 112, 172
Jersey Shore 117
John Pennekamp Coral Reef State Park 15
Jones, Malcolm, Jr. 70
journalism 6, 13–24, 54, 96, 97, 112; *see also* newspapers
Joyce, James 133
Juvenal 175, 176

Kafka, Franz 68
Kardashian, Robert 112
Kardashians 112, 113
Key West 36, 37, 119, 125, 126
"Key West: Smuggler's Island" 14
Kick Ass 22
"Killer: The Life and Death of a Cocaine Cowboy" 16
King, Stephen 9
Knight, Tony 96
Knight-Ridder 37, 96
Knopf, Alfred A. 8, 58
Knopfler, Mark 107
Koresh, David 83

Larson, Brie 140
Last Child in the Woods 155
Last Laugh Award 64
"Last of the Falling" 32
Latifah, Queen 115
Leno, Jay 133
Leonard, Elmore 11, 77, 116, 172, 174, 178
Lerman, Logan 140
Library of Contemporary Thought 25
Linley, Cody 140
Lippman, Laura 13
"Little Saboteurs, Puerile Politics: The Child, the Childlike, and the Principled Life in Carl Hiaasen's Ecotage Novels for Young Adults." 161
Lohan, Lindsay 113, 121
Lord of the Flies 109
Los Angeles Times 39
Louv, Richard 155
Lucky You 77–83, 86, 186
Lucky You (theatrical version) 83
Lupica, Mike 30
Lutz, John 172
Lyford, Connie 6, 10

Macbeth 103
MacDonald, John D. 4, 8, 163–165, 172
Madonna 133
Malone, Patrick 14
Maples, Marla 76
Marco Island 84, 170
marriage 6, 10
Married to the Mouse 28
Martin, Dean 181

Martin, Steve 133
Martinez, Gov. Bob 20
Maslin, Janet 11
Matthews, Francis 83
May, Elaine 4, 104, 163
McGee, Jim 16
McGee, Travis 1, 163, 164
McGuinn, Roger 10, 85
McVeigh, Timothy 83
Mehta, Sonny 8, 58, 186, 187
Mercury Outboards Bonefishing World Championship 9
"Metamorphosis" 68
Miami 57, 77, 119, 171
Miami Beach 117
Miami Herald 1, 3, 7, 8, 14, 15, 16, 18, 34, 77, 96, 172, 180
Mickey Mouse 25, 26, 59, 62
MidCurrent 9
Miller, Gene 14
Minnie Mouse 25, 26, 59, 62
Miranda, Miguel 17
"Miss Emory" pageant 6
The Monkey Wrench Gang 44, 45, 142, 151
Montalbano, William 1, 8, 14, 34–39, 94, 183, 184, 186
Moore, Demi 70
More Trash 5, 181
Morin, Richard 14
Moynihan, Daniel Patrick 19
Mutineer 10
My Ride's Here 10, 92

Naked Came the Manatee 77, 91
Naked Came the Stranger 77
"A Nation for Sale: Corruption in the Bahamas" 16
Native Tongue 8, 10, 25, 58–64, 67
Nature Girl 105–111
Neuharth, Al 7
New York Times 6
Newberg, Esther 39, 186
Newbery Honor Award 8
Newhart, Bob 181
Newman, Randy 11
newspapers 96, 97, 173, 177; *see also* journalism
Nichols, Mike 4, 104, 163
Nixon, Richard 6, 7, 13
North by Northwest 34
North Key Largo 15, 58, 60, 61, 116
"North Key Largo: The Last Stand" 15
Nyron, Neil 186

O'Connor, Flannery 177, 178
Orwell, George 13
Outdoor Life 5

Index

Paradise Screwed 23
Parker, David M. 172
Patterson, James 133
Pearson, Ridley 9
Pirates of the Caribbean 119, 121
Plantation 3, 181
Plantation High School 5
Politics and Film: The Political Culture of Film in the United States 70
Port Bougainville 15, 61
Potter, Harry 133
Powder Burn 34–36, 38
Presley, Elvis 93
Pulitzer Prize 13, 15

Quindlen, Anna 25

Razor Girl 125–132
"Read Together, Florida" 9
Reedy Creek Improvement District 28
Reiner, Rob 98
Reynolds, Burt 70
Richards, Keith 10, 133
Rivera, Geraldo 22, 55, 56
Robertson, Pat 76, 92
Robinson Crusoe 109
Rock, Chris 178
Rock Bottom Remainders 9, 10
Roof, Dylann 83
Room 140
Rose, Axl 114
Roth, Philip 43
"Rottweiler Blues" 10
Rowling, J.K. 133
Rushdie, Salman 133

Sachar, Louis 133
Sachs, Susan 14
St. Petersburg Times 7
Salinger, J.D. 5
Sanford, John 13
santeria 76
satire 1, 6, 11, 19, 21, 22, 50, 56, 58, 69, 94, 130, 131, 132, 165, 167, 174–179, 184
Savage, James 14, 17
Scat 145–151, 161
Scene of the Crime: The Importance of Place in Crime and Mystery Fiction 1
Scott, Willard 63
Seinfeld, Jerry 133, 172
"Seminole Bingo" 10
Seminoles 21, 106, 107
Shames, Laurence 172
Shea, Roz 39
Sheen, Charlie 115
Sherman, Alan 181
"The Short Happy Life of Francis Macomber" 89

Shriner, Wil 139, 140
Shulman, Neil B. 6, 182, 183
Sick Puppy 10, 83–91, 100, 104, 141, 146, 151, 170
Silas Marner 5
Silence of the Lambs 78
Silent Spring 159
Simpson, Jessica 115
Simpson, O.J. 112
The Sinners of San Ramon 39
Skin Tight 22, 52–58, 96, 98, 103, 116, 152, 183
Skink 4, 8, 46–51, 61, 62, 74, 76, 87, 88, 89, 90, 104, 105, 115, 116, 117, 118, 135, 151, 156–160
Skink—No Surrender 156–161
Skinny Dip 98–105, 171, 178
Slaughterhouse-Five 162
Snookie 117
South Beach 95, 117
Spears, Britney 113
Springsteen, Bruce 133
Standiford, Les 172
Star Island 111–118, 131, 152
Stormy Weather 71–77, 178
Strip Tease (book) 8, 64–71, 85, 110, 140, 171
Strip Tease (film) 70, 85
Sullivan, Ed 181
Survivor 109
Swift, Jonathan 11
Swiss Family Robinson 109

Tallahassee 20, 47
Tan, Amy 9
Tangerine 133
Team Rodent: How Disney Devours the World 25–29, 59
The Tempest 109
Ten Thousand Islands 107, 108, 111
Tennyson, Alfred 104
Tonight Show 181
Tourist Season 8, 17, 39, 40–46, 47, 54, 69, 84, 106, 136, 165, 186
Trap Line 36–37, 39
Treasure Island 109
Tropic 14, 16, 77
Trump, Donald 19, 76
Turow, Scott 9
Tustenuggee, Thlocklo 106
Twain, Mark 11, 13

University of Florida 6
Updike, John 133
USA Today 6

Vietnam war 4, 6
Vonnegut, Kurt, Jr. 162

Wainwright, Loudon III 83
The Washington Post 6, 13

Index

Watergate 6, 13
West, Adam 13
West, Nathanael 172
Westlake, Donald E. 70, 73, 176
What...Dead Again? 6
White, Randy Wayne 172
Willeford, Charles 172
Williams, Robin 178
Wilson, Charles E. 167
Winehouse, Amy 113

Winters, Jonathan 178, 181
Without Feathers 163
Wolfe, Linda 64
Wood, Ron 10
Woods, Tiger 31, 32
Woodward, Bob 97
writing 174–176, 181–187

Zevon, Warren 10, 92, 98

www.ingramcontent.com/pod-product-compliance
Lightning Source LLC
Chambersburg PA
CBHW032059300426
44116CB00007B/816